Securing the Commonwealth

Securing the Commonwealth

Debt, Speculation, and Writing in the Making of Early America

Jennifer J. Baker

The Johns Hopkins University Press
Baltimore

This book was brought to publication with the generous assistance of the Frederick W. Hilles Publication Fund of Yale University.

© 2005 The Johns Hopkins University Press
All rights reserved. Published 2005
Printed in the United States of America on acid-free paper
9 8 7 6 5 4 3 2 1

Johns Hopkins Paperback edition, 2008

The Johns Hopkins University Press
2715 North Charles Street
Baltimore, Maryland 21218-4363
www.press.jhu.edu

The Library of Congress has catalogued the hardcover edition of this book as follows:

Baker, Jennifer J., 1968–
 Securing the commonwealth : debt, speculation, and writing in the making of early America / Jennifer J. Baker.
   p. cm.
 Includes bibliographical references and index.
 Contents: Crisis and faith in the Puritan society—Making much of nothing in the Chesapeake— Benjamin Franklin's projections—Performing redemption on the national stage—Arthur Mervyn and the reader's investments—The medium between calculation and feeling.
   ISBN 0-8018-7972-8 (hardcover : alk. paper)
 1. American literature—Colonial period, ca. 1600–1775—History and criticism. 2. Politics and literature—United States—History—18th century. 3. United States—Intellectual life—18th century. 4. United States—Intellectual life—17th century. 5. Imperialism in literature. 6. Economics in literature. 7. Colonies in literature. I. Title.
 PS193.B35 2005
 810.9′3553—dc22   2005000734

ISBN 13: 978-0-8018-8969-1
ISBN 10: 0-8018-8969-3

A catalog record for this book is available from the British Library.

For my parents

Contents

Acknowledgments	ix
Introduction: Castle Building	1
PART I: New World Ventures	19
1 Crisis and Faith in the Puritan Society	27
2 Making Much of Nothing in the Chesapeake	43
PART II: The Price of Independence	63
3 Benjamin Franklin's Projections	71
4 Performing Redemption on the National Stage	96
PART III: Bonds of the New Nation	113
5 *Arthur Mervyn* and the Reader's Investments	119
6 The Medium between Calculation and Feeling	137
Epilogue: Headwork, Literary Vocation	157
Notes	169
Bibliography	193
Index	209

Acknowledgments

I am grateful for the intellectual and financial support that made this book possible. It began under the tutelage of two literary critics and a historian at the University of Pennsylvania. Elisa New's careful attention to rhetoric always reminded me that a scholar teaches. Christopher Looby taught me much about early American print culture and the role of language in the formation of a nation. Michael Zuckerman helped me tackle the daunting task of historical research and encouraged me to write for an audience beyond my own small circle of colleagues.

Michelle Burnham, Therese B. Dykeman, Stephen Fishbein, Mary Rose Kasraie, Jeffrey Richards, Joseph Roach, Lana Schwebel, Jason Shaffer, Timothy Sweet, Bryan Waterman, Eric Wertheimer, and Gregory Wolmart were patient readers and offered thoughtful responses to individual chapters. Lloyd Pratt, who read every page of the manuscript, sometimes several times, deserves special thanks. I appreciate, too, the professionalism and expertise of Michael Lonegro, my editor at the Johns Hopkins University Press, and Elizabeth Gratch, who copyedited the manuscript. Richard Beeman, with whom I first studied the intellectual history of the American Revolution, helped prepare me to write this book. Todd Gilman, at the Sterling Memorial Library at Yale University, facilitated my research at several turns and helped me put my hands on the microfilm of more than five decades' worth of letterbooks by Judith Sargent Murray. I profited as well from the opportunity to present material from this book to the Americanist Colloquium in the English Department at the University of Pennsylvania, the McNeil Center for Early American Studies in Philadelphia, and the Market Culture Colloquium at the Whitney Humanities Center at Yale University. Anonymous reviewers of the book manuscript, and of essays derived from it, offered valuable feedback, and I hope I have made good use of their advice. For their counsel and answers to assorted queries, I also thank Jean-Christophe Agnew, Jessica Brantley, David Bromwich, Ellen Cohn, Joanne Freeman, Laura Frost, Elliott Visconsi, and Sara Weber.

Several institutions provided financial support. A generous Benjamin Franklin Graduate Fellowship and an Andrew Mellon Dissertation Fellowship supported several years of research and writing at the University of Pennsylvania. A Kate B. and Hall J. Peterson Fellowship at the American Antiquarian Society in Worcester, Massachusetts, financed an invaluable month-long stay at its archive as I was beginning my research. A grant from the Frederick W. Hilles Publication Fund of Yale University provided financial assistance for the book's publication.

Portions of chapters 1 and 3 have appeared in earlier form in, respectively, "'It is uncertain where the Fates will carry me': Cotton Mather's Theology of Finance," *Arizona Quarterly* 56:4 (Winter 2000): 1–23; and "Benjamin Franklin's *Autobiography* and the Credibility of Personality," *Early American Literature* 35:3 (Fall 2000): 274–293. I am grateful for permission to use revised versions of this material.

Securing the Commonwealth

INTRODUCTION

Castle Building

> The Subject of *Paper Currency* is in itself very intricate, and I believe, understood by few; I mean as to its Consequences *in Futurum:* And tho' much might be said on that Head, I apprehend it to be the less necessary for me to handle it at this Time, because EXPERIENCE, (more prevalent than all the *Logic* in the World) has fully convinced us all, that it has been, and is now of the greatest Advantage to the Country.
> BENJAMIN FRANKLIN,
> *AMERICAN WEEKLY MERCURY*, MARCH 27, 1729

Modern readers of eighteenth-century American literature face a significant challenge: understanding a body of works thoroughly embedded in financial circumstances that were never their own. They have none of the experience with eighteenth-century paper currency that, according to Benjamin Franklin, makes tangible its benefits. Today's readers do have the advantage of hindsight and a rich historiography, but they must also work to picture what it must have been like to witness the advent and proliferation of paper money and banknotes. As Franklin intimates, few could understand, much less predict, how paper currency worked and why it rose and fell in value the way it did. To complicate matters, this currency was really just an instrument in a larger economic transformation that entailed a complex reconsideration of value itself. To talk of paper money and banknotes was actually to talk of a constellation of economic theories about risk taking, debt, and credit. Paper currency, issued in lieu of metal money not currently in hand, was a form of public borrowing, and this debt was itself an investment, a risk taken to reap future profit.

To date, readers of this literature have been able to imagine how speculative currencies, the rise of national banking, and the creation and deliberate maintenance of a public debt prompted anxiety and opposition. In many ways the rhetoric of this opposition was akin to that of English writers disturbed by the burgeoning public debt across the ocean.¹ Like their English counterparts, American opponents saw paper money and banking schemes as castles erected upon airy, rather than earthly, foundations. Such volatile schemes wreaked havoc and fostered the kind of society satirized in Hugh Henry Brackenridge's *Modern Chivalry*, in which people make promises they cannot keep and turn words into wind. That anxiety was a common literary response to an increasingly credit-based economy is one of the conclusions of Larzer Ziff's influential study of early American print culture, *Writing in the New Nation*. One signature of early American literature, Ziff writes, was the fear that personal "immanence" could be replaced entirely by textual "representation," thus creating a society in which people interact less with other individuals than with textual representations of those individuals in letters, pamphlets, newspaper pieces, and books. Ziff aptly attributes this fear to a new concept of personal wealth based on abstract forms of wealth, such as paper money, stocks, mortgages, and loans, rather than on the traditionally recognized real property of land.²

But the literature of colonial British America and the early United States records a concurrent response to such economic transformations. This alternative, and often counterintuitive, view saw the representative and unstable nature of paper currency as precisely its greatest asset. Public borrowing aroused suspicions in a Puritan and Yankee culture that emphasized frugality and moderation, in an agrarian South that exalted the self-sufficient patriarch, and in a Revolutionary culture that celebrated classical republican disinterestedness and the transcendence of market relations. And yet writers within all these social and intellectual circles imagined new modes of financial speculation and indebtedness as a means to build American communities and foster social cohesion. In this literature public debt figures as a varied resource for fledgling colonies, a tool for national independence, and a catalyst for sympathetic social interaction in the new nation.

Like the classical economists whose thinking prevailed by the end of the eighteenth century, the writers I examine believed that substituting paper for metal not in hand could be a means of economic growth, but they also hoped that the risks entailed in this substitution could foster colonial and national cohesion at times when the stability of those communities was at stake, binding people to their government as well as individuals to one another. Out of economic uncertainty, according to these writers, could come civic faith. When grasped in light of the era's economic thought, the claims of this literature reveal dramatic paradoxes. That debt might be an asset rather than a deficiency, that it might lead to independence rather than dependence, that it might be socially cohesive rather than divisive—these were claims that seemed incompatible with many of the existing views on debt. Yet experience, as Franklin writes, convinced these writers that such might be the case.

This rhetoric of advocacy adapted itself quite easily to various models of collectivity: the Puritan commonwealth, the republic of letters, the virtuous republic, and the benevolent society. The Marxist thought of the nineteenth and twentieth centuries would maintain that the mutually reinforcing nature of public credit and communality is one of capitalism's great illusions. Marx himself wrote that the modern state erects a "credo of capital" and deems the lack of faith in its credit machinery an unforgivable sin. A national debt, he added, was the only part of a nation's wealth which truly found its way into the collective possession because all the advantages that flowed from that debt system went straight into the hands of the capitalist class.[3] Another literary critic might indeed examine the contradictions of eighteenth-century writers' paradigms or see their literature as the rationalizations of a privileged class. I have chosen, however, to take these writers on their own terms, taking seriously their attempts to see a social dimension in an increasingly modern economy. I have read these works as investigations worthy of our investigation.

Although historians have shown that early Americans envisioned economic advantages deriving from paper money and collective debts, the central purpose of this book is to explain literature's participation in this imaginative process.[4] Part 1, "New World Ventures," examines the works of Cotton Mather and several Chesapeake writers who posited public debt as a varied resource capable of healing an economy but also consolidating a communal identity. Part 2, "The Price of Independence," details the importance of borrowing for national independence and reputability in Franklin's *Autobiography* and Royall Tyler's play *The Contrast* during the Revolution and shortly thereafter. Part 3, "Bonds of the New Nation," explains how Charles Brockden Brown and Judith Sargent Murray saw financial indebtedness as a basis for sympathetic relations in a social order that no longer enshrined classical republican virtue. Beginning with the first colonial currency issue in 1690 and concluding with the advent of national banking at the end of the eighteenth century, this book covers both colonial and early national experience and so uses the term *American* in both its pre- and post-1776 senses. Although the Revolutionary War marks an important turning point for this study, many of the intellectual trajectories are continuous over the century: colonial experience lay much of the groundwork for economic thinking in the revolutionary and early national eras.

Admittedly, this book is lopsided in its focus on commercially oriented writers. But I have felt justified in this emphasis because there has not been a full account of how these writers responded to, and participated in, the dramatic financial changes of the eighteenth century. Attending to this alternative view of public debt can change the way we understand the literary efforts of many familiar early American writers. In Cotton Mather's *Life of Phips,* for example, the tale of the colonial governor's search for sunken Spanish treasure does not, as readers have assumed, simply sanction self-interest and economic mobility. Rather, the story of the treasure hunt creates an allegory for governmental speculation and uses a Calvinist paradigm to tell a cautionary tale about the devastating communal effects of financial despair. Mather's eventual inclusion of this biography in his epic jeremiad, *Magnalia Christi Americana* (1702), has traditionally been understood as a forced attempt to rationalize the secularization of his colony. I would argue, however, that Mather saw economic speculation as inseparable from civic, moral, and even spiritual considerations.

This and other literary texts of the period often warrant rereading because one's critical vocabulary can shift once the economic preoccupations of early Americans are made more legible. Franklin's autobiography attempts to "represent" America not by recreating a putative ordinary experience but, rather, by acting as a "representative" on behalf of the new nation's fiscal experiments and vouching in writing for the promise of American speculations. In Royall Tyler's drama *The Contrast* "performance" is not simply a spectacle or charade but also a demonstrable action that fulfills a financial obligation and, in turn, further enhances one's credibility. And, while *sympathy* often refers in this literature to an affective or altruistic response to another's sufferings, it can also refer, in Alexander Hamilton's sense of the term, to a state in which one's economic interest is simply inseparable from another's.

A historicist reading of these works requires understanding how financial speculation was seen as essential to immigration, settlement, and national independence. A culture of speculation allowed for a more sanguine, one might say naive, view of capitalism's promise to promote simultaneously both individual opportunity and communal cohesion. When Franklin toured the factories of England, he was appalled by their conditions but confident that industrialism of that scale would never need to take hold in the abundant New

World. Defenders of speculation believed that stock-jobbing was a corruption of an otherwise valid business practice. And many hoped American slavery—the most sinister form of speculation, which saw human bodies as financial investments—would just disappear over time. Eighteenth-century advocates were certainly accused of being capricious or acting out of self-interest, but this accusation was countered by a rhetoric that emphasized the collective and publicly beneficial nature of public credit schemes.

This reading also requires understanding how early Americans thought about themselves *as Americans,* distinct from Europeans—even at a time when the term *American* designated a subset of English identity. The economic thinking of these writers was grounded in European thought, and yet these writers firmly believed that inhabitants of a colony within a mercantilist system understood debt differently from those living at the center of an empire. They considered the New World a peculiarly fertile ground for financial venture and a place that would attract those looking to use debt to exceed the limits of their own capital. They maintained that the American Revolution required novel financial measures. And, in the aftermath of political independence, they believed faith in public credit and the bonds between debtors and creditors would be all the more necessary—and all the more fragile—in a nation so in need of consolidation.

In tracing out points of contact between literary and economic culture, this book sharpens our sense of how early American writers perceived the civic function of language and literature in their communities. In *The Letters of the Republic* Michael Warner articulated what readers have long sensed about this body of writing: that post-Romantic conceptions of the literary do little to illuminate the writings of a community fully engaged in fighting an empire or creating a new government. *Literature* for eighteenth-century Americans meant writing and knowledge that was socially distributable, valued for its public utility rather than for what might be privately consumed or artistically appreciated. This public utility or civic capacity of early American literature was made palpable by economic experience. Writers saw their literary productions as potential economic interventions. They believed they could shape readers' perception of the state's credibility and thus affect the willingness of sellers to credit paper currency. They believed they could promote faith in the national debt or beseech creditors to act compassionately in hard economic times. Treatises, sermons, poems, novels, drama, and biography all worked to vindicate public debts by vouching for the promise of the community and its monetary experiments.

In my analysis terms such as *speculation* and *imagination* register the difference between this concept of literature and the one that would replace it in the following century. In the writing I examine, financial speculation is a cerebral operation. Like speculative thought in general, it is conjectural and formulated in the abstract (anticipating something yet to occur). Such speculation, however, is usually not personally creative or aesthetic. Consider, for example, this proclamation by one Massachusetts colonist, John Wise, in 1721: "*And I cannot think, but you will allow, so far as Imagination is necessary in raising the Glory, and value of a thing, the People of this Province are as capable as any other:* For that certainly we carry as much of the *Lapis Aurificus* or *Philosophers Stone* in our heads, and can turn other matter into Silver or Gold by the Power of thought as soon as any other People, or else I must own I have not yet Learnt the Character of my Country."[5] While Wise playfully compares the human head to the "philosopher's stone" of lore, the "power of thought" he describes is not transformative (or alchemical) so much as circumscribed by what he knows already and expects is possible in the future. That is, the colonists are "imaginative" not because they create a wholly new source of value but because they can form a mental concept of the traditional specie that is still forthcoming from the government. This imagination is a publicly serviceable procedure. It is not the indulgent "fancy" of a "castle-builder" who scorns "to be beholden to the Earth for a Foundation" in Richard Steele's *Spectator* 167.[6] But nor is it the celebrated castle building that is the hallmark of the creative mind in Henry David Thoreau's *Walden*. Neither frivolous fancy nor Romantic creativity, this mental substitution of paper for metal is "necessary" rather than inspired, collective rather than personal, and useful rather than aesthetic.

When in 1690 the Massachusetts legislature became the first government in the Western world to issue a paper money, private paper credit instruments circulated widely in European and imperial communities, usually in the form of promissory notes (personal promises to pay off a debt) and bills of exchange (instruments, akin to our modern-day personal checks, which drew from a third-party credit source). While the Massachusetts paper money, or "bills of credit," grew out of these already established private instruments, they were different in that they bore the promise of the government itself. Unlike individuals or private companies, the government could emit bills by fiat, backing them by legislative order rather than metal reserves and, in effect, creating value out of print itself. In 1694 the Bank of England would start loaning banknotes, but this institution, which provided the model for Alexander Hamilton's Bank of the United States a century later, was capitalized by private subscription, and its instruments were to be convertible at will for metal coins. In an effort to keep these distinctions in place, I have chosen to use the term *paper money* only to refer to government-issued bills of credit and not to banknotes, though both paper money and banknotes were forms of "paper currency" which functioned as exchange media.

The private commercial paper long in use by the time of the first Massachusetts issue had already given rise to a distinction between *cambia minutum* (exchange by coins or, literally, "pieces") and *cambia per litteras* (exchange by accounting or, literally, "writing"). From its inception, moreover, this distinction had had an ontological analog: metal was considered "real" and paper "imaginary."[7] What the Massachusetts bills threatened, in effect, was a potential erasure of this classic distinction and the creation of paper that acted *as money itself,* an imaginary that staked a claim to the real. The Princeton minister John Witherspoon wrote that "signs inconceivably facilitate commerce," and he marveled that people could "put any value [they] please in an obligation written on a few inches of paper, and can send it over the world itself at very little expence," but he drew the line at any paper instrument that was not readily convertible and used "the sign [of paper] separately from the standard [of coinage]." James Madison supported federal banking but believed "nothing but evil" would spring from "imaginary money." Noah Webster insisted that no paper "should circulate in a commercial country, which is not a representativ of ready cash." John Adams declared that every dollar issued beyond the exact quantity of gold and silver in the vaults represented nothing and was, therefore, "a cheat upon somebody."[8]

This distinction between representing and constituting money is not one with which buyers and sellers currently concern themselves. Americans today have no expectations that their paper money will ever be converted to metal or any other valuable commodity. Since 1971, when Richard Nixon officially severed all U.S. ties to a gold standard, no country in the world has used a commodity-based unit of currency. Before that year the U.S. and colonial governments had certainly suspended the specie standard, but these episodes were expected to be temporary. For Americans today *cash* only ever refers to paper greenbacks and metal coins of negligible material value, and *credit* refers to plastic credit and debit cards, personal checks, and layaway plans. But, for colonial and early national Americans, *cash* (like *money*) meant metal coins, and paper credit instruments were promises of forthcoming cash. Paper instruments usually circulated side by side with various kinds of foreign coins, and their value tended to suffer in the comparison.

Today buyers and sellers have other worries—stock market crashes, inflation, a weakened dollar overseas—but they do not worry that their greenbacks will be accepted only at a discount or rejected altogether. They do not worry that redemption might not occur or that the government will, as it did in eighteenth-century Massachusetts, revalue the bills already in circulation, replacing the "old tenor" of the original issue with the "new tenor" of its depreciated value and thereby reducing the redeemable amount (if, as often happened, an issue was being revalued a second time, the terms *old, middle,* and *new* would be used). Depreciation today is reflected in the cost of consumer goods: a dollar is still worth a dollar, but it buys less when prices go up. This shift is troubling in its own ways, but it does not appear, at least, that the government has suddenly changed the purport, or "tenor," of its words.

Eighteenth-century Americans, like their European counterparts, cared deeply about the moral and representational implications of their own monetary experiments. Yet the crucial distinction between constitutive and representative instruments could, in practice, be difficult or even impossible to discern because the stipulations and expectations with which instruments were issued varied markedly. The very terms I am using to draw this distinction are not easily separable. One might characterize bills issued with no collateral as an attempt to constitute or create value through legislation, but one might argue alternatively, as advocates did, that bills issued without collateral simply represent a value that does not exist for the moment but will (or at least could) sometime in the future. In other words, whether or not an instrument is convertible could depend on *when* one tries to convert it.

Perhaps it is safest to say that none of these instruments was intended to be irredeemable as they are today. Rather, those instruments not *immediately* redeemable or convertible at will for some kind of commodity (gold, silver, tobacco) were regularly criticized as air castles, alchemy, shadows, and deceit—particularly because even honest intentions did not always ensure full-scale redemption in the end. Perhaps all this sounds like philosophical hairsplitting, but it is important to emphasize how easily the monetary experiments gave rise to complex debates about the nature of reality, value, and representation. All of the writers I examine in this book maintained a traditional concept of reference and expected that monetary promises be based on a forthcoming tangible value: paper provided a less costly medium but was not itself a source of wealth. But these same writers also understood value as something provisional which might require time, public faith, and even the indulgence of creditors to materialize.

This notion of a scripted value not based on ready convertibility to metal was the culmination of earlier European experiences with coinage. Throughout the seventeenth century the continued acceptance of debased coins at face value undermined the notion that money derived its worth from either commodity value or legal designation, demonstrating, instead, the power of buyers and sellers to negotiate value in the act of exchange. When quantities sank low, coins, valued for what they could purchase, were esteemed at more than face value; when quantities rose, the same coins were undervalued.[9] These and other experiences prompted much debate between metallists, such as John Locke and David Hume, who maintained that money must essentially consist of or be backed by a commodity, and cartalists, such as William Potter, John Law, and James Steuart, who concluded that paper substitutes were not only acceptable but could profitably stimulate the economy by expanding the money supply.[10] England's Recoinage Act of 1696, through which debased coins were reminted so that a pound sterling corresponded with a designated metallic weight, was certainly a triumph for hard-money advocates, but the fact that debased coins had long circulated on par with standard coins offered unmistakable proof that money's nominal or face value need not correspond to its purity in order to gain currency. This passing of debased coins, as well as the introduction of banknotes and paper money, marked an important milestone in what Marc Shell describes as the overarching trend in Western monetary history: the increasing disjunction between "face value (intellectual currency) and substantial value (material currency)."[11]

The coinage crises revealed the monetary symbolism at work long before the introduction of public paper money. Only with the earliest coins, Shell observes, did exchange value derive entirely from the coins' material substance. Once the politically authorized value of a coin's inscription was no longer synonymous with its weight and purity, a new concept of monetary value emerged. Those inscriptions, originally intended only to provide official assurance of a coin's weight and purity, came to invest the coin with value itself. In the history of English coinage, for example, the "pound" originally designated a unit of weight but eventually became an imaginary unit of value completely detached from any material measurement. Therefore, "one pound sterling" in current coin was no longer the equivalent of a pound of silver plate. The "intellectual currency" invested by inscription, as Shell describes it, was always understood to operate symbolically, representing material substance as words represent things, and, as the case of the English pound indicates, the monetary symbol could easily become detached from its originally intended referent. (It is worth emphasizing as well that even the earliest coins, for which face and nominal value were matched, operated symbolically. While barter entails the exchange of goods for goods, a commercial transaction entails the exchange of goods for a designated medium of recognized purchasing power. The seller who receives the medium can then purchase what he or she desires. This medium, then, is not in itself the object sought and so assumes a symbolic role by standing in temporarily for the desired goods.)

What distinguished paper money from other forms of monetary symbolism, however, was the complete detachment of symbol and referent. Although a coin of precious metal operated within a symbolic economy, it was always simultaneously a commodity. Gold and silver were widely valued for their preciousness, and so, though coins did fluctuate in value according to market dictates, they always obtained acceptability and purchasing power (even the debased coin obtained a material value, albeit sometimes less than its inscribed denomination). Paper instruments, on the other hand, were of negligible commodity value; as promises of forthcoming metal specie, they were only a medium and wholly symbolic.

A modern literary critic's instincts might suggest that this financial mechanism provokes a crisis of language. Although this book is not primarily concerned with analogies between money and language but, rather, with a historicist reading of literature, it is worth stressing that paper money, viewed from a poststructuralist perspective, dramatizes transhistorically how all language works—as a symbolic system that can never fully close the gap between representation and reality.[12] In this light it is easy to imagine that writers would be unsettled by the new monetary mechanisms or be reluctant to relinquish the idea of a credit instrument that is itself a commodity or at least represents a commodity that can be produced at will. The critic's instinct would be confirmed, moreover, by one of the best-known commentaries on language and money in American literature. In his first book, *Nature* (1836), Ralph Waldo Emerson condemned unbacked paper currency as a moral corruption but also deployed it as a metaphor for all human words that have been detached from their origins in nature. Although it is beyond the chronological scope of my own study, Emerson's chapter on "Language" is worth quoting here, for it speaks of the very crisis that has been the focus of literary critics' work on money and language:

The corruption of man is followed by the corruption of language. When the simplicity of character and the sovereignty of ideas is broken up by the prevalence of secondary desires—the desire of riches, of pleasure, of power, and of praise—and duplicity and falsehood take place of simplicity and truth, the power over nature as an interpreter of the will is in a degree lost; new imagery ceases to be created, and old words are perverted to stand for things which are not; a paper currency is employed, when there is no bullion in the vaults. In due time the fraud is manifest, and words lose all power to stimulate the understanding or the affections.[13]

Later in his career Emerson's hostility toward the market would soften, and he would posit a much more dynamic concept of language, but here in 1836 the banknote captures his dismay over words that have detached from their original referent in the natural world. The publication of *Nature* coincided with the start of the Free Banking Era, three volatile decades during which unregulated "wildcat" banks filled the void left by Andrew Jackson's dismantling of the Second Bank of the United States. Although Emerson's concern is language, his banking metaphor, formulated during protracted bank wars, gold standard debates, and financial crises, also reveals much about his economic views. Currency, by implication, is a linguistic fraud that perverts the natural correspondence between "thought" and its "proper symbol."[14]

Emerson probably has in mind the hodgepodge of banknotes issued by state-chartered institutions and not federal notes or federal paper money (the latter had been outlawed by the Constitution and, but for a brief time during the War of 1812, would not be issued again until the financial crisis of the Civil War). Like earlier critics of paper money and national banking, however, he condemns the instrument for representing something that does not currently exist: a bullion that is not in the vaults.[15] The instrument is also analogous to a worn verbal cliché, which has, according to Emerson, lost "all power to stimulate the understanding or the affections."[16] The cliché continues to be circulated and accepted, despite the fact that it has been truncated or the original meaning lost over time: when, for example, "happy as a clam at high tide" is shortened to "happy as a clam," it means something not because the shortened expression is intelligible (why are clams necessarily happier than other creatures?) but simply because it has gained currency as a phrase. A debased coin or a paper instrument also continues to circulate simply because it has gained acceptance among buyers and sellers—and not because it obtains value in any way that is tangible or legitimate for Emerson.

If readers made assumptions about eighteenth-century economic thought based on Emerson's *Nature*, they would not be entirely wrong. *The Anarchiad* (1786–1787), a mock-epic poem published serially by the Connecticut Wits (David Humphreys, Joel Barlow, John Trumbull, and Lemuel Hopkins) in the aftermath of Shays's Rebellion, launches a similar attack on the use of legal language to transform paper into a medium of exchange. This celebrated political satire attacked rural supporters of paper money and called for a new constitution and stronger federal government equipped to regulate the nation's finances. Modeled, in part, after Alexander Pope's mock-epic *The Dunciad*, the poem offers a fiscal warning of mythic proportions which forebodes a reign of allegorical tyrants, such as Chaos, Night, and Anarch, if the rage for paper money is not curtailed. *The Anarchiad* depicts paper advocates as duplicitous upstarts, but equally villainous are the local courts that have mandated the acceptance of devalued currency at face value. In an apostrophe to paper instruments Anarch revels wickedly in the transformative power of legal language:

> Fair from the Gen'ral Court's unpardon'd sin,
> Ap'st thou the gold Peruvian mines within;
> Wak'd to new life, by my creative power,
> The press thy mint, and dunghill rags thy ore.

Anarch's constitutive "creative power" entails a licentious use of law and letters alike. While the press transforms toilet rags into money, legal tender laws render "fair" the "unpardon'd sin" of roguery and turn debtor crews into "licens'd villains": "Their ears, though rogues and counterfeiters lose, / No legal robber fears the gallows noose."[17] That such instruments "ape" gold—the verb connoting a clumsy imitation of a social better—suggests again that paper is mere fakery and also the instrument of provincials on the make.

"Self-taught" and "unletter'd," advocates of paper money are said to pervert meaning for the sake of their own social climbing. The double-layered allusion to Pope and Milton's *Paradise Lost* also reinforces the satire's larger concerns that paper money violates a putative linguistic integrity. In a passage borrowed directly from the fourth and final book of *The Dunciad*, Chaos speaks an "uncreating" word that reverses the genesis of the "new-born state":

> Thy constitution, Chaos, is restor'd;
> Law sinks before thy uncreating word;
> Thy hand unbars th'unfathom'd gulf of fate,
> And deep in darkness 'whelms the new-born state.[18]

In Pope's satire the speaker laments the death of Logos: while God's creating Word called forth the world and wrought coherence out of chaos in Genesis, words in Pope's England have only "uncreating" powers. Pope's satiric lament, based on a similarly uncreating act by Milton's Chaos, was aimed at London's deteriorating educational and literary institutions.[19] The satire of *The Anarchiad* predicts that paper credit schemes in the United States will bring a similar kind of linguistic apocalypse. Because the very genesis of the newborn state of the United States, like God's creation of the world, was enacted through words, such corruption would be particularly devastating to a nation so conceived in language. Chaos has been lamentably restored, the stanza suggests, and only the reversal of his uncreation, by way of a legitimate restoration of law and letters through a national Constitution, will bring an end to darkness.[20]

Like Emerson, the Connecticut Wits decry the detachment of credit instrument from bullion and, more generally, the detachment of the linguistic sign from any substantial referent. I have lingered over these examples because this extrication of money from material backing—if only temporarily—was actually a key advantage in the eyes of advocates. The experience of the coinage crises in the 1690s demonstrated how monetary symbols might retain value despite a detachment of face value from collateral, but Law, Steuart, and classical economists Adam Smith and David Ricardo went one step farther in arguing that this detachment could actually fuel economic expansion.

In his famous critique of mercantilist banking in *The Wealth of Nations* Smith explained this link between inconvertibility and economic expansion. He argued that a bank, rather than maintain a one-to-one ratio between metal reserves and circulating banknotes, could use a one-to-four or one-to-five ratio, keeping on hand only enough reserves to meet redemption needs and then reinvesting the rest for additional profit. Complete convertibility, he emphasized, was actually the mark of a stagnant economy, and, if banks could free up metal languishing as "dead stock" in the vaults, that money could do double duty in circulation (Smith's concept of "multiplicative banking," which Steuart had proposed a decade earlier, was essentially that of modern-day banking, in which the entirety of deposits are not kept in house but reloaned with interest). "By substituting paper in the room of a great part of this gold and silver," Smith wrote, a nation could "convert a great part of this dead stock into active and productive stock."[21] Or, as Benjamin Franklin had put it earlier in 1729, "Money which otherwise would have lain dead in [bankers'] Hands, is made to circulate again thereby among the People: And thus the Running Cash of the Nation is as it were doubled."[22] While Smith insisted that banknotes have some measure of backing and be convertible on demand (he did not, like Franklin, advocate paper currency that was issued without reserves), he maintained that a measure of inconvertibility could facilitate growth.[23]

This paradigm of multiplicative banking offered a way to exceed the limits of existing capital, and limited capital was the problem by which early American communities defined themselves. Public credit schemes were largely understood as a "necessity" in the specific eighteenth-century sense of the term: a measure prompted by pressing economic constraints and a paucity of monetary options. In early American communities that lacked the capital and infrastructures of Europe, borrowing was unavoidable, and writers understood that projects such as immigration, community building, and the Revolutionary War itself were made possible by risk taking. Paper instruments were needed to supplement dwindling coinage supplies, provide start-up loans, and foster colonial and national self-sufficiency. Poor Richard may have warned that "he that goes a borrowing goes a sorrowing," but he directed that warning to those who sought to buy luxuries, or "superfluities," on credit.[24] Franklin's autobiography, on the other hand, teaches the importance of responsible borrowing for both the individual and nation lacking start-up capital (not enough attention has been paid to the way the literature of this period distinguishes between reckless and prudent forms of borrowing). At the age of twenty-three, during his own rise on credit, Franklin wrote of the "nature and necessity" of a paper currency in his adopted colony of Pennsylvania, emphasizing that borrowing was not necessarily the indulgence of the profligate but a legitimate tool for individuals and communities working to overcome economic restrictions.

Not everyone so readily distinguished, as Franklin did, "superfluous" and "necessary" uses of credit. As the socioeconomic stereotypes of *The Anarchiad* make clear, what credit advocates saw as a necessary means of exceeding economic limitations—or of simply subsistence—their opponents might see as overreaching. To the latter, financial castle building could threaten deeply held values by removing incentives for manual labor and failing to recognize the solidity of land-based wealth. Railing against land speculation and lottery tickets in 1797, one anonymous essayist wrote: "If thou hast a wife and children, who depend on thy daily labour for their support, read only half the history of poor Sancho's disappointments, and thou wilt never leave thy family to go in search of adventures, or quit the honourable post of honest industry from the delusive hope of becomeing a governour. Thy little farm is of more consequence to thee than a million acres of the new emission of counterfeit land; and a cottage in the woods is much better than a castle in the air."[25] According to this essay, the pragmatic Sancho of the first book of *Don Quixote* provides the most reliable model for the venturesome man. The writer warns the dreamer not to lose everything in search of wealth and status—not necessarily bad advice—but does not contemplate less reckless forms of castle building or their usefulness to those who have not even the means to possess a little farm.

Still, to describe such debt as "necessity" tells only part of the story, for it was also understood not as a stopgap measure for those with limited cash but as a government's tool for long-term economic growth. What many Americans today might share with their eighteenth-century counterparts is the sense that any kind of national debt ideally ought not to exist. Until recently, a digital National Debt Clock ticked away in midtown Manhattan, frightening passersby with estimations of a multitrillion-dollar debt and the share each American family bears of this burden, and politicians use the relative size of the national debt to assess the state of the union. But Hamilton, the architect of U.S. national finance and a very different kind of credit advocate than the Shaysite, called a well-managed national debt a "national blessing," and the accumulation of debt has been used strategically by the U.S. government ever since.[26] Although the mark of insufficient capital, public credit could be a tool for expansion rather than mere survival; in addition, well-executed borrowing might increase the government's credit rating in the eyes of citizens and other governments—and so increase chances of borrowing again in the future. Hamilton stressed that the debt not be "excessive" (and he would certainly consider today's debt excessive), but the fact that he would insist that some measure of debt be intentionally maintained was surprising in his time and, for the economic layperson, perhaps still so today. Hamilton, who worked as a child for a struggling family business and then became a clerk in a St. Croix trading company around the age of twelve, hardly represented all of his generation. His was a commercial mindset that threatened the agrarian values his opponents enshrined, but his financial plan for the new United States nevertheless institutionalized a concept of debt which found consistent expression in literary and intellectual circles.

Many writers I examine also perceived the instability of credit schemes and their reliance on popular opinion as a communal resource. Witherspoon warned that the "essential defect" of monetary signs was their dependence "ultimately on the faith or credit of the persons using or answerable for them," and he worried that paper signs not secured by property were insufficiently protected against risk.[27] Others, however, believed that the reliance on faith, rather than material backing, could potentially confirm governmental authority. If credit was generally the trust one placed in a person's integrity and commercial credit was the trust one placed in a person's ability and willingness to meet financial obligations, *public* credit was the trust one placed in a government's ability and willingness to do so. What initiated public credit was a debt, and hence a limitation, on the government's part—public money and banknotes were often referred to as "public securities" because they represent a pledge or surety of future payment—but public credit was nevertheless an expression of confidence in the government's reliability. The greater a government's public credit, the more it could borrow and borrow on advantageous terms. In actuality many people accepted the terms of public borrowing only grudgingly because they had no choice, especially when the acceptance of currency was mandated by legal tender laws, but in the era's writing the sustained circulation of securities nevertheless figures as a testament to the colony's or nation's viability.[28]

The instability of unbacked currency could also intertwine personal and civic interests in beneficial ways. By making personal assets contingent on the larger economy, public credit structures invested people financially and emotionally in their community's welfare. This concept of communal investment took different forms and could accommodate radically opposed economic philosophies.

On the one hand, those who understood the market as driven by profit motives and competition maintained that these schemes could benefit the community. If an individual's personal assets were tied to the fate of the market, that individual would have an incentive to care about the larger community and the success of its credit instruments. Public credit structures could harness self-interest for communal purposes, and for this reason, Hamilton declared, a national debt would be the "cement of our union."[29] On the other hand, those who advocated the kind of "moral economy" E. P. Thompson describes, in which civic benefit is thought to derive from the suppression of self-interest, believed that governmental credit schemes bestowed on individuals the responsibility of upholding the credit of their communities. Instead of commodity backing, paper instruments relied on governmental sanction and the faith of buyers and sellers, and this faith was itself considered an expression of public-spiritedness. Individuals who refused to accept paper money were often publicly denounced as enemies of the community, as when Philadelphia's Committee of Inspection and Observation demanded in 1776 that Thomas Rogers and Joseph Sermon be "precluded from all trade or intercourse" for refusing wartime bills.[30] In this episode wartime exigency took precedence over free trade, making it just one of many instances when sellers were reprimanded for acting according to their own interests.

Marx would say that Rogers and Sermon were guilty of violating the "*credo* of capital"—the blind faith in a nation's credit machinery. As Marx would have predicted, the writers here created and endorsed various creeds to contend with the unpredictable and often volatile economic climate of their time. Paper credit schemes defined the boundaries of a community—quite literally because, unlike metal, paper was not universally accepted and often could only circulate where it was originally issued—but they also defined a community by soliciting, and even exacting, commitment. Sometimes this commitment was linked explicitly to religious faith, as in the case of Cotton Mather's Puritan society: not surprisingly, the jeremiad Sacvan Bercovitch has described could be used to chastise colonists for their foundering financial faith and simultaneously stir them to action. Sometimes this commitment was part of the more general civic religion we associate with a figure like Benjamin Franklin. Sometimes this credo expressed a faith in human benevolence: more of a bystander than public advocate of public debt, Judith Sargent Murray looked optimistically for a way to find social connections in webs of financial obligation. While the works of these and other writers reflect a consistently Anglo-American perspective, they also indicate the range of promises that credit systems held out to people of various regions, philosophies, and socioeconomic backgrounds. But they do much more than offer a glimpse of early Americans' views of credit, for they tell us something about how these writers understood the civic function of their literary efforts. Theirs is a literature that attempts to secure the commonwealth—economically but also socially—in times of profound insecurity.

Part One / New World Ventures

> My Name *Old Tenor* is, 'tis true, I own,
> And by that Name have many Years been known.
> *But what alas! is all this Stir and Noise!*
> *Have I not been quite just unto your Cause?*
> Indeed I've help'd the *Poor Man* in Distress,
> And eas'd the *Widow* and the *Fatherless.*
> I've built you Houses, for to keep you warm,
> And bought you Cattle for to plow your Land.
> When in Distress, a helping Hand I've been,
> And purchas'd Things to carry you to your End.
> JOSEPH GREEN, "THE *DYING SPEECH* OF OLD TENOR," 1750

> Who can desire more content, that hath small means; or but only his merit to advance his fortune, than to tread, and plant that ground he hath purchased by the hazard of his life?
> JOHN SMITH, *DESCRIPTION OF NEW ENGLAND*, 1616

> This indented Bill of Two Shillings & Six Pence shall pass Current for the Sum herein mentioned in all Payments according to the Directions of an Act of Assembly of Maryland.
> MARYLAND BILL OF CREDIT, ISSUED 1733

When the colony of Massachusetts began retiring its bills of credit on March 31, 1750, under order from British Parliament, the printer Joseph Green issued a ballad broadside applauding the role those bills had played in six decades of colonial settlement. Green's "Dying Speech of Old Tenor," sung by an anthropomorphized paper bill, reminds colonists that bills of credit provided debtor relief, helped fight their wars, built homes, and put coats on their backs. While the ballad admits that the value of these bills was inflated and manipulated to serve "the worst of Mortals," it also insists that the benefits made those risks worthwhile.

Like Green, the New England and Chesapeake writers with which I begin this book imagined colonial bills of credit to be hardworking and productive. The benefits that accrued from public debt, however, were social as well as economic. In Massachusetts Cotton Mather and some of his fellow Puritans hoped that a paper money reliant on public opinion would exact renewed commitment to the New England way. In Maryland and Virginia writers urged their colony to replace tobacco money with paper money, thus preserving nature's bounty but also fostering an increasingly literate republic of letters in which citizens could think abstractly and use writing, rather than tangible materials, as their medium of trade. Colonial writers in both regions worked to project an economic future but also to imagine a new civil order.

What these different writers shared was a tendency to see the colonies' economic ventures as the product of New World experience. While each writer wrote with his particular regional concerns in mind, all viewed public credit experiments from the perspective of one living at the edge of an empire. It was from this colonial perspective that they conceptualized not only the economic potential of their communities but also the constraints placed upon that potential by British trade regulations.

In the program of British mercantilism the North American colonies were repositories of raw materials as well as a market for England's manufactured goods. Through this system England sought to accumulate a more favorable balance of trade, the settlement of which would require the shipment of metal specie from colony to metropolis. In response to this policy, colonial governments looked to paper as a plentiful medium of exchange that might increase commercial fluidity, stimulate trade, and reduce the need for inconvenient forms of barter. The claim that mercantilist policy did in fact drain away specie was roundly rejected by many opponents of paper money (and continues to be disputed by historians today); nevertheless, the era's pamphleteers frequently depict a colonial economy sapped of its monetary lifeblood with each shipment of specie to England. "The blood and vital Spirits of the Body-politick, (I mean the Medium of Exchange)," one colonist proclaimed in 1720, "is so near exhausted as portends a *Certain, & Speedy* dissolution."[1]

To cope with their chronic shortage of monetary media, colonists relied on barter, IOUs, coins of European countries, and various experimental media— wampum in New England, tobacco in the South, playing cards in Canada—before turning to government-issued paper instruments. By the middle of the eighteenth century all nineteen British American colonies in continental North

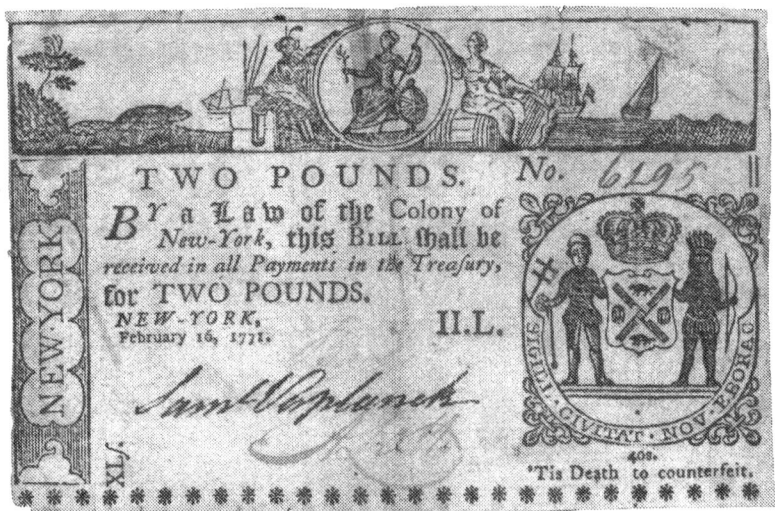

Figure 1. These bills, issued by colonial New York, align credit use with New World enterprise. In the 1771 bill (*top*) an American Indian (at center left) and the figure of Commerce (sitting on a shipping barrel to the right) flank the figure of Britannia; ships and a beaver symbolize the fur trade and transatlantic commerce. In the 1775 bill (*bottom*) the Latin motto proclaims, E PARVIS GRANDIS ACERVUS (A Massive Stack from Small Things). Contrary to those critics who denounced paper credit as worthless, the agricultural metaphor and image implies that it can spawn production. Courtesy of Special Collections, University of Notre Dame.

America, from Newfoundland to West Florida, had developed paper monetary systems of one kind or another.[2] For want of "Europe's long accumulations, especially of cash and other liquid capital," financial historian Bray Hammond writes, Americans had to "invent, improvise, covenant, and pretend" to find a way of financing enterprise.[3] When the British Parliament's "Bubble Acts," initially designed to curb speculative practices after the South Sea Bubble fiasco, were extended to British America at midcentury (resulting first in the 1750 retirement of bills in New England), proponents defended paper instruments as an invention spawned by colonial necessity.[4]

Europe's romance of the New World must only have reinforced this impulse to experiment with monetary media. Consider, for example, the shipwrecked Robinson Crusoe's response to finding "Thirty six Pounds value in Money" aboard his damaged ship: "I smil'd to my self at the Sight of this Money, O Drug! said I aloud, what art thou good for? Thou art not worth to me, no not the taking off of the Ground, one of those Knives is worth all this Heap; I have no Manner of use for thee, e'en remain where thou art, and go to the Bottom as a Creature whose Life is not worth saving."[5] Here the European finds himself extricated from the marketplace of the Old World, tempest-tossed onto a landscape that is strange and, as such, capable of repositioning familiar objects in new light. Encounters with non-European cultures expose him to different value systems (like many European explorers, Amerigo Vespucci marveled that seemingly trivial objects such as bird feathers, fish bones, and colored stones were prized by indigenous people, while the wealth that Europeans enjoy, "such as gold, jewels, pearls, and other riches, they hold as nothing").[6] Moreover, in a landscape lacking the technologies of home, the European needs to revalue materials according to how they might enhance his chances for physical survival: on Thomas More's isle of Utopia, a fictitious landscape inspired partly by Vespucci's narrative, iron emerges as the more useful—and thus valuable—metal, while gold and silver are revealed as substances long overvalued by "human folly."[7]

These moments of insight about value are often fleeting. While Crusoe does gain new appreciation for the utility of a knife, he cannot finally leave the coins behind—despite the fact that they will have no purchasing power on what he assumes is an unpopulated island (Vespucci assumes the locals' love for colored stones is naive, and it is never clear in More's often flippant account whether Utopia is utopian at all). Nevertheless, these encounters ask readers, if only momentarily, to question their attachment to familiar commercial media. To do so emphasized for the novel's reader that the New World might foster, and even require, new ways of conceptualizing money's operations. While colonists would not relinquish their attachment to metal, the new landscape had helped them appreciate other forms of value. There was no gold and silver on the eastern seaboard of North America, but surely corn, tobacco, beaver pelts, land, and entrepreneurial energy counted for something.

The process of immigration, and the narratives devised to represent that process, must also have reinforced for colonists the central role of indebtedness in the New World enterprise. Readers of North American settlement narratives and promotional tracts know how consistently they embrace the language of potential and opportunity. It is worth emphasizing, however, how often such narratives see debt as the first step to realizing that potential and acting on that opportunity. In William Bradford's account of the Plymouth colony the Puritans must brave rough waters and a hostile wilderness but also submit to an arrangement with London merchants in order to finance their journey. This business venture made possible a religious venture but kept the colony in debt for twenty-five years.[8]

In the next century J. Hector St. John de Crèvecoeur's "What Is an American?" would proclaim that the archetypal American not only forms "schemes of future prosperity" but is shrewd enough to understand that indebtedness might convert dreams into reality.[9] The turning point in the immigrant's efforts to acquire independence is his discovery that credit is a resource:

> He looks around and sees many a prosperous person who but a few years before was as poor as himself. This encourages him much; he begins to form some little scheme, the first, alas, he ever formed in his life. If he is wise, he thus spends two or three years, in which time he acquires knowledge, the use of tools, the modes of working the lands, felling trees, etc. This prepares the foundation of a good name, the most useful acquisition he can make. He is encouraged, he has gained friends; he is advised and directed; he feels bold, he purchases some land; he gives all the money he has brought over, as well as what he has earned, and trusts to the God of harvests for the discharge of the rest. His good name procures him credit.[10]

The momentum of Crèvecoeur's language, particularly in the string of declarative sentences ("he is advised," "he feels bold," "he purchases some land," etc.), conveys exuberance but also suggests that the immigrant follows a swift trajectory from poor European to American freeholder. It is entrepreneurial energy, captured in Crèvecoeur's verbs, that "prepares the foundation for a good name," and it is this good name that then "procures him credit." The money he has brought with him is not sufficient to cover all costs, and so credit makes possible his acquisition of a land deed, which, in turn, transforms him into "an American, Pennsylvanian, and English subject."[11] When Crèvecoeur concludes the essay with the story of Andrew the Hebridean, the realization of the immigrant's dream is illustrated with a line-by-line account of his assets totaling 640 Pennsylvania dollars. The debts have been discharged, and he has begun to save.

This entrepreneurial, risk-taking, and venturesome personality was not a New World invention. It was a European one characteristic of the commercial classes in those societies dating back hundreds of years, but the manifestation of entrepreneurial values in America was remarkable, as James Henretta writes, "in the extent of their influence and in the relative absence of a countervailing (if not predominant) ethic of aristocratic leisure and gentility."[12] What may have been limited to the bourgeois class in Europe was characteristic of a much wider range of experiences of white Europeans in the New World.

Potential is perhaps never so obvious as when it has been thwarted, and so some of the most compelling examples of this entrepreneurial paradigm appear in the narratives of those individuals for whom opportunity was either not available or only available in limited form. Recalling the origins of his renaming in a 1798 memoir, the former slave Venture Smith observes that the enslaved African is a means, and not an agent, of New World speculation because the slave purchaser makes an initial outlay of capital with the expectation that a lifetime of uncompensated labor will render his investment profitable: "I was bought on board by one Robertson Mumford, steward of said vessel, for four gallons of rum, and a piece of calico, and called VENTURE, on account of his having purchased me with his own private venture."[13] Although Smith's intellect and savvy eventually procure his freedom, the narrative replicates a New World success story with important differences. The hero of Smith's narrative—described in the editor's preface as "a Franklin and a Washington" destitute of education and broken by hardships—always reminds readers that the African cannot pursue enterprise as a white man could.[14] Entrepreneurial immobility is the gauge by which the slave's bondage is measured.

Similarly, the abolitionist rhetoric of Olaudah Equiano, another slave who undertook business speculations to emancipate himself, gains power through its variation on the New World paradigm. Like many slave narratives, Equiano's *Interesting Narrative* is structured around a model of bondage and redemption that is spiritual, financial, and physical. Equiano, who uses a speculator's vocabulary to describe his "projects" and "schemes" for freedom, begins with a start-up loan from his master (one-half puncheon of rum and one-half hogshead of sugar), earns petty cash as a trucker of goods, and eventually saves enough to purchase his freedom.[15] The narrative culminates in his business success and conversion to Christianity, but there is one crucial difference between Equiano's enterprise and that of the Hebridean immigrant or indentured servant. Unlike Crèvecoeur's immigrant, Equiano cannot assume that his debts can be easily tallied and discharged. He borrows to launch a business enterprise, but, even once he has made profits and paid back the loan, buying out the bondage of slavery itself remains a matter of his master's discretion. New World chattel slavery was distinct from prior forms of slavery in its construction of bondage as an inherited and *permanent* condition. After much struggle Equiano is finally granted the opportunity to purchase his freedom, and yet such a purchase would have been unthinkable for most of the patriarchal planters in the southern colonies. Rhys Isaac's remarkable study of eighteenth-century Virginia indicates the extent to which this planter's status rested on the idea that the slave's bondage was not redeemable by any quantifiable amount of money. The notion of disbursement would have undermined the planter's sense of independence because it implied that lower-status individuals could discharge their obligations by mere payment. This slaveholding mentality would preclude any possibility of a slave undertaking and paying off a quantifiable amount of debt.[16]

That the slave, the most unlikely of figures to benefit from Atlantic opportunity, could construct a biography around this model of enterprise illustrates how powerful and pervasive was the concept of *potential* in narrating New World experience. The importance of potentiality cannot be overemphasized. Cotton Mather thought his colony had strayed from the mission of its founders but still believed in the prospect of its renewal. He believed the colony's collective debts might inspire this renewal on economic as well as moral and civic fronts. Writers in the Chesapeake, in contrast, were troubled not by declensional fears but by the still inchoate nature of their frontier communities. They hoped to realize for the first time the region's economic, cultural, and literary promise, and they saw paper money as the investment necessary for the task.

CHAPTER ONE

Crisis and Faith in the Puritan Society

Cotton Mather envisioned a New England economic community governed by the Golden Rule rather than the quest for gold. He believed—as John Winthrop and his grandfather John Cotton had—that individuals could be bound together through ties of financial obligation, and he wondered if public paper finance could help foster these communal bonds. In unprecedented ways paper bills of credit drew people into a tangled web of mutual obligations through which one person's default or refusal of credit might trigger a string of repercussions for the rest of the exchange community. In addition to providing much needed funding, these bills could potentially benefit the commonwealth by making individual interests inseparable from the welfare of the larger economy.

Mather's economic vision was born of declensional fears. He believed the community's backsliding had begun when the Puritan virtues of industry, frugality, and enterprise spawned widespread prosperity shortly after the first migration. While this wealth was not in itself wrong, there was no way to ensure that it would not subsequently give rise to self-interest and divisiveness. New England history, Mather wrote in *Magnalia Christi Americana,* had verified the "Old Observation" that, when religion begets prosperity, the daughter often destroys the mother.¹ Like the specifically American jeremiad Sacvan Bercovitch has detailed, Mather's call for a new kind of marketplace was lamenting but essentially optimistic about the community's moral and spiritual potential. The rhetoric of public credit lent itself to his conjunction of self-chastisement and renewal.

Mather explicitly outlined his hopes for religious, social, and economic renewal in *Theopolis Americana, Lex Mercatoria, Some Considerations on the Bills of Credit*, and other essays. But his biography of William Phips, the colonial governor whose tenure coincided with the first issue of Massachusetts paper bills, dramatizes in literary fashion how economic and religious faiths might bind a collective. The biography presents financial outcomes as providential dispensation and posits that ventures, like life in a predestinarian world, must be sustained by conviction. Readers have long viewed this tale as a story of Phips's entrepreneurial self-making, but it is also a story of economic commonwealth that applauds commitment to the colony's financial ventures.

Public Debt and the Theopolis Americana

In *Theopolis Americana* (1710), one of his best-known treatises on business ethics, Mather called for the establishment of an American economic community modeled after the City of God. In this theopolis mutual benefit would replace private gain. "The Street must have no *Dirty Ways of Dishonesty* in it," he wrote, and the dealings of a righteous buyer or seller were to be so above reproach that he might willingly make them as "Transparent" as "Glass."² In a sermon entitled *Lex Mercatoria* (1720) Mather insisted that a Christian "must rejoyce in the Prosperity of his Neighbour" and adhere to the following code: "I am so to Deal with another man, that the man with whom I deal may be benefited as well as myself."³

The reciprocity Mather imagined was based on a binding relationship between parties in the act of exchange. In *A Man of his Word*, published in 1713 apparently in response to rampant loan defaults, he warns that breaking a vow to man is akin to breaking a vow to God. Christ's example, however, proved that poverty was "not a Thing always Forbidden of God," and Mather did not rule out the possibility of financial reprieve. Christianity demanded charity, and the New England project, as envisioned by Winthrop's "Model of Christian Charity," was to be governed by laws of mercy as well as justice. So, in another essay, *Fair Dealing between Debtor and Creditor* (1716), Mather advocated the following guideline: if a man is able to pay, he must; if he is unable to pay, his creditor must show compassion. While Mather worried over broken promises, he also believed that the merciful renegotiation of such promises helped strengthen communal ties.[4]

In this paradigm of godly capitalism public paper money might serve a singular role. The first such money was issued by the colony's cash-poor legislature to cover William Phips's costly and unsuccessful military expedition to Quebec in 1690. These bills of credit were IOUs, paid out to soldiers and military suppliers in lieu of metal cash. They were intended to bear interest and circulate only until their retirement. Yet, while bills specified a conversion date, after 1715 the colonial legislature often delayed calling them in for conversion or called them in only to redistribute them.[5] This and subsequent issues were intended to be short-term and redeemed for coinage within a few years, but, in fact, people usually redeemed them for tax credit instead. In 1712 the Massachusetts government declared bills to be "legal tender," thereby making it illegal for a creditor to refuse a bill for payment—and forcing colonists to contend with the notion of a currency justified by law rather than material backing.[6]

Over the course of his lifetime Mather's views on paper money were not entirely consistent, particularly because political loyalties, rather than economic principles, often governed his public statements on monetary policy.[7] It would be difficult to extract a single economic outlook from his writings because theory often gave way to unapologetic pragmatism. Mather nevertheless regularly praised money, particularly paper money, as the mark of a progressive society. In *The Christian Philosopher* (1721) he writes that men remain "brutish and savage" in societies where money has not been introduced.[8] And in *Some Considerations on the Bills of Credit Now Passing in New-England* (1690), an early treatise that coincides with the composition of *Phips*, he heralds paper money as an innovation made possible by literacy and education. Metal money is simply a symbol of exchange necessitated by an "ignorance of Writing and Arithmetick," and therefore the spread of writing and reckoning skills discharges metal money of any "Conceited necessity." An educated society, he argues, can just as easily settle debts through units of accounting.[9]

Such accounting offered the added advantage of abstracting monetary value, and Mather seems to have liked the idea that paper money dematerialized exchange and eliminated its grubbier aspects: "Do not *Bills* Transmit to Remote Parts," he asks rhetorically, "vast summs without the intervention of *Silver*?"[10] Mather also hoped that money made of paper rather than precious metal would discourage the love of mammon and hoarding (Gresham's Law held that the more materially valuable the monetary medium, the more likely it would be saved rather than recirculated). The anonymous author of a later pamphlet, *New News from* Robinson Cruso's *Island* (1720), made a similar case for paper money by associating hard-money advocacy with a love of gold which necessarily corrupts virtue: "Nature, in the production of Gold (as one ingeniously observes) seems to have presaged the *Misery of her Lovers,* by making the place where it grows barren of Herbs, Plants, &c. intimating thereby that in the Minds where the *Desire* of this Metal shall *take Birth,* no Sparks of *Honour* or *Vertue* shall remain."[11] Seeing the landscape itself as indication of a greater design, the writer argues that the love of gold crowds out human virtues just as the raw metal makes the land barren of vegetation.

In *Some Considerations* what appeals perhaps most to Mather about paper money is the fact that each issue will be, in effect, a collective debt: "*All the Inhabitants* of the Land, taken as one Body are the *Principals,* who Reap the *Benefits,* and must bear the *Burdens,* and are the Security in the *Publick Bonds.*"[12] According to a pamphlet by the Puritan John Wise, public credit structures had invested people with the responsibility of upholding them. "Out of Love to your Country, and the Civil Well-being of it," Wise wrote in 1721, "Ponder these things Wisely; and be perswaded to keep up your noble Fund." Through civic-minded deliberation—not solipsistic flights of fancy—people could render bills "as good as Money."[13]

As one might expect, opponents to paper money also invoked the "love of country" in their rhetoric. While advocates insisted that bills would foster a more charitable commonwealth by providing much needed debtor relief, opponents feared that paper money would facilitate corruption and allow debtors to take advantage of their creditors in inflationary times. In particular, the introduction of public paper money also provoked many colonists' concerns over the community's moral status. This money, emitted without metal backing to defray public expenditures, constituted a communal debt—a debt because it promised something the government did not, at the moment, have in its possession. Printed promises that were not immediately convertible seemed to stake false claims to value and cast doubt on the integrity of the government. Essentially a measure to buy time until the colony could procure funding, paper money also aggravated fears that the community was backsliding with each generation. Writing about the colony's debts, one anonymous pamphleteer proclaimed, "we had found an easy way of paying for them, and shuffling the Saddle off our own backs, on to our Children; when the Debt was to be paid, it was but raising so many Thousand Pounds to be paid in such Years to come."[14]

Despite these differences of opinion, both opponents and supporters of paper bills used the currency crises to resist laissez-faire economics and urge a return to an economy regulated for the common good. As Perry Miller noted long ago, writers on both sides of the debate couched their treatises in the form of a jeremiad.[15] Opponents called upon consumers to foster husbandry and resist importing foreign luxuries in order to help Massachusetts balance its trade deficit with the mother country.[16] Meanwhile, those who supported paper currency insisted that the bills *would* work once properly combined with economic restraint and self-sufficiency.

Opposition to public paper money focused on the practical matter of economic feasibility, but it also touched on concerns of a distinctly Puritan theological nature. When Wise wrote with amazement that "by the Power of Thought" alone the community could "conclude" the bills "to be as good yea better than [metal] money," he intended for paper bills to be a medium and not a source of value itself.[17] The minister Thomas Paine, however, accused Wise of investing mere paper with undue worth in ways analogous to the Catholic insistence that the wine and bread of Communion were substantially the body and blood of Christ. Although not an opponent of paper bills in general, Paine advocated a more conservative plan than the one proposed by Wise. Punning on his adversary's surname, Paine dismissed Wise's thinking as "the Product of a too exorbitant Fancy": "[Wise] will tell us that [the bills'] Credit may be kept up by the *power of a* Wise *Imagination,* pag.44. (Just like the Popish Doctrine of *Transubstantiation; Crede quod edes, et edes,* say they.) And we may with the same reason say of any other of our Affairs, *Believe that they are well, and they are and shall be so.*"[18] Paine's charge that Wise advocates a Popish alchemy is clearly informed by a Protestant poetic. He reminds his readers that the paper instrument only metaphorically stands in for, and does not become, the metal that is the basis of monetary value.

Credit schemes and currency of fluctuating value also touched a specifically predestinarian nerve. These financial mechanisms were consistent, in fact, with a larger uncertain world, as financial redemptions seemed as unknowable as spiritual redemptions. Max Weber's famous argument that Puritans looked to their own material blessings to discern whether they were saved or damned should not obscure the extent to which an illegible and volatile credit-based economy seemed only to withhold clues, offering no consolation to the individual looking to know the status of his or her soul.[19] An economy increasingly based on intangible and abstract forms of wealth, such as paper money, seemed to undermine many Puritans' search for answers.

This impact would have been most keenly felt by "preparationist" Puritans, who, as Janice Knight explains, considered conversion a gradual and always *provisional* process for which faith and worldly conduct might be relevant (as opposed to "spiritists," who insisted instead on God's immediate, unconditional, and knowable granting of grace). This preparationism, which was enshrined in Mather's *Magnalia Christi Americana* and ultimately came to represent Puritan orthodoxy in subsequent American historiography, generated the anxiety that Weber saw as the driving force behind Calvinist commercial energy. To the "preparationists," while nothing was proof positive of the grace of God, the lack of solvency was often the mark of sin. People fell into debt because they could not control their appetites for luxury or their desires to exceed their rank in a divinely ordained social order. For these people the attempt to discern outward manifestations of God's will was complicated, to say the least, by the advent of paper credit systems that increasingly redefined wealth as a function of appearance and perception. Insisting that credibility have a tangible, material basis, preparationists might have argued that indebted persons could rely on visible signs of wealth which were, in reality, empty. If people succeeded by manipulating their own credibility in the marketplace, rather than by sheer industry, even the identification of the reprobate—as those who lacked industry—was a difficult task.[20]

This is not to say that preparationists would necessarily have been opposed to public paper money but just that its mechanisms would have resonated with their own spiritual uncertainties. In fact, it is precisely because of its preparationist sensibilities that Mather's *Life of Phips* can envision an unstable public credit system that tests and demands commitment to the commonwealth in beneficial ways. Drawing from a traditional Puritan analogy between financial and spiritual redemption, Mather's biography solicits faith in the New England project by illustrating how despair—one not unlike religious despair—can devastate communal credit structures. It ultimately offers a lesson to assorted readers—readers of credit bills, readers of providential dispensation, and readers of the biography itself—on how to maintain faith in the face of unknowing.

Phips, Redemption, and the Recovery of Treasure

William Phips's military leadership and royal governorship coincided with a series of pivotal moments in Massachusetts history, including Indian wars, military ventures in Canada, the Crown's revocation of the colonial charter, the colony's overthrow of the Andros government, the Salem witchcraft trials, and, of course, the colony's first experiments with paper money. As a result of this timing and Phips's direct involvement in some of these episodes, the biography, first published separately in 1697 and included in the *Magnalia* in 1702, allows Mather both to memorialize an individual and to reflect more generally on the tumultuous events of the previous decade. Theories abound about why Mather would have seen fit to include an extensive biography of a backwoods fortune hunter in his ecclesiastical history, and some readers have speculated that the biography is Mather's justification of New England's secularization at the close of the seventeenth century and of his own family's close relationship with the Phips government.[21] Without dismissing these possibilities, my own reading of the biography suggests that Mather might also have imagined that *Phips* could address the colony's economic concerns in much the same way as his essays.

Built into this biography is the story of the colony's first paper money. Far from an incidental detail, this story helps establish Phips's civic-minded character and buttress the biography's call for public-spiritedness. Readers of *The Life of Phips* have largely focused on the biography's other financial venture, Phips's discovery of a Spanish shipwreck and almost forty thousand pounds of silver and gold. This feat, which brought knighthood, a private fortune, and the Massachusetts governorship to a man of obscure origins, has led Bercovitch and other readers to see the biography as a prototypical "New World success story."[22] It is necessary, however, to attend to the way Mather tells of *two* financial ventures in this biography: Phips's oceanic treasure search but also the colony's speculative paper money.

Both are speculative ventures that could enrich or impoverish, and both require the ongoing faith of those involved in order to keep the project afloat. The impatient sailors, "weary of their unsuccessful Enterprize," succumb to temptations of mutiny and piracy and, as a result, almost bring down the ship.[23] Likewise, a lack of faith in paper bills by soldiers and civilians threatens to dismantle the colony's financial structure. Fear of imminent ruin becomes a self-fulfilling prophecy, as panic itself has the power to devalue credit: "Many People being afraid," Mather writes, "that the Government would in half a Year be so overturned, as to Convert their *Bills of Credit* altogether into *Wast Paper,* the *Credit* of them was thereby very much impaired" (*LP* 206). Those soldiers who do not abandon the assault on Quebec, despite much "dis-spiriting Information" (199), earn Mather's praise and provide a model for bill holders who need to do their share in supporting the war effort.

Resistance to despair is vital to both financial projects. Phips, whose outlook on life is summarized by a motto from a Dutch coin—"Incertum quo Fata ferant" (It is uncertain where the Fates will carry me)—must endure his unknowing (*LP* 161). While searching for treasure, he must quell the mutinous impulses of his impatient crew and steer clear of the giant "boilers," or submerged coral reefs, which might sink the ship. This resistance to despair, moreover, must occur without any guarantees of success. In Mather's scenario the *presumption* of success is as financially destructive as loss of faith. The sailors make the mistake, in fact, of taking the first signs of sunken treasure as a guarantee of success, turning "their *Despondencies* for their ill success into *Assurances,* that they had now lit upon the *true Spot* of Ground which they had been looking for" (167). When they return to the Captain's table to report their good news, Phips, by contrast, expresses "his Resolutions to wait still patiently upon the Providence of God under these Disappointments" (168). The lack of faith leads to financial panic and devastation, but assurance is an equally dangerous temptation. Nothing, ultimately, can guarantee the redemption of a speculative project.

Mather saw such economic faith as particularly necessary in the fledgling New England community. Phips, a man of "Enterprizing *Genius*" who could "*prudently* contrive a weighty Undertaking, and then patiently pursue it unto the End" (*LP* 161), is equipped with the necessary entrepreneurial outlook to serve self and society. In his *Essay upon Projects* (1697) Daniel Defoe also held Phips up as the exemplary "projector" who forms schemes for personal gain and civic benefit, crediting Phips's sea venture for inspiring the creation of the Bank of England and funding numerous financial projects in England. According to Mather, Phips tried to make his economic faith a model for others to emulate as well: during the credit crises in Massachusetts, especially, Phips's readiness to exchange his own metal cash for colonial bills served as an example for the rest of the community. He writes admiringly, "General *Phips* was in some sort the *Leader;* who at the very beginning, meerly to Recommend the *Credit* of the *Bills* unto other Persons, chearfully laid down a considerable quantity of *ready Money* for an equivalent parcel of them" (207).

The manner in which this resistance to despair resonates with theological language merits special scrutiny. The pagan Fates on Phips's Dutch coin parallel a Christian providence that defies human understanding, and Phips's resistance to financial despair resembles a religious conviction. Mather renders financial conundrums part of a larger inscrutable Puritan world, and the effect is an exemplum that could apply to religious or economic scenarios.[24] Mather reminds the reader that all faith must be granted in the face of uncertainty.

The story of Phips's treasure hunt draws from a Puritan convention of figuring grace as the discovery and recovery of treasure. Mather followed this convention in other writings, such as his 1726 funeral elegy for Elizabeth Cotton, in which he likened election to the opening of a "rich cabinet" and the exposure of the "jewels" that are the "peculiar treasure of the Almighty King."[25] Readers of Edward Taylor's poetry will also recall that his preparatory meditations figure the unregenerate soul as a dust-laden pearl or rusty metal that is finally retrieved from the corporeal cabinet, unlocked by God's key, and cleansed by Christ's love. The removal of rust, a corrosive substance that evokes the transience and perishability of the flesh, offered a particularly dramatic image of regeneration.[26]

The discovery of treasure was just one of many staple metaphors that Mather might draw from the language of finance. Images of payment or sudden outpourings of wealth had long suited the Puritan notion of a covenant of grace, through which Christ's sacrificial death redeems the debt of human sin for the elect, and just a few samples of Taylor's poetry show how adeptly the language of finance could be adapted for preparationist meditation. Of Christ Taylor writes, "He's Cancelling the Bond, and making Pay: / And Ballancing Accounts: its Reckoning day." Grace is an equal exchange, a "Heavenly trade" that dissolves the debt of human sin. "I am thine, and thou art mine indeed," the speaker says as he imagines the reciprocity of grace, "Propriety is mutuall." In another meditation the saving grace of Christ's love unleashes the blood that will pay for human sin, and the speaker juxtaposes an image of Christ opening the faucet of his own blood to a settlement of a debt in a shop or countinghouse: "Hence Love steps in, turns by the Conduit Cock: / Her Veans full payment on the Counter drop." In yet another, Communion wine has replaced Christ's blood, and an unstopped river of liquor, given to the regenerate at the Lord's supper, flows freely and "costs us nothing."[27] If grace entails an ongoing communion between God and the elect, circulation hindered or contaminated marks the sinful state. The channel between a depraved human and God remains blocked until grace unleashes an effortless liquidity that is both fiscal and physical.²⁸ The metaphor is twofold, as solvency—both the capacity to dissolve and become liquid as well as the capacity to pay all legal debts—figures the moment of grace.

Built into this metaphor of riches is also the possibility of their being counterfeit, and in this way the metaphor is particularly serviceable for Mather's biography, which warns repeatedly that faith not give way to the presumption that redemption will occur. The sixth meditation of Taylor's first series provides a fitting example of this figure: the speaker beseeches God to make him a coin in God's hand and inscribe him as authentic and inimitable, but this coin can also always bear a false exterior. It is the "Counterfeted Coine" of the reprobate that is exposed on Reckoning Day,²⁹ and Meditation 6 opens with the speaker agonizing over the possibility that his own face value, like a counterfeit coin, only belies a debased interior:

> Am I thy Gold? Or Purse, Lord, for thy Wealth;
>   Whether in mine, or mint refinde for thee?
> Ime counted so, but count me o're thyselfe,
>   Lest gold washt face, and brass in Heart I bee.
>   I Feare my Touchstone touches when I try
> Mee, and my Counted Gold too overly.³⁰

The recurrence of the words *count* and *counted* evoke the Puritan preoccupation with self-assessment. The human attempt to discern worth—always a suspect enterprise—stands in sharp contrast to God's ultimate judgment of a soul. Although the speaker has been "counted" as gold, by himself or his peers, God's recount must determine whether he does, in fact, number among the worthy. Punning with the word *o're*, the speaker acknowledges that God will ultimately decide his worthiness (i.e., count him "over") but still cannot resist expressing his hope that he will be considered worthy (like "ore" that contains precious metal). The speaker's touchstone, rubbed against alloys to determine their gold content, tests (or "tries," in metallurgical parlance) not only the speaker but his "Counted gold"—those outward signs of goodness which he has quantified in an attempt to glimpse the fate of his soul.

Understanding the preparationist's use of such financial metaphors is crucial to understanding the biography's depiction of Phips's success. After days at sea, during which he must endure numerous trials and resist despair, treasure is finally revealed to Phips: "Thus did there once again come into the light of the Sun, a Treasure which had been half an Hundred Years *groaning under the*

Waters: And in this time there was grown upon the Plate a Crust like *Limestone,* to the thickness of several Inches; which Crust being broken open by Irons contrived for that purpose, they knockt out whole Bushels of rusty Pieces of Eight which were grown thereinto" (*LP* 168–169). According to Kenneth Silverman, Mather possessed one of these very pieces-of-eight.[31] A gift from Phips himself, the coin hung on his library wall for nearly thirty years, suggesting perhaps that the minister valued it more for its symbolic significance than for what it could purchase. In this passage the tempestuous sea voyage finds a striking parallel in Mather's account of the *Mayflower* migration in his biography of William Bradford, but here he has added the financial trope: the retrieval of corroded coins from their limestone encasement, the rescue from darkness and torpor, suggesting a transformation from depravity to grace. The discovery of treasure fulfills a financial speculation and redeems the promise of fortune on which the royal sea venture was initially premised, but the reader can find spiritual meaning in the scene as well. According to Mather, the "trials" and "mortifications" of past failures prepared Phips for his eventual success (257).

Understood in light of this figurative convention, Phips's discovery of treasure takes on new significance. This treasure can only be obtained through a faith that rests somewhere between the dangerous extremes of assurance and despair. While Philip Gura believes Mather's treatment of the treasure hunt endorses the "sinful folly of a man's seeking filthy Spanish lucre off the West Indian islands," the treasure hunt is also crafted in such a way to showcase an exemplary faith.[32] This episode speaks to quotidian anxieties about the economic fate of the New England project by speaking to larger, more familiar spiritual conundrums. It teaches that one's religious faith occupies a middle ground that Jonathan Edwards would later describe as the "just medium between the two extremes of self-flattery and despondence" but also that financial faith occupies this ground as well.[33] The sailors on board Phips's ship fluctuate between "assurances" and "despondencies," but Phips, who maintains a position between both, provides a model for Mather's readers.

Undoubtedly, this biography reflects the stresses of modernity on Puritan orthodoxy. But it is not the secularized theology found in the works of Daniel Defoe or Benjamin Franklin, which arguably replicate the conversion narrative in form more than anything else. In both *Robinson Crusoe* and *The Autobiography* the sea voyage is governed by a "providence" that is also a secular "fortune," but it would be a mistake to assume that Mather's concept of providence is devoid of religious import. As numerous sermons will attest, Mather, whose own son Increase drowned at sea, agonized over the meaning of natural disasters and, in particular, the storms that caused shipwrecks. In a sermon following a 1723 storm that brought "incomputable" losses in both money and human lives, Mather wrote, "WHEN we are visited with *Natural* STORMS, [*As we are at this Moment!*] the *Way* of the Glorious GOD, is to be considered in them."[34] Sea perils symbolized the general precariousness of human life, the ease with which one blast of heaven might enrich or impoverish.

Whereas Edward Taylor's poetry posits that the poetic conceit in its literal form is ultimately secondary—the image of gold may convey grace, but the actual money of earthly transaction is the mark of depravity—Mather's use of treasure imagery can be strikingly literal and, as a result, intimately engaged with the economic concerns of his time. For Mather it is not enough to say that such correspondences between matter and spirit are figurative devices, for he believed that they inhered in God's providential design. As a result, fiscal-spiritual analogies took on remarkable significance in a colonial community burdened by public debts. Mather was not alone in this respect. Between 1690, the year of the first Massachusetts issue of paper money, and 1751, the year the Currency Act retired the last of the colonial bills, religious and financial conundrums inspired strikingly similar language in the literature of Puritan New England. Most notably, during the Great Awakening, as opponents of a controversial Land Bank worked to undermine public confidence in the newly issued banknotes, critics of the revivals simultaneously accused ministers and their followers of spiritual counterfeiting.[35] While I do not want to minimize the rhetorical uses for which such language was deployed, I would emphasize how readily financial outcomes were interpreted as providential dispensation.

Mather's 1714 pamphlet *Pascentius: A* Very Brief *Essay upon the Methods of Piety* illustrates how financial metaphors could take on literal significance in hard economic times. In his aim to promote pious patience among those who suffer, Mather draws an analogy between God's promise and a bill of credit (and, by extension, between providential dispensation and the conversion of that bill to metal cash), and he urges readers to accept the promise until it can be realized: "The *Promise* of GOD is a *Bill of Credit,* not inferiour to any Coin of *Silver or Gold;* and it will do for us when we must say with him of old, *Silver & Gold have I none.*" But the header on each page of the pamphlet reads, "How to Live in Hard Times," and Mather's essay is specifically concerned with those suffering economically in Massachusetts. When Mather warns that "A *Fearful*

Apprehension, that God cannot or will not *Provide* for us, is the most likely Way to be Left *Unprovided* for," he speaks of provisions that include material wealth.[36]

Given this literalism, Mather's treasure-seeking tale would seem to highlight a very Puritan paradox governing the text: namely, that Phips's financial success could be interpreted as a reward for his faith. Mather's story comes dangerously close to positing a covenant of works by which one can simply attain material and spiritual rewards through diligence. I say "close" because I find that the biography continually manages to counter this implication. In *Pascentius*, an essay that asks, "*What is the* GOOD, *which we are to* Do, *that so* GOD *may Do Good unto us, and give us Food & Gladness?*" the equation of diligence and reward is unqualified; however, this biography is more complex. While Phips simplistically wonders what he "*should do to be saved*" (*LP* 187), other moments in the narrative attest to the futility of such calculation. While Phips's success potentially suggests that faith brings reward, the rest of the narrative repeatedly emphasizes that faith must nevertheless be granted *in the absence* of any certainty.[37]

I would say, in fact, that one of the biography's main concerns is the world's inscrutability and the danger of human devices contrived to cope with unknowing. The flat, blank surface of the ocean and the "thick fog" that throws the sailors into a "new Perplexity" suggest that the world is indecipherable in the eyes of a preparationist Puritan. The starving sailors stranded at Antecosta must drop their fishing hooks in the water without knowing whether they have, in fact, "any prospect of catching anything" (*LP* 215). Phips was reportedly fond of telling a story of a hermit who, "being vexed with Blasphemous Injections about the Justice and Wisdom of Divine Providence," traveled with an angel that "*he might see the hidden Judgments of God*" and ultimately discovered that justice was simply not readily apparent to the human eye. At the conclusion of this tale Mather again uses a spatial metaphor—in which divine providence is a depth that is humanly unfathomable—in order to reiterate that Phips's faith confronts both entrepreneurial unpredictability and spiritual uncertainty. "Thus General *Phips*," he writes, "though he had been used unto Diving in his time, would say, *That the things which had befallen him in this Expedition, were too deep to be* Dived *into!*" (203–204).

This outlook also carries consequences for Mather's treatment of other episodes in his colony's recent history. Consistent with his resignation to unknowing, Phips puts an end to the witchcraft debacle by insisting that even the *likelihood* of possession is not a firm basis for conviction and that such judgment about the status of another's soul is forbidden. Under Phips the accused must be cleared because the courts find it "impossible to Penetrate into the whole Meaning of the things that had happened" (*LP* 246). As Mitchell Breitwieser observes, "probability"—a concept that denied complete certainty but nevertheless provided enough foundation for conviction—had long been used to justify the legal proceedings of these trials. Phips, however, rejects probability as a concept too dangerously close to assurance.[38]

Other moments in the biography also condone Phips's acceptance of unknowing. The "Presumptuous and Unwarrantable Juggle" of the astrologer's predictions is likened to Satanic arrogance, and the art of prognostication is condemned because it risks revealing "*Future* or *Secret* Matters unlawfully enquired after" (*LP* 264). Phips, despite the fact that many of the predictions have already come true, wisely rejects the temptation to believe the astrologer. Among these predictions is a financial forecast—at the age of forty-one the governor would find a second and even greater sunken treasure than the first—but Phips treats this divination with the same "Pious Neglect" as the others, resolving that he can count on neither the perishable treasures of forthcoming wealth nor the durable treasure of eternity. In response to the predictions, Phips reportedly says to Mather, "I believe Satan might have leave to foretel many things, all of which might come to pass in the beginning, to lay me asleep about such things as are to follow, especially about the main Chance of all" (266). Phips will not be lulled into a false security about what the future will bring. The term *main Chance*—meaning the most important thing risked or at stake—reinforces the notion that there are no complete hedges against contingency. The phrase, commonly used to designate the major financial risk of a project or the fortune risked by an entrepreneur, refers here to Phips's ultimate fate.[39] He will not, in other words, bank on either a long life or spiritual salvation.

Phips's resignation to economic uncertainty carries moral and social consequences. Breitwieser argues that Phips's "assertion of uncertainty" is not, in fact, antinomian piety but, rather, a precursor to Franklinian pragmatism. He considers this "epistemological humility" to be "a *denial* of the assertion that God clearly sponsors the use of authority to prescribe the proper shape of life and to proscribe others."[40] Relinquished from agonizing over something he can never discern anyway, Breitwieser concludes, Phips is free to chart a life according to his own desires. I believe, however, that this interpretation runs the risk of reading Phips's epistemological surrender as a rationalization of unleashed free enterprise. The sixty sailors stranded at Antecosta, who make up a "sort of *Commonwealth*," illustrate for Mather the devastating effects of unleashed self-interest (*LP* 209), and he condemns the sailor who eats more than his fair share. Similarly, the biography, like *Some Considerations*, emphasizes that the uncertainties of public finance, rather than encouraging unchecked economic liberalism, might make people feel obligated to support credit schemes.

The resistance to despair in the face of precariousness is the lesson of Mather's biography. Such resistance, the mark of both civic duty and religious conviction, also extends to readers themselves, for, by implication, Phips's confrontation with uncertainty also serves as instruction on the reading process itself. Early in the narrative Mather acknowledges that a complete relation of Phips's trials would "Tire the patience of the Reader" (*LP* 162), as if to acknowledge that readers, like the sailors on the ship, may succumb to impatience. Readers may also have to confront doubts because the biography's didacticism has required a measure of mythmaking. In ways that prefigure Franklin's equation of the life as lived with the life as written, Mather acknowledges his own authorial power in reconstructing or "resurrecting" Phips so that his "*Infirmities may be Buried*" and "*Virtues and Graces may Supervive*" (*LP* 273). The need to provide a model of religious and financial faith takes precedence over truth telling, and it is equally imperative that readers credit what has been presented to them. That Mather begins this narrative with a letter from Nathaniel Mather vouching for its credibility as history is not surprising in itself, for such prefaces were in keeping with the literary conventions of the day. Given the subject and purpose of this biography, however, Nathaniel Mather's pledge that Mather's history will deliver is significant. Readers of both the letter and the representative life are aligned with readers of credit bills and encouraged to read with a necessary suspension of disbelief. A half-century later, defending the revivals against the charge of spiritual counterfeiting, Jonathan Edwards would call for a similar suspension of scrutiny. In his "Faithful Narrative of the Surprising Work of God" he writes, "I thought it might not be beside my duty to declare this amazing work, as it appeared to me, to be indeed divine, and to conceal no part of the glory of it, leaving it with God to take care of the credit of his own work, and running the venture of any censorious thoughts which might be entertained of me to my disadvantage."[41] Because only God can ensure the credibility of these appearances, the narrator of the revival episodes must venture to declare the amazing work "as it appeared" to him. Edwards's account is a "faithful narrative" not because, as one might expect, it corresponds precisely (or faithfully) to a reality but, rather, because it is articulated with faith, with skepticism held in check.

The *Life of Phips* instructs readers on how to cope with epistemological anxiety, and this instruction ultimately applies to the biography itself. Both the fictional life and the process of reading that life are invested with consequences for the larger community. I would not, as other critics have, go so far as to say that the biography advances an Enlightenment secular morality as a replacement for religious piety because I believe it presents civic-mindedness as inseparable from faith.[42] Mather champions public-spiritedness in the marketplace, like his more secular successor Franklin, but he does not detach this virtue from the imperatives of Puritan piety. To Phips, in fact, Mather gives the very praise he would also give to John Winthrop: he is a man who can transform the "old *Heathen* Virtue of PIETAS IN PATRIAM, or LOVE TO ONES COUNTRY" into a "Christian" virtue (*LP* 174). The stories of the colony's and Phips's financial ventures demonstrate that public service can be imbued with faith. In this biography economic confidence is a version of faith precisely because economic outcomes are providential and beyond human knowing. To have such faith is itself a public act, a contribution to a commonwealth that is faltering yet capable of regeneration.

CHAPTER TWO

Making Much of Nothing in the Chesapeake

When the printer William Parks established the first paper mill in Virginia in 1744, a poet named Joseph Dumbleton responded with a paean to papermaking and printing. First published in Parks's *Virginia Gazette*, the poem celebrates the printer's creative capacities:

> Tho' sage Philosophers have said,
> *Of nothing, can be nothing made:*
> Yet *much* thy Mill, O *Parks,* brings forth
> From what we reckon *nothing worth.*[1]

Parks's mill, which makes paper from rags, overturns Parmenides' proclamation "ex nihilo nihil fit." Dumbleton uses an epigraph from Ovid's *Metamorphoses*, "In nova, fert Animus, mutates dicere formas, Corpora" (Of bodies changed to various forms I sing), to provide an alternative philosophy and applaud two transformations: not only does the mill turn worthless rags into paper, but the writer or printer then invests this paper with literary value. The mill makes much of rags, and the writer and printer make much of rag paper. Everyone profits in the ideal economy imagined in this poem. Townsfolk happily receive "hard Cash" for their "soft Rags"; Parks reaps "Quires" from "Tatters"; and, most significant, the community enjoys access to various written and printed texts, including love letters, poetry, political tracts, and the *Gazette* itself.[2]

This poem, produced at a moment when the Chesapeake colonies were self-consciously striving to create their own literary, political, and economic cultures, celebrates the transformative power of writing and print. The paper becomes socially meaningful—as literature and as communication—only once the "Substances of what we think" are allowed to "live in *Ink*" on its surface.[3] Dumbleton's poem illustrates a tendency among Chesapeake writers to imagine that a thinking population could use the printed word to make much of nothing. In a similar maneuver Ebenezer Cooke's 1730 *Sotweed Redivivus* proposes that a thinking population use the printed word to create a cost-effective paper currency. In Cooke's poem the much made from nothing is not simply this new exchange medium but also the various social and cultural benefits that he imagines will come with an economically fortified community. Paper currency is the means by which an inchoate frontier settlement might become an advanced society. Although eclipsed today by Cooke's earlier and more raucous satire, *The Sot-Weed Factor*, this later poem warrants consideration by anyone interested in the Chesapeake's development, for it illustrates how writers imagined that investing in a public debt might consolidate a regional identity.

While Massachusetts paper money assumed a place in that colony's narrative of heyday, decline, and potential renewal, Cooke and other Chesapeake writers saw these financial measures as part of a much more straightforward narrative of progress.[4] According to this narrative, Maryland's and Virginia's long use of tobacco as its medium of exchange had encouraged excessive cultivation of the sot-weed from the start: the region's markets were glutted, its soil and natural beauty depleted, its economy stagnant and undiversified. By substituting paper for tobacco money and reducing their production of tobacco, however, the colonies might extricate themselves from allegedly primitive forms of barter and preserve nature's bounty. The economic reform brought by paper money also promised to foster the pursuit of higher arts. In an attempt to combat the economic problems of Maryland and Virginia, writers had taken up their pens, but, while economic debate had sparked a regional literature, it also highlighted the need for permanent economic reform to free up energy for more diverse kinds of writing.[5] Paper money was the brainchild of the region's writers, but it would hopefully make possible their turn to more elevated subjects befitting increasingly sophisticated communities.

Assessing the Ailing Body Politic

Dumbleton's celebration of his community's resourcefulness was part of a social transformation in the Chesapeake in the first half of the eighteenth century. Since their founding, Virginia and Maryland had lacked the communities and social institutions of the Middle Colonies and New England. Early populations had been largely male indentured servants who came in search of economic opportunities in agricultural production and had little interest in establishing families, towns, or any permanent ties to the region. As a result of several demographic shifts and the replacement of European servitude with African slavery, however, white colonial societies began to cohere at the end of the seventeenth century. Jack P. Greene writes that the concentration of wealth in the hands of large-scale planters also created a class of elites who were invested in emulating English society in the colony—rather than simply making money and returning to England—and who "threw themselves into its 'improvement' with a public spiritedness and a sense of community and corporate responsibility that had been rare among earlier generations."[6]

Civic leaders in the Chesapeake saw the establishment of a local printing press as a crucial step in this transformation. In 1726 Thomas Bordley, a leader in the Maryland Assembly, engaged Parks to print the province's laws and legislative proceedings in the hopes that access to such publications might change the ignorant Marylander into the kind of informed "Commoner, so much esteemed in *England.*" In particular, Bordley wanted to give freeholders the information necessary to evaluate their government and determine whether their "*English* Liberties were asserted or Neglected" by their legislative representatives.[7] The *Maryland Gazette,* the newspaper Parks launched a year later in Annapolis, continued in this vein, not only informing readers of local issues but also publishing solicited opinions, foreign news, and local belletristic offerings. In 1730 Parks opened a press and bookstore in Williamsburg and began publishing a similar vehicle, the *Virginia Gazette.*

This so-called spirit of improvement was brought to bear on the region's economic problems. Maryland and Virginia had found themselves far too dependent on tobacco crops and without a sufficiently fluid medium of exchange. The earlier promotional literature of Thomas Hariot, John Smith, and George Alsop had depicted for English readers the region's abundant natural resources, and it would seem that the Chesapeake would not require the kind of credit mechanisms which had emerged in the relatively resource-poor regions of New

England. But, as in all parts of British America, coins did not linger long in these colonies, and so both Maryland and Virginia had resorted to making tobacco the official circulating medium of exchange. This policy motivated excessive cultivation of the crop, which glutted the market, drove down its price, and exhausted much of the region's soil. The editions of local newspapers still extant today indicate that the dwindling price of tobacco inspired a large portion of the literary endeavors that found their way into print, as essayists and poets weighed in on the question of how to combat the depreciation and wean the colony off a single-staple system.

One of the first productions of Parks's Williamsburg press, a 1730 poem by J. Markland called "Typographia," credited the printer's art with creating a class of informed freeholders in Virginia capable of economic problem solving. Dedicated to William Gooch, the governor who initiated the regulation of tobacco prices in that colony, the poem identifies print as the means for enlightened self-governance:

>   Great REPRESENTATIVE!
> What Thanks shall we return? What Honours shew?
> To whom our *Staple* does its Being owe,
>   By whom our Hopes revive:
>   By whom all *Arts* recov'ring live,
> That erst like drooping Plants had dropt their Head,
> And once again, with native Vigour thrive:
> From whom VIRGINIA's Laws, that lay
>   In blotted *Manuscripts* obscur'd
>   By vulgar Eyes unread,
> Which whilome scarce the Light endur'd.
> Begin to view again the Day,
>   As rising from the Dead.
> For this the careful *Artist* wakes,
>   And O'er his countless Brood he stands,
>   His numerous Hoards,
>   Of *speechless* Letters, *unform'd* Words,
>   *Unjointed* Questions, and *unmeaning* Breaks,
> Which into Order rise, and Form, at his Commands.[8]

In an act reminiscent of the biblical account of creation, the artist-printer Parks forms order from chaos. Using the "countless Brood" of printing types that would otherwise remain "speechless letters" and "unform'd words," he creates words on the page. He ushers the written law, previously obscured in largely unread manuscripts, into the light of day. Print has helped publicize and thereby implement Gooch's famous Tobacco Inspection Act, which aimed to reduce glut and eliminate poor-grade tobacco by requiring inspections of all crops. Properly publicized, the law has revived the staple of the colony but also "all *Arts*" that, like a tobacco plant itself, have been flagging.[9]

In Maryland debates over the tobacco problem filled the local *Gazette*: though it would soon broaden, Capper Nichols writes, the "roots" of literary culture in this colony were "inextricably entwined with the 'sotweed.'"[10] The literature generated by this controversy was indication of the colony's advancement but also a reminder of its unrealized potential. Addressing Parks in a 1726 proposal for a new tobacco law, one anonymous writer declared that, while the conveniences attending a press in an infant country were obvious to all, one advantage had hitherto gone unnoticed: its ability to facilitate conversation in a community of reticent individuals. A press, he wrote, could "make Publick the Thoughts of any Well-Wisher of his Country, where he endeavours to discover any Thing that may be for a general Good, which is the only End the Author of this following Piece aims at."[11] Beyond the immediate task of enabling economic reform, a press could empower colonists to act on behalf of the commonwealth.

Sotweed Redivivus was one of the region's more notable attempts at economic intervention, and the poem must be understood in relation both to the ongoing conversations in the *Maryland Gazette* as well as to Cooke's earlier poem. *The Sot-Weed Factor*, the 1708 poem for which Cooke is primarily known and the inspiration for John Barth's 1960 comic novel of the same title, features a merchant-speaker who satirizes the dysfunctional economy and judicial system of the colony. *Sotweed Redivivus*, a sequel of sorts published twenty-two years later, revives the speaker as a merchant-turned-poet who champions a remedy to heal the ailing body politic: namely, a diversified economy made possible by government-issued paper currency. The first poem is comic satire and the second more of an economic treatise, thinly veiled as poetry, which proposes a solution for the problems depicted two decades earlier.

Both poems respond to economic woes and confirm Nichols's theory that such problems gave rise to Maryland's literary publishing. But the second poem, in particular, illustrates how this literary flourishing depended on a class of reading freeholders ready to debate how the state might handle those troubles.

Speaking of his paper money project, one of the planters of *Sotweed Redivivus* declares himself such a freeholder:

> And with Submission to the State,
> I have a Project in my Pate,
> May prove the Making of this Land,
> If executed out of Hand;
> Which is to give my Fancy vent,
> Within my *Pericranium* Pent.[12]

While the term *project* traditionally connoted suspect financial scheming and cheating, Daniel Defoe's *Essay upon Projects* (1697) redefined projection as a potentially honest and valuable form of speculation which could benefit a community: by applying the speculator's foresight and resourcefulness, individuals and groups could envision future public improvements and then take steps to realize them.[13] Like Defoe's projects, the planter's project is intended for public benefit. It is the product of fancy in that it is innovative; however, it is emphatically not frivolous but, instead, performs serious work on behalf of the colony.

To understand how the second poem envisions economic reform, one must revisit the conclusion of the first one. The earlier picaresque narrative poem, first published in London in 1708 and reprinted in slightly modified form by Parks's Annapolis press in 1730, mocks the provincial manners of Maryland. Likely based on Cooke's own trip to Maryland to settle an estate he had inherited, the poem portrays a landscape filled with crude food, promiscuous women, duplicitous planters, and a corrupt legal system.[14] One of the most significant markers of Maryland's barbarity is its monetary system. At the conclusion of the poem the factor finds himself empty-handed because a Quaker planter has reneged on his promise to remit tobacco in exchange for goods already received. The factor sues his adversary, but his hired lawyer, a "quack" who takes bribes, achieves only a hollow legal victory, as the Quaker planter is ordered to reimburse him in "country pay," or plantation products equivalent in value:

> Now Court being call'd by beat of Drum,
> The Judges left their Punch and Rum,
> When Pettifogger Docter draws,
> His Paper forth, and opens Cause:
> And least I shou'd the better get,
> Brib'd *Quack* supprest his Knavish Wit.

> So Maid upon the downy Field,
> Pretends a Force, and Fights to yield:
> The Byast Court without delay,
> Adjudg'd my Debt in Country Pay;
> In Pipe staves, Corn, or Flesh of Boar,
> Rare Cargo for the *English* Shoar.[15]

The speaker concludes that he has been unfairly treated because he is an outsider, and no justice will have "the Heart" to "give his Verdict on a Stranger's part." But one of Cooke's own footnotes indicates that by Maryland law people could settle debts in country pay, and therefore the speaker's primary disadvantage as a "stranger merchant" lies, instead, in the fact that these pipe staves (the wooden slats used in casks, barrels, and hogsheads), corn, and boar flesh cannot be marketed in England, making them far more valuable to colonists than to merchants. Pipe staves would not be worth transporting on their own, and the corn and boar meat would be too perishable to survive the long journey (even preserved in brine, boar would have found a small market in England).

The speaker's criticism, then, implies not simply that the court is corrupt but that its institutionalized methods of barter, or country pay, are primitive. In the poem's final lines the curse that the speaker hurls at Maryland is also the curse of barter itself:

> Raging with Grief, full speed I ran,
> To joyn the Fleet at *Kicketan;*
> Embarqu'd and waiting for a Wind,
> I left this dreadful Curse behind.
>
>   May Canniballs transported o'er the Sea
> Prey on these Slaves, as they have done on me;
> May never Merchant's, trading Sails explore
> This Cruel, this Inhospitable Shoar;
> But left abandon'd by the World to starve,
> May they sustain the Fate they well deserve:
> May they turn Savage, or as *Indians* Wild,
> From Trade, Converse, and Happiness exil'd.[16]

The speaker condemns Maryland to savagery and isolation from the world of trade, and, in fact, he would have understood these conditions to be the result of barter exchange itself. What the speaker describes would not be barter by everyone's account, for, though there is no medium of exchange in use, the payment of commodities has still been calculated in monetary units. The speaker also does not see (or does not mention) that all of Maryland's foreign trade worked similarly: the exchange of manufactured goods for tobacco is simply a form of barter more convenient for him (usually colonists, rather than merchants, were the ones who suffered, since, under the British monopoly, they had no other market and often had to accept unnecessary luxury goods in exchange for the factor's tobacco).[17] Nevertheless, the poem presents country pay as a uniquely primitive mode of exchange, and these final lines are the basis for the second poem's call for reform.

Critics have remarked on the poem's condemnation of Maryland's provincial ways, but they have not attended to its relevance to the sequel's treatment of commercial exchange. This ending voices a concept of barter which will be the starting point for Cooke's advocacy of a dematerialized medium of exchange in the later poem. This concept of barter was central to early American thinking on paper money and later to the classical economist's account of modern capitalism.[18] With the division of labor, in Adam Smith's history, individuals had to "truck, barter, and exchange" to get what they need, and eventually a common equivalent was needed to negotiate exchange because labor—the real measure of exchangeable value—was too difficult to gauge.[19] Widely valued, transportable, and easily divisible, precious metals served this office well and made possible long-distance trade, and this trade eventually gave rise to the bill of exchange, an even more transportable medium than metal coin.

According to this historiography, the commodity value of a coin ensured that buyers and sellers would esteem it, but the coin's primary value lay in its symbolic function. Contemporary theorist Jean-Joseph Goux writes that such media only represent the absent objects of buyers' and sellers' desires, negotiating the conflicts between exchange parties that cannot offer what the other really wants (in this formulation the miser is one who has lost sight of money's representational function).[20] Or, as Georg Simmel wrote in *The Philosophy of Money* (1907), the commercial medium is the "third quantity" that gauges the relative values of what each party seeks to acquire. This "proportion" marked a watershed moment in the "development of the purely symbolic character of money": "One of the greatest advances made by mankind—the discovery of a new world out of the material of the old—is to establish a proportion between two quantities, not by direct comparison, but in terms of the fact that each of them relates to a third quantity and that these two relations are either equal or unequal."[21] Here the "old world" is a repository of familiar materials—gold, silver, leather, paper, tobacco, beads, shells—which might be transformed into newly symbolic media.

Colonial and early national pamphleteers consistently chronicled this introduction of a common equivalent in their own monetary tracts (and often linked explicitly this new world of symbolic money with the geographic New World) because the symbolic nature of metal money laid the groundwork for their advocacy of paper forms. Material value led buyers and sellers to honor the coin's symbolism; however, they reasoned, if esteem could be generated by promise or by law or by public support, any material might substitute for metal. To be convincing, this argument needed to address the claim, which Marx has since made familiar to contemporary readers, that only a commodity could express value and serve as a common equivalent in commercial exchange.[22]

For this reason Benjamin Franklin's *Modest Inquiry into the Nature and Necessity of a Paper-Currency*, a 1729 essay that was reprinted in Chesapeake newspapers, emphasizes that the medium symbolically "*is* whatsoever it will procure." Whether gold, silver, copper, or tobacco, this medium becomes "to those who possess it . . . that very Thing which they want because it will immediately procure it for them." It is "Cloth to him that wants Cloth, and Corn to those that want Corn."[23] Franklin's essay as well as Cooke's *Sotweed Redivivus* both claim that paper currency can free colonists from the constraints of barter, giving them the means to acquire what they truly need rather than what their exchange partner has to offer at the moment. Franklin's theory must have appealed to those Marylanders who were dismayed to be paid with worthless tobacco. Fittingly, when Parks reprinted Franklin's essay in the July 22, 1729, edition of the *Maryland Gazette*, the prefatory remarks heralded it as a work "so nearly adapted to the Circumstances" of Maryland that it would certainly "be of service" to the colony.

Another advocate of paper money, the Virginian Peyton Randolph argued that, with "respect to trade or debts," a currency could be made of anything so long as it functioned effectively as a unit of accounting. Writing in 1759, Randolph posed this rhetorical question:

> I will now ask where is the material Difference between one Kind of Currency and another with Respect to Trade or Debts; but I bar the Man of miserly Habits from giving any Answer at all, he is first for the most Part a Stranger either to Trade or Debts, because he can scarcely trust himself, how then will he trust an-

other. Again, the Wretch conceives such an inexpressible Pleasure in the counting and poring over his Golden Guineas, that I much question whether double the Sum in Bank-Bills would purchase them. 'Tis to the *rational Trader* alone that I apply, and such Merchants ought to be deemed; to them therefore I address myself, and I am persuaded I have their true Answer in this Memorial.[24]

Men of miserly habits cannot grasp the medium's symbolic function. They are governed not only by an unprincipled desire for gold—and the pleasure that comes with counting guineas—but by an inability to think rationally. In this essay commodity money appeals to base impulses, while paper money appeals to reason and trust. Cooke's *Sotweed Redivivus* draws similar distinctions, heralding a paper medium as the innovation that can cure the ills of a crude and dysfunctional economy. The printing press that can create enlightened public discourse can also create this cure.

Cultivating Resources

While *Sotweed Redivivus* has none of the biting satire of its predecessor, it is a sequel in that it attempts to undo the curse of the first poem. Many readers have concluded that Cooke's sudden shift from mockery to boosterism reflects the fact that he eventually embraced his identity as a Marylander when he settled in the province permanently. Indication of this change seems to have come years earlier when Cooke drafted a number of prefaces for a revised second edition of *The Sot-Weed Factor*. Drawing various analogies between tobacco and his own verse in all four drafts, Cooke promises to omit the curse on the colony, hoping that this "second crop" will prove "merchantable ware" and not be blasted again by a storm of criticism.[25] No second edition exists today, but a "corrected and emended" third edition of *The Sot-Weed Factor* appeared in Cooke's *Maryland Muse* collection of 1731. The new ending contains no curse but only a tempered warning that young merchants collect *before* paying out in goods and the following benediction:

> AND may that Land where Hospitality,
> Is every Planter's darling Quality,
> Be by each Trader kindly us'd,
> And may no Trader be abus'd;
> Then each of them shall deal with Pleasure,
> And each encrease the other's Treasure.[26]

This innocuous "third crop" replaces the curse with a wish for reciprocal trade and all-around prosperity.[27]

Although the economic advice of *Sotweed Redivivus* is clearly formulated with a planter's interests in mind, it presents itself as a public-spirited endeavor of potentially widespread and beneficial consequences. The poem features not a picaro but a concerned citizen who debates the colony's economic woes with a planter, dramatizing the very discursive means by which the colony might address these problems. As the planter himself acknowledges, these debates replicate the kind of public discourse which has filled the pages issued from Parks's press:

> I wish my Country very well:
> And tho' the PRESS with Schemes does swell,
> To make us thrive at Home the better,
> As P.P. tells us in his Letter,
> If *Planters* would be rul'd by me,
> I will their best Physician be:
> Prescribe the Means, wou'd, I am sure,
> If rightly apply'd, work a Cure.   (SR 20-21)

Like the poem itself, the planter's proposals to cure economic woes take a rightful place alongside those cures proposed by "P.P." and other pseudonymous contributors to the *Maryland Gazette*. The planter's project, after all, has been "Exactly copy'd from his Mind" in the second canto of the poem (10). In ways similar to the schemes that have addressed the government's inability to control price depreciation, Cooke's poem, subtitled "The Planter's Looking-Glass," holds the mirror up to the state for examination.

Sotweed Redivivus grounds its remedies in a crucial distinction between tobacco as commodity and tobacco as medium—or, in local parlance, between a "trade crop" and "money crop." It is the same distinction Franklin made in his well-known pamphlet "between Money as it is Bullion, which is Merchandize, and as by being coin'd it is made a Currency."[28] The source of the province's problems, according to Cooke, is its reliance on a staple that functions both as a commodity and as a medium. Since the initial settlement of the colony, tobacco had been the medium with which the government paid clergy and officials and also with which colonists settled local debts and paid their taxes. Although this practice made sense, given the difficulty of keeping metal coins in local circulation, it also encouraged endless cultivation of the crop. When

William Jennings Bryan fought the gold standard in the 1890s, he argued that money was a creature of law and could not be brought into existence like wheat or manufactured goods. But, in fact, for Marylanders and Virginians currency could be brought into existence with devastating consequences, as the sharp rise in supply, much of it of a poorer quality, drastically reduced its purchasing power.

Exacerbating this problem was the fact that planters chose to use their best products as merchandise to sell overseas and their inferior products as currency for local payments. All forms of currency would fluctuate according to the market, but, as the purchasing power of the tobacco currency diminished dramatically, the use of this medium began to look less like monetized exchange, in which the medium leads to the acquisition of the desired object, and more like barter that left people holding goods they could not use. Foreign trade was already essentially conducted as barter, since colonists traded their tobacco for whatever English goods were brought ashore by merchants, and now local trade began to seem similarly cumbersome. Exchanging tobacco currency simply *was* barter, one London ship owner exclaimed in a 1729 issue of the *Maryland Gazette:* "Indeed, we think it will be the Interest of your Province, that all Debts be contracted in Money; it is now Time to leave off the old Way of Barter."[29] This writer proposed that Maryland "turn Tobacco Debts into Money Debts" to help eliminate trashy tobacco.

Writers whose remedies appeared in the pages of the *Maryland Gazette* often hoped that London merchants could be persuaded to do their part in keeping tobacco prices from sinking. *Sotweed Redivivus,* however, proposes that the Maryland Assembly take it upon itself to ensure that the quantity, quality, and price of tobacco stay elevated. By printing and loaning out a paper currency, the local government could relieve colonists of their need to pay debts in tobacco (the government, in other words, would undertake a debt in order to provide this relief). This substitution of paper money debts for tobacco debts would, in turn, curtail the production of the staple and encourage farmers to grow other crops, such as hemp, which might improve the land. Other governmental efforts, such as limiting tobacco cultivation and requiring "inspection notes" for any tobacco sold as merchandise, would improve the quality and, equally important, provide assurance of that quality in the eyes of buyers.

In *Sotweed Redivivus* the advantages of a relatively worthless medium, such as paper or nonprecious metal, are numerous. For one thing, as the planter's discussion of copper, tin, and brass coins emphasizes, a less valuable medium promised to stay put in the colony. Invoking Gresham's Law, Cooke's planter forecasts that such coins

> Not subject to be clipt by Shears,
> Like Yellow-Boys, have lost their Ears;
> But as a Free-born Subject range,
> Of different Size, for ready Change.   (*SR* 5)

A less desirable medium than gold or silver would protect coins from clipping and hoarding, freeing them for easy circulation. In canto 3 Cooke's planter observes that, while any moidores, pistoles, and cobbs brought "hither, from the Mines of Spain" would be unlikely to remain within the colony, "*Copper-Coin,* like vagrant *Cain,* / Wou'd never wander into *Spain,* / Or long in Misers Bags remain" (26). The logical extension of this theory is clear: if copper remains local, then so will paper.

A paper medium, which had absolutely no value as merchandise and would not likely be readily accepted outside the colony, came to be considered by many as the only medium not susceptible to hoarding or drainage. Decades later, during the Revolutionary War, a congressional circular would subscribe to a similar logic and depict the national paper money as a friend who never abandons: "Let it also be remembered that paper money is the only kind of money which cannot 'make to itself wings and fly away.' It remains with us, it will not forsake us, it is always ready and at hand for the purpose of commerce or of taxes, and every industrious man can find it." Here the readiness and availability of worthless paper far outweighs the commodity value of metal stored mysteriously beneath the earth's surface. If Britain loses its colonial territory and trade monopolies, it will have to discharge that debt by "taxes to be paid in specie, in gold or silver, perhaps now buried in the mines of Mexico or Peru, or still concealed in the brooks or rivulets of Africa or Indostan" (ironically, the victorious United States found itself in the same predicament after the war and, under Hamilton's financial plan, paid off the war debt in part through excise taxes levied on farmers). The circular's rhetoric invests paper money with the anthropomorphic virtue of loyalty, but it is the paper's availability, or human "readiness," which is to keep it in American hands. The difficulty of extracting gold or silver (it is only "*perhaps* now buried" and, unlike paper, is not available to "every industrious man") makes it valuable but also infuriatingly elusive.[30]

By replacing tobacco money, a paper medium would also reduce the region's cultivation of a crop that was considered devoid of any socially redeeming value. Tobacco was the drug that poisoned the human mind and body as well as the body politic. Unlikely to foster industry or civic service, it was the one staple in British America, David S. Shields observes, that "defied heroic treatment" and remained conspicuously absent from the georgics of the time.[31] Tobacco's close association with slave labor also made it morally suspect. The crop required an extraordinary investment of manpower, and the drive to put more land in cultivation had quickly prompted importations of African slaves. During the reign of Charles I, Cooke's planter recalls in canto 2, the stinking weed was tended by "*Scotch, English,* and *Hybernians* wild, / From Sloth and Idleness exil'd" until these European hands were replaced by Ethiopians from "scorching *Africa*'s burnt Shore" (*SR* 11). Cooke's condemnation of tobacco slavery seems to stem not from a sense of its inhumanity but, rather, from the fear that it will remove all incentives for industry among the European colonists. The Scottish, English, and Irish planters were exiled from sloth presumably to assume an industrious life in the colonies, but they have been increasingly replaced by slaves. Those white planters who do tend tobacco have no incentive to labor diligently when they are paid in "*Indian* Weed" that "will not answer Need" (13).

Perhaps most important, *Sotweed Redivivus* imagines that a paper medium will reduce the need for endless land clearing and the waste of natural resources (it would be more than a century before paper made from wood pulp would be widely used in North America). Cooke's prefatory remarks open with a striking anti-pastoral image that will become crucial once the monetary debates commence. When the author invokes the Pierian Muses and heads off to the forest, he finds that the landscape offers no inspiration:

> *To* Battle-Town, *the Author took his Way,*
> *That thro' thick Woods and fenny Marshes lay,*
> *And mangled Oaks, laid blended on the Plains,*
> *Cut down for Fuel by unthinking Swains.*
> *At Ax and Hoe, like Negroe Asses tug,*
> *To glut the Market with a poisonous Drug:*
> *Destroy found Timber, and lay waste their Lands,*
> *To head a Troop of* Aethiopian *Hands,*
> *Worse Villains are, than* Forward's Newgate *Bands.*   (*SR* iv–v)

This landscape has been ravaged by slash-and-burn modes of land clearing, first used by Algonquin tribes for subsistence farming and then deployed with devastating effects by colonists on a large scale. The villainous swains, who tug, glut, and mangle, "waste" resources in more than one sense of the term: destroying the land but also failing to put timber to constructive use. Later in the poem Cooke's planter will propose that timber, as well as the colony's iron, hemp, and flax, be used more resourcefully for shipbuilding. Such "floating Castles," as he describes them, are not capricious visions but viable ventures that could reduce the colony's cost of doing business. Adopting a mode of land clearing which is shortsighted and regrettable, such unthinking swains only

> *Will by their Heirs be curst for these Mistakes,*
> *E'er* Saturn *thrice his Revolution makes;*
> *Whose thriftless State, this* Looking-Glass *is meant,*
> *By way of Metaphor, to represent:*
> *Wherein the* Planter *may his Fate behold,*
> *By sad Experience, has been often told.*
> *It's Industry, and not a nauseous Weed,*
> *Must cloath the* Naked, *and the* Hungry *feed.* (v)

The term *thriftless* condemns those wasteful tendencies evident in the ravaged landscape, but the original meaning of this word—fecklessness or inefficacy—applies to Cooke's description as well. The colony is wasteful as well as impotent.

Virginia's first locally produced history, Robert Beverley's *History and Present State of Virginia* (1705), similarly locates the origins of the region's economic troubles in its initial dependence on tobacco and its failure to realize the land's potential. In his account Beverley emphasizes that the soil has always supported a variety of flora, but from the first days of settlement colonists have neglected to nurture this bounty. In his study of American georgics Timothy Sweet observes that the one specimen missing from Beverley's extensive catalog of natural bounty is tobacco itself, as if to emphasize that the staple actually undermines the colony's prospects for agricultural diversity. "No Seed is Sowed there, but it thrives," Beverley writes of the fertile soil, "and most Plants are improved, by being Transplanted thither. And yet there's very little Improvement made among them, nor anything us'd in Traffique, but Tobacco."[32] Beverley also emphasizes that colonists, in their single-minded focus on tobacco cultivation, have not promoted the settlement of towns and the division of labor. Urban communities, he argues, are capable of supporting the cloth industries linked to hemp, flax, cotton, silk, and wool production and thereby alleviating their dependence on the English cloth trade, but no single family could carry out all the steps in cloth production. Therefore, by "reason of the unfortunate

Method of the Settlement, and want of Cohabitation," they cannot profitably use these crops that "might otherwise supply their Necessities, and leave the Produce of Tobacco to enrich them, when a gainful Market can be found for it."[33]

Beverley depicts with urgency a colony that has wasted its God-given resources and repeatedly relapses "into the Disease of planting Tobacco."[34] In the final paragraph of the history his account of the colonial past aims at bringing about reform in the future: "Thus they depend altogether upon the Liberality of Nature, without endeavouring to improve its Gifts, by Art or Industry. They spunge upon the Blessings of a warm Sun, and a fruitful Soil, and almost grutch the Pains of gathering in the Bounties of the Earth. I should be asham'd to publish this slothful Indolence of my Countrymen, but that I hope it will rouse them out of their Lethargy, and excite them to make the most of all those happy Advantages which Nature has given them; and if it does this, I am sure they will have the Goodness to forgive me." This sponging is not an exploitation of natural resources per se but an exploitation unaccompanied by commensurate improvement of the land.[35] While Beverley never explicitly links such wastefulness to Virginia's monetary problems, he and his readers understood that the colonists' unwillingness to cultivate cloth-related crops only increased their debt to the metropolis and furthered London's mercantilist efforts to accumulate specie. Devoting just one short chapter to Virginia's monetary customs, Beverley laments, "The Inconveniences to *Virginia*, by the drawing away all the Specie, are inexpressible."[36]

William Borden, a North Carolina pamphleteer who published with Parks's press, makes a similar case for paper currency in a neighboring colony that also used a tobacco medium. In *An Address to the Inhabitants of North-Carolina* (1746) Borden proposed that this new paper medium might rejuvenate the rivers of nature's bounty which would otherwise, if "continually running out on every Hand," eventually "be drain'd dry." Using elaborate analogies between the life systems of humans and animals, Borden warns North Carolina not to become like caterpillars who depend "for Food on the Leaves thereof, which come by Nature, (without any Cultivation or Propagation of their own)" and "often times eat themselves out and perish." A medium of "no intrinsick Value," he argues, will prevent hoarding and spur both industry and husbandry. The colony's natural resources, which long "served the Inhabitants in the Infancy of the Province, as well for a *Medium* as for Food and Raiment," have "had their Time" and "are almost eaten out and gone."[37] Borden asks rhetorically, "Is there not then a Duty incumbent upon us, to emulate or strive to excel the Catterpiller, in labouring to encourage and assist each other, to cultivate and propagate something, substantial, in lieu thereof?" An intervention made possible by the collective will and wisdom of rational freeholders, a paper medium will facilitate the production of new crops to replace those used for food and raiment. But, more so, it will make wasteful "money crops," those crops produced solely to provide an exchange medium, unnecessary altogether.[38]

Cooke, Beverley, and Borden condemn the way in which land has been wasted, but in Cooke's understanding this destruction has also depleted the region's main source of poetic inspiration: it is not coincidental that the poet-speaker is looking for the Pierian Muses when he finds the mangled oaks left behind by tobacco cultivation. Poetry is also endangered by ecological destruction in the work of another Maryland poet, Richard Lewis. His "Food for Criticks," an eclogue that appeared in Parks's *Maryland Gazette* and was reprinted in Philadelphia and Boston, opens with claims that the American bard need not look to the Golden Age because his native landscape provides far more beautiful subject matter: the "fam'd castalian or pierian well" presumes no more to tell of "ancient streams"; instead, it confesses the superiority of Pennsylvania's Schuylkill River. Yet, while Lewis encourages local poets to take their models from the spirits, or "vocal shades," of the American forest, he also acknowledges that this resource may disappear. The poem turns alarmist and finally laments the waste of hunters who, "arm'd with fire, endanger ev'ry shade" in order to gratify their impulses for luxury (Maryland passed its first deer preservation act in 1730). As the "pretty songsters breathe their last," the fount is at risk of running dry. Only the "more humane" can "taste nature's bounty" and also "admire her bloom," and by the final lines the poem reverses its opening claims by calling for a return to the gentler temper of Eden and the Golden Age.[39]

For Cooke and Lewis poetry faces yet another danger, for, so long as literary energy is tied up coping with economic problems, letters will never thrive there.[40] In Lewis's preface to his 1728 translation of a Latin poem, for example, a conventional apology for the work's inferiority takes a peculiar regional turn. Lamenting that his English translation will necessarily lack the life and energy of the original Latin, he draws a telling comparison between the cultures of the classical past and the colonial present:

There Painture breathes, *There* Statuary lives,
And Music most delightful Rapture gives:

> *There,* pompous Piles of *Building* pierce the Skies,
> And endless Scenes of *Pleasure* court the Eyes.
> While *Here,* rough Woods embrown the Hills and Plains,
> Mean are the *Buildings,* artless are the *Swains:*
> "*To raise the Genius,*" WE no Time can spare,
> A *bare Subsistence* claims our utmost Care.⁴¹

Although the gauge of excellence here is the lyric of "fair Italian Plains," the high standards of England have surely contributed to such feelings of inadequacy. Preoccupied with economic survival, Marylanders stand no chance of producing art that is comparable. Lewis, who favored the initial development of industrial arts, notably shipbuilding and linen manufacture, and eventually of the fine arts, thanks Benedict Leonard Calvert for his attempts to "add new Life to [the] declining Trade." Less concerned here with preserving the woods than clearing them for more refined buildings, he hopes that "Arts Polite" will "shine in this Domain" once the colony is released from its economic constraints.⁴² In Cooke's preface as well there is a hint of regret that literature has by necessity been pressed into service exclusively for economic problem solving. Immediately after encapsulating the proposed remedies that will be the subject of his poem, he announces that the "thread-bare theme" of economic reform (it was, in fact, the most recurring topic of Parks's *Gazette*) did "never drink of the Castalian Springs" (*SR* vi).

If Cooke, Lewis, and other writers published by Parks were part of a self-conscious flowering of writing in the Chesapeake, these apologies convey nevertheless a frustration with the still crude state of letters. Cooke's poem looks forward to a time when literate freeholders in a republic of letters might solve their economic problems and thereby enable the pursuit of other intellectual endeavors. The planter, who has a "Project in [his] Pate," represents the freeholder who might use ingenuity for the particularly cerebral task of coining paper money. He agrees with the poet-speaker that money, whether in "Tan-Pit coin'd, or Paper-Mill," can be invested with value, adding that it matters not what "Sort of Mine" it issues from, "since ev'ry Thing / Is worth no more than it will bring" (*SR* 3–4). And yet this planter might still be exceptional in his ability to make this substitution. Elsewhere in the poem, for instance, one esquire contemplates the proposed paper money and claims he could not vote

> For such an odd contriv'd Intention,
> As e'er was laid before Convention:

> Alledging, *Planters,* when in drink,
> Wou'd light their Pipes with Paper Chink;
> And knowing not to read, might be
> Impos'd on, by such Currency.   (7–8)

Illiterate planters are not the only ones unprepared for monetary change. The "Convention" before which this "odd contriv'd Intention" is laid is not simply the Maryland Assembly but custom itself. Even the literate may have difficulty accepting this new way of carrying on trade.

The problem, then, is a cyclical one. The remedy of paper currency requires literacy, yet, if Marylanders are consumed with staying afloat economically, they may never have the opportunity to become literate. The poet-speaker urges Maryland to defy convention and venture to use paper currency and other economic reforms to break the cycle. He concludes the poem by warning his audience to "be advis'd" and heed his exhortation:

> Begin, be bold, old Horace cries,
> And bravely venture to be wise.
> In vain, he on the Brook Side stands,
> With Shoes and Stockings in his Hands;
> Waiting 'till all the Stream be past and gone,
> That runs, (alas!) and ever will run on.   (*SR* 28)

Horace, a carpe diem poet, calls for bold initiative but still waits tentatively by the brook for his chance to cross. The stream "ever will run on," and the more he waits the more time simply will be lost. There will be no perfect time for Maryland, and the colony must act now.[43]

In 1733 a proposal similar to the one recommended by Cooke was eventually enacted. Ninety thousand pounds in paper bills were printed and loaned to planters, who could use them in lieu of tobacco to pay local debts. The government, in other words, went into debt by printing unbacked currency and then loaned that currency, at interest, to individual debtors.[44] Although the issue did provide debtor relief and was eventually redeemed, it was not until the Tobacco Inspection Act of 1747 that the government effectively kept tobacco prices elevated.[45] Cooke's poem foresaw some of the means by which Maryland would remedy its woes, but much of its vision remained unrealized, particularly because the institution of slavery only became more entrenched in the regional economy.

Because Cooke's economic program was not realized, the poem remains an act of projection. Although its intricate economic concerns are not legible to most modern readers, its forward-looking impulse reveals much about this moment in the Chesapeake. The poem records a community in transition, trying to shake its status as provincial and imagine a new kind of thinking population. In this vision paper money is a tool for economic and cultural progress, one that will diversify the economy, free people from necessity, and let arts thrive. But, just as important, paper money, like the pamphlets, *Gazette* essays, and the poem itself, is the resource of a community that has begun to understand the power of print.

Part Two / The Price of Independence

> This BILL entitles the BEARER to receive EIGHT *Spanish milled* DOLLARS, or the Value thereof in *Gold* or *Silver*, according to a Resolution passed by CONGRESS, at York-Town, 11th *April*, 1778.
> CONTINENTAL BILL, ISSUED APRIL 11, 1778

> I had the honour of being born (God be thanked) not in England, but in America; not in a petty island, a cage for slaves, and a nursery for banditti and cutthroats, but in the centre of the vast continent of North-America, whose boundless and unexplored regions are fit to be inhabited only by such free and uncontrouled souls as mine! America! where enterprizing genius may perambulate without the least restraint.... My father's name (for I undoubtedly had one) was *Liberty*.
> THE ADVENTURES OF A CONTINENTAL DOLLAR, UNITED STATES MAGAZINE, JUNE 1779

> If the history of commercial banking belongs to the Italians and of central banking to the British, that of paper money issued by a government belongs indubitably to the Americans.
> JOHN KENNETH GALBRAITH, *MONEY: WHENCE IT CAME, WHERE IT WENT*

In a speech on the national debt in 1787 one Massachusetts politician proclaimed that states "become respectable on the same principles by which the character of individuals is maintained."[1] A year later Noah Webster insisted that governments and individuals be held to the same standards of behavior with respect to their debts: for governments "to compel individuals to perform contracts and yet break their own solemn promises; to punish individuals for neglect, and yet set a general example of delinquency, is to undermine the foundation of social confidence, and shake every principle of commutativ justice."[2] Politicians and writers who did not agree on what exactly should be done to maintain their character did at least agree that a state's credibility and a man's credibility rested on similar grounds. This equation stands behind two of the era's most famous literary treatments of personal credit: Benjamin Franklin's *Autobiography* and Royall Tyler's *Contrast*. Their stories of individual heroes offer instruction on how the state might come of age and secure its reputability through responsible indebtedness.

Like Franklin's autobiographical persona and Tyler's Colonel Manly, the new nation achieved success through borrowing: almost $450 million in unbacked state and federal currencies as well as $12 million in foreign loans.[3] When the thirteen colonies sought independence, the Continental Congress justified a national paper money in 1775 as an experimental medium necessitated by the novel and exigent circumstances of a revolution. Given the extent to which Britain's revenue system had incensed colonists, the Congress was reluctant to raise funds by levying taxes. Fiat currency that quickly depreciated in the hands of its holders *was* a form of taxation—one that hit hardest those who were cash poor and forced to use them while their value was low—but this measure was much easier to justify in theory.

The decision to use paper money to fund the war was also based on a conviction that the public debt that had earlier facilitated colonial settlement could now be pressed into service for revolutionary purposes. The textual history of another ballad broadside by Joseph Green confirms that colonists saw settlement and national independence as parallel experiences. In its first incarnation, entitled "A Mournful Lamentation for the sad and deplorable Death of Mr. Old Tenor," the ballad eulogizes the departed persona of old-tenor money for his role in colonial settlement:

> To fruitful fields, by swift degrees,
> > He turn'd our desart land:
> Where once nought stood but rocks and trees,
> > Now spacious cities stand.

A half-century later the ballad, renamed "A Mournful Lamentation On the untimely Death of Paper Money," was recycled and the earlier praise replaced:

> He rais'd and paid our Armies brave.
> > To guard our threaten'd State;
> Whose val'rous Deeds their Country save,
> > And num'rous Foes defeat.

In this "doleful tale" the assassins who have killed off Paper Money fail to appreciate the work he can perform. Marx identified public debt as the modern nation-state's primary tool for colonial expansion, but here the instrument of Britain's expansion is deployed, instead, for colonial rebellion and independence.

This was not the first time paper money had been hailed as an instrument of independence. Because British mercantilist policy was designed to accumulate a favorable balance of trade that would have to be settled by the shipment of specie out of the colonies, paper had seemed a viable alternative to metal media that might free the colonies of their trade debt to the mother country. Britain had always prohibited colonial governments from declaring any medium "legal tender" (legally mandating its acceptance, or "currency"), and, in the minds of colonists, the mother country's attempts to regulate colonial currency, via the Currency Acts of 1751 and 1764, was proof that Britain conspired to hinder their economic growth and reduce them to financial dependence. To make matters worse, the Stamp Act of 1765, which required that all public documents be affixed with tax stamps shipped from London, applied to financial instruments and undermined the benefits of paper as a cheap and plentiful commercial medium. In the years leading up to the Revolution, the printing of various colonial bills became symbolic of, and instrumental in, the move for political independence. A national Continental currency, issued to pay for soldier's salaries and military supplies, provided much of the underwriting for the risky, but potentially profitable, venture of insurrection.[4]

Yet, while it was understood as an instrument of independence, paper currency also prompted debates over the extent to which a hefty public debt would compromise the nation's vitality and self-determination. What did it mean for the new nation to define itself through staggering loans from Spain, France, and Holland as well as loans from soldiers who served in exchange for paper money IOUs? Those who had supported the public debt, especially hard-money advocates who accepted it as an emergency measure, now wondered aloud when these loans would be paid. Revolutionaries who had been inspired by visions of a virtuous republic began to grow disenchanted. Many of them saw the fulfillment of fiscal obligations and the fulfillment of the republican vision as inseparable. Debts threatened to undo newly won independence and cast suspicion upon the country's honor, and, so long as they lingered and accrued, the promises of revolutionary times would never be realized. This irony was keenly felt, and some of the rhetoric surrounding war finance attempted to recast dire necessity as ingenuity: boasting that America had brilliantly created money to fund its independence, Thomas Paine wrote in 1778, "We are rich by a contrivance of our own."[5]

Figure 2. Wartime bills often proclaimed themselves instruments of liberation. The "Sword in Hand" bill (*top*), which was engraved by Paul Revere and issued in Massachusetts, features a soldier holding the Magna Charta and the words "Issued in defence of American Liberty." Beneath it is a counterfeit of Revere's forty-eight-shilling bill (the warning frequently printed on bills, "Death to Counterfeiters," was not always a deterrent). In this counterfeit, as in the original, the soldier's Magna Charta has been replaced by the Declaration of Independence. Courtesy of Special Collections, University of Notre Dame.

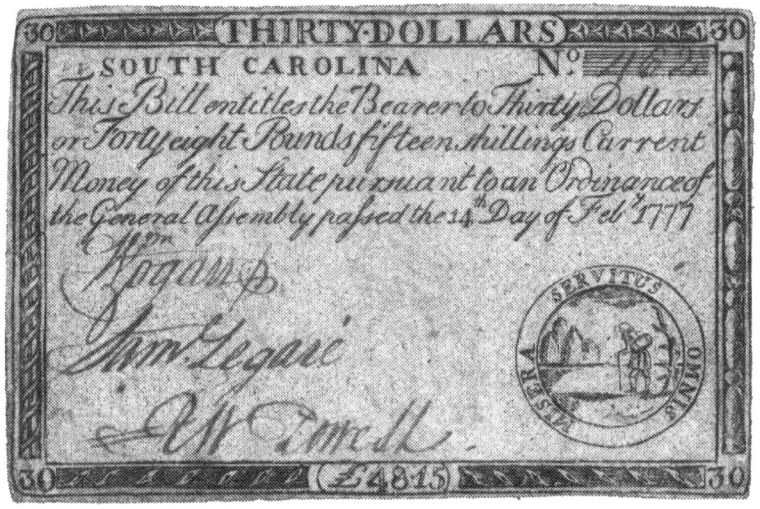

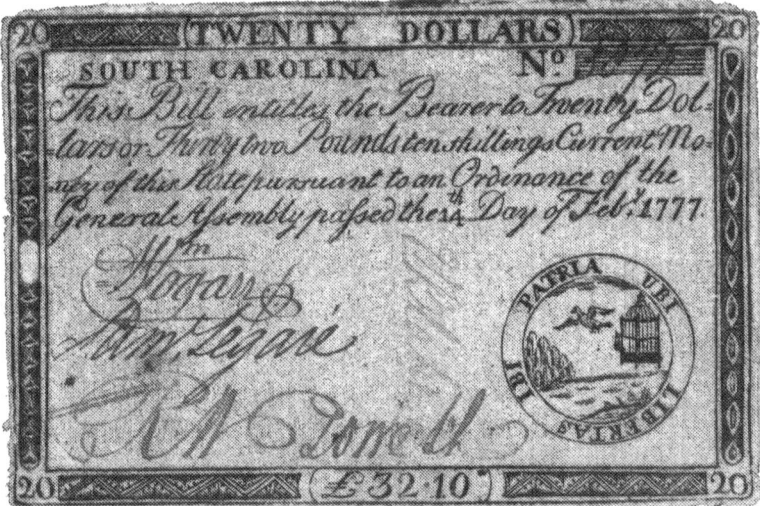

Figure 3. Like the "Sword in Hand" bills of Massachusetts, these 1777 South Carolina bills celebrate freedom. One announces, SERVITUS OMNIS MISERA (All Forms of Slavery Are Wretched), and the other features a bird fleeing a cage and the motto, UBI LIBERTAS IBI PATRIA (Where There Is Liberty, There Is Homeland). Courtesy of Special Collections, University of Notre Dame.

This carefully crafted rhetoric also emphasized that paper money revealed a popular sovereignty at work. Praising the war debt, one anonymous writer declared in 1787 that the "faith of the people" themselves had "impressed" the bills with their value.[6] According to Paine, the colonists could choose to credit the monetary symbols of their own making rather than the empty symbols of monarchical power. At first glance this rhetoric of volition might seem inconsistent with the fact that currency fluctuations could make the consequences of one's actions impalpable and apparently beyond the reach of individual estimation or control; after all, in such a volatile credit system, one's destiny would seem a function not of agency but of impersonal economic forces. Rhetoric and reality might be easily reconciled, however, if one saw this volition as necessarily *collective*. Otherwise powerless people, that is, could effect change by acting in concert with one another.

David Ramsey's 1789 *History of the American Revolution* seems particularly intent on highlighting the role of patriotic human agency in the wartime economy:

> That the endangered liberties of America ought to be defended, and that the credit of their paper was essentially necessary to a proper defence, were opinions engraven on the hearts of a great majority of the citizens. It was therefore a point of honor and considered as a part of duty, to take the bills freely at their full value. Private gain was then so little regarded, that the whig citizens were willing to run all the hazards incidental to bills of credit, rather than injure the cause of their country by under valuing its money. Every thing human has its limits. While the credit of the money was well supported by public confidence and patriotism, its value diminished from the increase of its quantity. Repeated emissions begat that natural depreciation, which results from an excess of quantity.[7]

A witness to the new nation's growing pains, Ramsey sought to construct a history of consensus and chose not to dwell on unpatriotic behavior. Although he is correct in pointing out that the issues did not depreciate noticeably at first, he describes only the "great majority of citizens" exhibiting honor and duty in their handling of public credit bills and says nothing of the creditors who refused to accept them in transactions and stockjobbers who purchased them at discount with the hopes of redeeming them at full value later. What is most curious here is how Ramsey accounts for the eventual depreciation of the bills. Admirable patriot activity (the willingness to "take the bills freely" and "run all the hazards") gives way to a depersonalized, even organic, process in which repeated emissions, with no apparent human cause, "begat" a "natural depreciation." Ramsey suggests that, because "every thing human has its limits," even the patriots' noble attempt to uphold the value of Continental bills could not stave off the inevitable forces of supply and demand. This distinction between different kinds of depreciation also governed a congressional circular letter to citizens in 1779. According to the circular's logic, "natural" depreciation results from too large an issue of bills and "artificial" depreciation from the "distrust (however occasioned) entertained by the mass of the people either in the *ability* or *inclination* of the United States to redeem their bills."[8]

But, according to a classical economic model of the market, even the so-called natural depreciation was the collective effect of individual human desires and decisions, for it was precisely because such individuals feared for their own purses and undervalued the bills that they sank in value. In this understanding all depreciation is artificial in the sense of being man-made. In Ramsey's account, which simultaneously emphasizes and de-emphasizes human agency, a curious mixture of two economic models emerges. When Ramsey showcases the patriotism of the Revolutionaries, he invokes a model of moral economy, which assumed that individuals were capable of and accountable for effecting market change. When, on the other hand, he wants to downplay the colonists' self-interest and describe an organic process free of human intervention, he invokes the mysterious yet predictably self-regulating mechanism that Adam Smith had dubbed the "invisible hand."

The congressional circular understood depreciation to result from popular "distrust" in the "ability" or "inclination" of the government to redeem its bills, and for this reason the government would need to provide people with the necessary assurances. Good intentions were not sufficient if the government did not also make visible those intentions through regular redemptions, or "performances." Such performances, in fact, could transform a public debt into a permanent means of bolstering federal credibility. Erected in 1791, the new nation's banking plan called for the complete redemption of wartime money but also *ongoing* strategic borrowing that would showcase the government's ability to undertake and discharge debts. According to this plan, the new nation would earn points each time it paid off a loan.

If this seems strange, consider that today credit-rating institutions grant higher scores to individuals who have successfully assumed mortgages and car loans than those who have never had to rely on borrowing. Or consider even the equation of borrowing and masculine bravado in Theodore Dreiser's novel *The Financier* (1912). Speaking with the man whose daughter he will eventually take as mistress, Cowperwood explains that risk is an entrepreneur's opportunity to prove himself to others: "I want to bid for five million," he says to Butler. "I only want one million but I want the prestige of putting in a bona fide bid for five million. It will do me good on the street."[9] Cowperwood performs sexually—seducing Butler's young daughter and fathering two children with a wife whose previous husband could sire none—but he also performs as a borrower. He bids for more loans than he needs—loans that others would never dare take on—because they will bolster his reputation. For Cowperwood borrowing is merely the price of self-determination: an ongoing dependence through which, paradoxically, he hopes to empower himself.

They are hardly Frank Cowperwoods, but Franklin's autobiographical persona and Tyler's Colonel Manly demonstrate the empowering effects of assuming arrears. In Franklin's account of a young man's coming of age, indebtedness provides the means for his own self-determination, and he uses this model, in turn, to solicit the reader's faith in the nation's own rise on credit. And, in the most popular native drama of the republican era, Colonel Manly's comic triumph suggests that both the manly man and the viable nation prove themselves as borrowers.

CHAPTER THREE

Benjamin Franklin's Projections

Benjamin Franklin's *Autobiography* teaches the value of a good credit rating. Hard work is well and good, but sometimes loans are necessary. So, the Franklinian persona, who carts his printing papers through the streets in a wheelbarrow just to assure other tradesmen that he is industrious, repeatedly reminds his reader that reputation, in an economy based on credit, is an asset in itself. In what are now frequently cited words Franklin recalls, "In order to secure my Credit and Character as a Tradesman, I took care not only to be in *Reality* Industrious and frugal, but to avoid all *Appearances* of the Contrary."[1]

Written at a time when American public credit was tenuous both at home and abroad, this memoir simultaneously comes to concern itself as much with the new nation's credit rating as with Franklin's own reputation. Like Franklin's widely influential *Nature and Necessity of a Paper Currency,* the *Autobiography* articulates profound faith in debt as the means by which individuals and also communities can advance themselves. Franklin's *Autobiography* is a tale of his own rise to wealth and social prominence and a more speculative archetype of the success other American tradesmen might achieve, but it also illustrates how America might rise on credit in ways similar to the entrepreneurial individual.

The rhetorical strategies of Franklin's *Autobiography* are governed by a conviction that debt could be a resource for the individual as well as the commonwealth. But it is also the case that understanding Franklin's autobiography as a voucher for national credibility leads to a new understanding of its autobiographical persona. Scholars have consistently characterized Franklin as a writer who fashions a depersonalized self in order to represent a putatively universal American experience, but, in fact, Franklin vouches for America precisely by exploiting the specifics of his own remarkable career and reputation. This concept of representation was reinforced by a philosophy of public credit through which prominent individuals vouched for governmental credibility, for Franklin believed that public credit would have to rely upon "individuals of established reputation," as Alexander Hamilton put it, "conspicuous for probity, abilities and fortune."[2] In this sense the *Autobiography* claims representative status not as a text that is indicative of ordinary American experience but, rather, as a story of *extra*ordinary success which vouches for, or represents as an advocate might, the new nation and its promise.[3] In this autobiography it is personality, and not a depersonalized self, which works to enhance American credibility.

Rising on Credit

As Franklin was a young entrepreneur launching himself through start-up loans and friendly letters of introduction, the colonies were using paper credit instruments to fund their own speculative ventures. Shortly after his arrival in Philadelphia in 1723, the colony of Pennsylvania introduced its first paper money by lending interest-bearing bills to debtors willing to use their own lands for security. Although public money in Franklin's native Massachusetts had eventually aggravated that colony's financial problems, Pennsylvania currency was well managed and suffered little long-term depreciation.

Franklin's *Nature and Necessity of a Paper-Currency* claimed that such credit was vital to American enterprise. Because an increased availability of credit would drive down the interest rates and provide cheaper credit to those without capital, colonial governments—for only the cost of the paper on which the money would be printed—could help launch the laboring classes, attract new immigrants, and stimulate exchange and real estate development. If the colonies were to draw immigrants intent on advancement, Franklin wrote, credit would have to be readily available. The immigrant or upstart must first become dependent to creditors in order ultimately to become independent.[4] Franklin considered paper money a resourceful innovation and a necessary substitution that could compensate for the colonies' and young nation's lack of metal wealth. He dubbed it an "excellent Machine for Settling a new Country" which could facilitate individual enterprise and promote the economic welfare of communities.[5] The colonial landscape had yielded little silver or gold, he wrote in a defense of American paper money presented to British officials in 1767, and an "Imitation of the Bank of England, where every Bill is payable in Cash upon Sight," was simply "impracticable."[6]

To be sure, Franklin's advocacy of paper credit was never unqualified. He lamented the "evil" of depreciation which would accompany excessive and mismanaged emissions. While he believed that creditors could help support unbacked bills, he also believed these bills would eventually, at a future time, need to be redeemable for something of value—or, if they remained in circulation, they would need to retain their purchasing power. And, even though popular opinion could sustain the fiction that the bills were, even at the moment of their issue, worth their "proclaimed" value, he acknowledged that severe depreciation made redemption increasingly impossible and weakened the creditor's confidence.

Notwithstanding these problems, paper money was a mysteriously effective mechanism in Franklin's view. It was "understood by few," as he wrote in the *American Weekly Mercury* in 1729, and yet capable of sustaining an undertaking as costly as a full-scale war. Writing from his ministerial post in Passy, France, Franklin marveled at all that Revolutionary currency could accomplish: "The whole is a Mistery even to the Politicians; how we have been able to continue a War four years without Money; & how we could pay with Paper, that had no previously fix'd fund appropriated specifically to redeem it. This Currency, as we manage it is a wonderful Machine."[7] Curiously, Franklin does not say whether *he* fails to understand paper currency along with the French, just as fifty years earlier, in the *American Weekly Mercury,* he does not say whether he numbers among the mere "few" who understand Pennsylvania money. But he also makes irrelevant the question of his own comprehension, for his point is precisely that one need not understand this mechanism in order to appreciate its benefits.

Franklin understood that some observers would find this mysteriousness disconcerting and be reluctant to credit something they could not understand. As one of the men who selected the mottoes for the first series of Continental dollars in the spring of 1775, Franklin worked hard to craft a rhetoric that would convince buyers and sellers to put faith in the venture. Taking full advantage of the fact that Continentals were not only a source of revenue but also a medium on which Revolutionary rhetoric might circulate, he chose mottoes and images that might favorably influence public opinion of the war.[8] The series of ten denominations, each bearing a distinct image and Latin text, all speak, in one way or another, to the importance of the colonial cause and the promise of the American future: SUSTINE VEL ABSTINE (support or leave) presents an ultimatum for the British; DEPRESSA RESURGIT (Tho' oppressed it rises) predicts American victory; and MAJORA MINORIBUS CONSONANT (the greater and smaller ones sound together) envisions an American consensus akin to musical harmony.

As the bills are themselves a reminder that independence will carry a price, mottoes often combine optimism with a candid acknowledgment that war is costly. On the two-dollar note, the engraving of a hand threshing wheat and the phrase TRIBULATIO DITAT (tribulation improves) emphasizes that strength will come only with struggle, and on the seven-dollar note the engraving of a tempest and the single word SERENABIT (it will clear up) predict victory only after the colonists have weathered the storm of war. Although these two mottoes make unqualified predictions about American success, another bill, bearing the motto EXITUS IN DUBIO EST (the end is uncertain), offers a frank reminder that the colonist must act without complete assurance of victory. To accept a Continental dollar was, in effect, to gamble on the country's future because buyers and sellers generally believed that only American victory would ensure that bills would be valuable after the war (to the dismay of many, these bills severely depreciated despite victory, though other instruments were eventually redeemed with interest). With uncertainty an inevitable part of the process of political change, Franklin likely saw the optimism of this monetary rhetoric as a risky but necessary speculation.

Franklin's efforts to uphold the new nation's currency were not limited to his selection of mottoes. In an attempt to vouch for the bills' credibility and influence how readers would interpret their rhetoric, Franklin also penned an essay for the *Pennsylvania Gazette*, entitled "Account of the Devices on the Continental Bills of Credit," to explain their meaning to the public. The essay suggests that popular opinion can help determine whether the bills' values and the mottoes' predictions of Revolutionary success will eventually be realized. Franklin offers a translation of the Latin, an analysis of the translation and images, and a lesson on how to read a financial instrument. He assumes the posture of an objective observer, claiming only to give "Conjectures of their Meaning" for the simple reason that "No Explanation of the Devices on the Continental Bills of Credit [has] yet appeared,"[9] but his interpretation is clearly calculated to inspire confidence in both the bills' promises and the war effort championed by the mottoes.

In the image of a busy beaver on the six-dollar note, for instance, Franklin sees a glimpse of American perseverance and financial independence from British trade regulations:

> Another had the figure of a *beaver* gnawing a large tree, with this motto, PERSEVERANDO; *By perseverance*. I apprehend the *great tree* may be intended to represent the enormous power Britain has assumed over us, and endeavours to enforce by arms, of taxing us at pleasure, *and binding us in all cases whatsoever;* or the exorbitant profits she makes by monopolizing our commerce. Then the *beaver*, which is known to be able, by assiduous and steady working, to fell large trees, may signify *America*, which, by perseverance in her present measures, will probably reduce that power within proper bounds, and, by establishing the most necessary manufactures among ourselves, abolish the British monopoly.[10]

Franklin makes clear that he can only *venture* an interpretation, attempting to "apprehend" what "may be intended" by the image and what will "probably" occur in the future. Even though he cannot speak definitively about the future, Franklin nevertheless publicly extends his credit to the Revolutionary cause and, in turn, to the credit of the bills on which the rhetoric appears. As a speculative act in a time of crisis, the analysis demonstrates the extent to which one must be willing to take risks in order to support public credit.

Franklin's "Account of the Devices" indicates that he saw his writing as a means to effect economic change. In the *Autobiography* he also points to several instances in which his own published words operated similarly. He recalls that his "well receiv'd" 1729 pamphlet on paper currency helped convince the Pennsylvania legislature to issue more money, and this emission (in addition to landing Franklin a printing contract for the currency issue) provided much needed financial relief for the colony's debtors (*ABF* 53). He also writes that the reduction of the colonial trade deficit in Pennsylvania (and, as a result, the increase in metal currency available for trade in the colony) was attributed by

Figure 4. The mottoes on these Continental dollars, which Franklin probably helped select and later interpreted for the public, predict success but also emphasize that Americans must endure uncertainty. The first three offer assurances: SERENABIT (It Will Clear Up), TRIBULATIO DITAT (Tribulation Improves), and PERSEVERANDO (By Perseverance). The last, however, concedes, EXITUS IN DUBIO EST (The End Is Uncertain). Courtesy of Special Collections, University of Notre Dame.

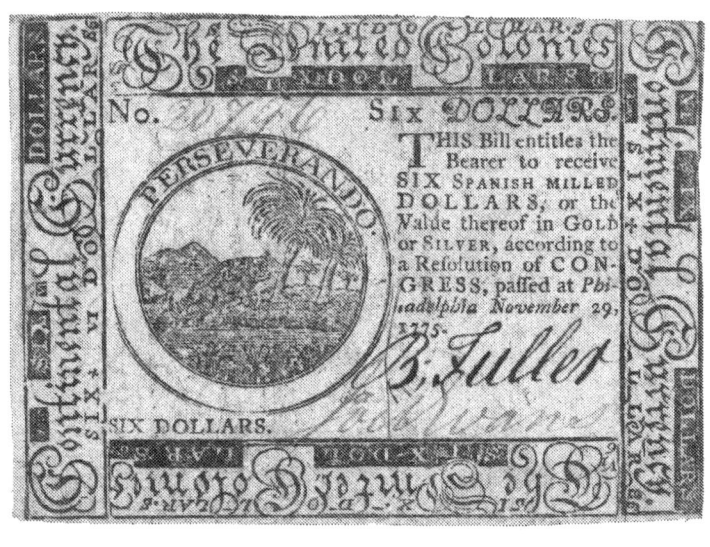

many to his aphorisms' sage advocacy of industry and frugality in "The Way to Wealth."

These convictions would only have been reinforced by a political climate in which print media influenced public credibility and monetary value. As historians have observed, both the Declaration of Independence and later the U.S. Constitution were written, published, and circulated largely to help establish national credibility and procure much needed European loans for the fledgling nation (such loans, it was assumed, would then strengthen public confidence in the feasibility of independence and raise currency values at home). Charles Beard went so far as to argue that the Constitution framers were "public creditors" who had invested in the private but government-chartered Bank of North America and who hoped the document would enhance the value of their own holdings. Other historians since have argued that the theory is overwrought in attributing one motive to all framers, but Beard is essentially correct in acknowledging the interdependence of print media, public credibility, and currency values. His thesis also identifies the capacity of public finance to transform individual bill holders into public investors and to make private and civic interests ultimately inseparable.[11]

It is instructive, then, to understand Franklin's essay, as well as the *Autobiography*, in the context of a literary culture in which writers often worked to support public credit. Thomas Paine, for example, deployed print media to combat monetary problems during the Revolutionary conflict. Many of his *American Crisis* papers written during the Revolution, particularly numbers 3, 5, 7, 9, 10, 13, and "The Crisis Extraordinary," address the concerns of colonists and soldiers over depreciated currency and mounting war debts. Paine's rhetoric responds by emphasizing that the nation's debts are nothing compared to the rewards and are beneficially "circulated within," unlike Britain's arrears, he argues, which accumulate as the government pays out the salaries of foreign soldiers. Paine appeals to his reader's reason, crunching the numbers to show what a sound investment war will be for the nation, but he also simply beseeches readers to ignore their doubts. The support of currency, he writes in his third pamphlet, goes "hand in hand with the suppression of disaffection and the encouragement of public spirit." Paper money is not "easy" credit but a test of a community's convictions. Paine presumes a reader who can effect economic change: "I call not upon a few, but upon all: not on *this* state or *that* state, but on *every* state: up and help us; lay your shoulders to the wheel."[12]

Even Paine's pamphlets not explicitly concerned with wartime finance use an idiom of investment and work to elevate morale at a time when financial support for the war was precarious. Paine began writing his first and most famous *Crisis* pamphlet, for example, at the early signs of currency depreciation, in December 1776. Reportedly composing on a drumhead by the light of campfire as he accompanied George Washington and the troops on their retreat across New Jersey, he stressed that freedom comes only at a price: "These are the times that try men's souls. The summer soldier and the sunshine patriot will, in this crisis, shrink from the service of their country; but he that stand it *now,* deserves the love and thanks of man and woman. Tyranny, like hell, is not easily conquered; yet we have this consolation with us, that the harder the conflict, the more glorious the triumph. What we obtain too cheap, we esteem too lightly: it is dearness only that gives every thing its value."[13] In this pamphlet Paine identifies panic as a "touchstone of sincerity and hypocrisy" which brings the true character of men to light. Elsewhere he labels doubt as a "species of infidelity" and claims that the fulfillment of expectation depends on popular backing: "Those who expect to reap the blessings of freedom, must, like men, undergo the fatigues of supporting it." The financial metaphors carry literal significance, for Paine writes of a crisis that is simultaneously psychological and economic. Hard times lead to low morale, which in turn sinks bills deeper and jeopardizes the entire movement for independence. Paine's speculations are necessary because, by instilling confidence, the pamphlets might eventually make possible the realization of their own projections.[14]

A similar sense of self-fulfilling prophecy informs David Humphreys' 1782 address to disheartened and impoverished soldiers who had been paid in increasingly depreciated Continentals. Writing in 1782 for the express purpose of inspiring soldiers, Humphreys finds resource in the recollection of a glorious past and "the anticipation of the future."[15] His promise of forthcoming redemption and his exhortation to wait patiently for that redemption apply both to the promise of the Continentals and, more generally, to the promise of the new nation: "The mild temperature and serenity of the air, the salubrity of the climate, the fertility of the soil, the luxuriance of its products, the extent of territory, and the amazing inland navigation, which those boundless lakes and immeasurable rivers will open—cannot fail, one day, to render that garden of the world equal to the representation given of it, in the conclusion of the poem."[16] Humphreys' preface sees a latent prosperity in the landscape of America: fertile, navigable, and seemingly limitless, it will eventually match the "representation given of it" by the poem that follows. His poetic forecast of the garden, however, will only be realized "one day," and the fact that such fulfillment is necessarily deferred for the moment is itself a source of motivation.

In this passage financial faith and the reader's suspension of disbelief are intimately related. Marc Shell has argued that the faith one brings to the reading of literature is similar to the act of crediting monetary instruments: "Credit, or belief, involves the ground of aesthetic experience," he writes, and what confers belief in credit instruments "also seems to confer it in art."[17] But, in the case of Humphreys' address, the two modes of belief are not simply analogous but, in fact, mutually reinforcing. The poem's projections of fertility work to inspire the soldiers' financial faith; likewise, the financial faith, which is necessary to keep the war going, might make the realization of the poetic dream possible. When and how Humphreys' vision will be realized is less important than the motivation that comes with its futuristic orientation.

Like Paine's and Humphreys' wartime writings and Franklin's account of Continental devices, the *Autobiography* posits a reader whose suspension of disbelief can help fulfill the text's projections: taken as true, the memoir might inspire enterprise, encourage much needed immigration, or bolster the public confidence and the financial structures premised on such confidence. According to the narrative's logic, then, the process of realizing its promised life actually begins with a faithful reading of the *Autobiography* itself.

This faithful reading would be crucial in the years after the Revolutionary crisis. In the postwar years people such as Paine and Humphreys opposed paper money (though not readily convertible banknotes), and, like many, they thought it was time the nation reckoned with its debts. As Franklin took up part 2 of his memoirs in Passy, France, in 1784, he had just spent years using his own name to lobby the French government for crucial war loans to the United States. During this time his primary responsibility was the maintenance of the nation's name abroad, and complicating this task was the depreciation of various paper credit instruments weakening the government's credibility at home. "I cannot," he had anxiously written about mounting French loans, "suffer the Credit of our Country to be destroyed."[18] It is against this backdrop that Franklin resumes his memoirs at Passy, and the *Autobiography* eventually takes its more public turn using the story of the young Franklin's rise on credit to advocate the nation's rise on credit and to "represent," as Humphreys says, its latent prosperity.

Credible Selves

When Franklin's adversaries responded to his "Account of the Devices," they condemned him for using print to fashion a textual self that belied a putative real self—in much the same way they condemned paper money for misrepresenting wealth. These and other writings suggest that opponents of paper money consistently characterized its supporters as upwardly mobile individuals inclined to use writing and print to manage their public self-presentations: they were, according to this logic, manipulators of credibility, both monetary and personal. These opponents were threatened by the concept of a self fashioned through writing or print, rendered anonymous, depersonalized, and, in Larzer Ziff's formulation, removed from immanence. While Franklin understood the power of such depersonalized selves, he also understood that in insecure financial times people wanted the concrete assurances of individuals. For this reason it is worth examining some of this oppositional rhetoric before turning to the *Autobiography,* for it helps explain why Franklin would have felt the need to establish a "credibility of personality" as a way of authorizing his own representation of American credit.

One telling attack on Franklin's essay, entitled "Considerations on the Use and Abuse of Mottos," implies that Franklin is an imposter who fashions himself as learned. The essay barely mentions fiduciary matters, focusing instead on attacking improperly educated writers who speak only a smattering of Latin and clichés distorted to serve their ulterior motives: Franklin's selection and subsequent analysis of the Latin mottoes on the Continental dollars is reduced to self-serving pretense. Satirizing Franklin's use of aphorisms, the writer also presents a list of vices and for each finds a truncated, decontextualized line of biblical Scripture which appears to condone the action but in fact has been manipulated in order to rationalize bad behavior.[19]

Another response to Franklin's essay, entitled "Representation and Remonstrance of Hard Money. Addressed to the People of America," also aligns the advocacy of paper money with social posturing. This address to "the people," spoken by the persona of Hard Money itself, acknowledges the importance of public opinion, yet the essay insists that accurate assessment is the prerogative of an elite class of "reading men" who are "able to conceive that first appearances are oftentimes deceitful, and that *all is not gold that glitters.*" To this critic there is likely little distinction to be made between Franklin and someone like the notorious eighteenth-century confidence man Stephen Burroughs. In his memoirs Burroughs recalls the dreams of social mobility unleashed when he witnesses the ultimate manipulation of value, a metal counterfeiter's manufacture of easy money: "I saw, in my own imagination, my fortune certainly made," Burroughs recalls. "Not a doubt remained in my mind of becoming the richest man on the continent of America." Paper money advocates might argue that Burroughs distorts the initial logic behind credit, for he creates unauthorized money that constitutes theft rather than borrowing. But, in the minds of its opponents, even legitimate paper money was a counterfeit like the one Burroughs admires—a pretense of material value which is not present or tangible.[20]

In "Representation and Remonstrance of Hard Money" Franklin's upstart machinations are also facilitated by his knowledge of printing. Drawing on the traditional distinction between "real" metal money and "imaginary" paper money, the writer implicates paper instruments in a larger print culture that distorts value by rendering it synonymous with public perception. In this essay unbacked paper money, depicted as the brainchild of Franklin and the embodiment of Franklinian strategizing, emerges as a national version of the upstart's textual management of reputation. Metal specie is personified as a man of substance, honorable birth, and fluency in all languages (metal's widespread acceptability making it universally conversant). The Continental, by contrast, is the obscure child of a Philadelphia printer and given to "affecting an importance, as if he had been equal to the *solid coin*."[21]

Two anonymous responses to this essay, written in the persona of the Continental Dollar, applaud currency as the product of an enlightened republic of letters. In one the Continental Dollar declares, "If a *Printing-office* was the place of *my nativity,* so has it been of the noblest productions that ever blessed or adorned the world." In another he boasts, "I am by the mother's side of the family of *Paper;* a family that has been of more service to the commonwealth of letters than all of the name of Hard-Money that ever have existed." Yet an exchange in the *Worcester Magazine* in 1786 and 1787 illustrates how paper currency raised fears that print media could stand in for personal presence and mislead readers.[22] In the September 1786 issue of this magazine an article appeared defending the devalued (and, as a result, much maligned) Continental dollars that had been issued to fund the Revolutionary War. Adopting the persona of "Paper Money" and speaking on its own behalf, the writer takes credit for having funded the war and claims that the "death" of Paper Money (i.e., its rapid devaluation) was a necessary sacrifice made for the defense of the colonies. Yet in the November issue Paper Money rescinds this claim. The speaker states that "falsehood, arrogance and pride were apparent" in the earlier essay and confesses that Paper Money is, in fact, "a tool of knavery, dishonesty, fraud, and injustice." In the January 1787 issue, however, Paper Money once more speaks up, this time claiming that the November article was submitted by an "impostor" and reiterating the claims of the first essay.[23] At this point the reader cannot discern who is, in fact, the real Paper Money, and the whole interaction implies a clear analogy between a counterfeited credit bill and a forged text. An article and credit bill are representations of, respectively, an author and metal wealth, but both representations by their nature—as texts produced in generalized, reproducible print—are susceptible to illicit imitation.

As Franklin knew through personal experience, printing made possible mass-produced, uniform instruments—and that standardization would give the instruments a necessary legitimacy—but the general and reproducible nature of print also facilitated counterfeiting because one only needed to procure or copy the engraved plates in which the original was set in order to duplicate the text. Franklin, who was awarded the contract to print issues of Delaware, New Jersey, and Pennsylvania paper bills, was keenly aware of these risks. In order to safeguard against counterfeiting, he designed a method of "nature printing," which used the imprint of a single leaf on each of the denominations as a kind of thumbprint or touchstone of authenticity. Like all currency printers, Franklin also had to work under the watchful eye of an appointed official, and he was required to destroy any unused surplus and give all printing plates to the treasury once the run was complete in order that they not be used illegally.[24] Advancements in printing technology facilitated the production of credit instruments, but they also made that production more vulnerable to corruption.

Franklin would have understood both the power and risks of substituting texts for money and people. The depersonalization brought about by print media was certainly liberating for a class of people who could not use social status to procure favorable evaluations. Government-issued credit instruments transformed the act of exchange in the sense that the government's word, rather than that of the buyer, was pledged, relieving low-status individuals of the burden of proving their credibility.[25] Consider, for example, the response of one planter in neighboring Maryland to his legislature's decision to issue circulating "tobacco notes" in exchange for produce. In the April 5, 1753, issue of the *Maryland Gazette*, he writes, "the Advantage of having Tobacco Notes in my Pocket, as giving me Credit for the Quantity mentioned in them wherever I went, and that I was thereby at large to dispose of them when, to whom, and where I pleased; whereas, before this Act, my Credit could not be expected to go beyond my own Neighborhood, or, at farthest, where I might be known." Yet, while the government-issued notes assure others that the planter's credit is good, hence freeing him to conduct business in areas where people do not know him personally, who assures others that the government's word is good? Distinguished individuals, Franklin suggests, could serve this function.

Readers have readily seen that Franklin was empowered by his creation of personae through writing, but they have paid less attention to Franklin's belief that these textual selves might at times be of limited effectiveness. In the early parts of *The Autobiography* Franklin portrays himself as a young man who profitably manages his public presentation through writing: he submits essays to the *New-England Courant* anonymously, to cite one well-known example, so that his brother will not dismiss them on the basis of the author's youth (here he "disguises" his handwriting, but print would have accomplished this anonymity as well). But, although the Franklinian protagonist repeatedly masks himself in this way as a young man, this practice ceases once he retires from printing and becomes a spokesman for governmental credit and other public projects. Franklin would have understood that public credibility required immanence: known, prominent people who would promote currency or make a point of publicly accepting bills as a show of support. Such personalized vouchers on behalf of civic ventures attempted to restore the tangibility many perceived had been lost with geographic expansion and the growth of print. For this reason the latter part of Franklin's *Autobiography*, covering his public service after retirement, features a public spokesman who is supposedly unmasked rather than disguised (he may be no less a rhetorical construction, but he is not presented as such to the reader). I would go so far as to say that the *Autobiography* is itself Franklin's attempt to counter the kinds of anxieties expressed by his adversaries. It is a personalized voucher that trades on his name, his prominence, and his success story.

The Autobiography

Franklin's tales of his early financial entanglements illustrate the necessity of credit for the young tradesman, and, when the memoirs assume their more public orientation, the particulars of this early entrepreneurial experience ultimately legitimate the nation's experiments with public debt. In keeping with the text's mission to provide a conduct manual for the young tradesman,

Franklin's early fiscal history teaches two important lessons: that a certain measure of start-up debt is necessary and that the patient debtor (as well as the investor) can ultimately reap reward. In these entanglements Franklin himself is often the unfortunate victim of loan defaults. Collins and Ralph, both chronically insolvent, eventually renege on their obligations to Franklin. Governor Keith, who offered to write Franklin letters of introduction with which to purchase start-up materials for his printing business, strings him along with deferrals: the young Franklin is "appointed to call at different times, when [the letters] were to be ready, but a future time was still named" (*ABF* 31), and ultimately Keith defaults on this promise altogether.[26] Yet Franklin expresses little indignation over these incidents. Recounting his trip to London, for example, he regrets his unwise decision to lend money to Ralph but emphasizes that he "lov'd him notwithstanding" and that his time in the city had allowed him to acquire a different sort of capital, namely advantageous conversation and personal connections (40).

Franklin's sympathetic treatment of the chronically overextended here may have much to do with the fact that he is simultaneously recollecting his own early struggles with debt: in order to lend money to Collins, he himself dipped into money he was holding for Vernon—committing what he described as "one of the first great Errata" of his life—and he too needs to defer his creditor until he can acquire the funds for repayment (*ABF* 27). It is only through indebtedness, moreover, that Franklin is able to launch himself because Meredith's father provides the funding for Franklin's first printing business, and, when this backer balks on half the amount, two friends (William Coleman and Robert Grace) come forward with assistance. Praising his first printing client, George House, as a valuable patron, Franklin recalls that "the Gratitude [he] felt towards House" made him "often more ready than perhaps [he] should otherwise have been to assist young Beginners" (47). Despite the common characterization of Franklin as a self-proclaimed self-made man, he repeatedly acknowledges that his initial success could not have been possible if financial backers and customers had not been willing to invest in him. While the *Autobiography* does, as J. A. Leo Lemay writes, record a progression from dependence to independence, Franklin never loses sight of the fact that dependence—in the form of start-up loans—is the necessary first step for the entrepreneur.[27]

The young Franklin is not an irresponsible debtor, like others in the memoir, and he impresses on his reader that he went to great pains to repay every loan with interest (he even notes that he repaid his brother, with a gift of new printing type, for the services lost when he broke his apprenticeship and fled to Philadelphia).[28] As Franklin comes of age, then, those loans mature as well, and he makes payment. But, even despite what surely would have been disapproval of Keith's irresponsibility, Franklin nevertheless identifies with the logic of the governor's promises: "But what shall we think of a Governor's playing such pitiful Tricks, and imposing so grossly on a poor ignorant Boy! It was a Habit he had acquired. He wish'd to please everybody; and having little to give, he gave Expectations. He was otherwise an ingenious sensible Man, a pretty good Writer, and a good Governor for the People" (*ABF* 33). With no assets Keith has only promises to give, but even his *promises to provide* such a letter are suspect. Franklin does not condemn these promises because they are, at least, an act of resourcefulness. His very use of the word *expectations*, a traditional term for the projected earnings of a financial investment, suggests that Keith's optimism and promises derive from an entrepreneurial spirit.

From Keith's constant stalling, moreover, Franklin learns that the debtor can use polite language to buy time. In one telling instance Keith satisfies Franklin temporarily by sending, through a secretary, the "civillist Message in the World" (*ABF* 31), and Franklin applies this lesson when Mr. Vernon comes calling for his money: "Mr. Vernon about this time put me in mind of the Debt I ow'd him: but did not press me. I wrote him an ingenuous Letter of Acknowledgments, crav'd his Forbearance a little longer which he allow'd me, and as soon as I was able I paid the Principal with Interest and many Thanks" (51). The savvy manipulation of language—condemned by his adversaries as a tool of the parvenu—is crucial to Franklin's maintenance of his own credit. The letter's "ingenuous" language, which defers rather than confronts, only looks ingenuous because, even at a young age, Franklin was savvy enough to renegotiate a loan. From this encounter Franklin also learns that the patient investor reaps rewards. As interest is the creditor's due, Vernon's willingness to extend the line of credit not only enables Franklin's eventual success but also proves profitable for the lender. Recounting the story of Thomas Denham, Franklin reiterates this point: "He had formerly been in Business at Bristol, but fail'd in Debt to a Number of People, compounded and went to America. There, by a close Application to Business as a Merchant, he acquir'd a plentiful Fortune in a few Years. Returning to England in the Ship with me, He invited his old Creditors to an Entertainment, at which he thank'd them for the easy Composition they had favor'd him with, and when they expected nothing but the Treat, every Man at the first Remove found under his Plate an Order on a Banker for the full Amount of the unpaid Remainder with Interest" (*ABF* 39). The account of Denham is yet another of Franklin's archetypal success stories (even making literal the figurative immigration of Franklin's arrival in Philadelphia). Once Denham achieves his American success, the patient creditors who "favor'd him" with "easy Composition" (*composition* referring here to a mutual agreement or settlement) are duly rewarded.

Another, and perhaps the most dramatic, illustration that patience can bring reward—and, conversely, that doubt can preclude profit—is Franklin's story of the "croaking" Samuel Mickle. Franklin recalls his early years in Philadelphia:

> This Gentleman, a Stranger to me, stopped one Day at my Door, and ask'd me if I was the young Man who had lately opened a new Printing-House: Being answer'd in the Affirmative, he said he was sorry for me; because it was an expensive Undertaking, and the Expense would be lost, for Philadelphia was a sinking Place, the People already half Bankrupts or near being so; all Appearances of the contrary, such as new Buildings and the Rise of Rents, being to his certain Knowledge fallacious, for they were in fact among the Things that would soon ruin us. And he gave me such a Detail of Misfortunes now existing or that were soon to exist, that he left me half-melancholy. Had I known him before I engag'd in this Business, probably I never should have done it. This Man continu'd to live in this decaying place, and to declaim in the same Strain, refusing for many Years to buy a House there, because all was going to Destruction, and at last I had the Pleasure of seeing him give five times as much for one as he might have bought it for when he first began his Croaking. (*ABF* 47)

According to historical records, Mickle was actually a real estate developer who bought property in the city well before this incident took place in 1728. If Franklin embellishes the facts, he does so to craft a lesson for the entrepreneur and especially the recent immigrant. While the pessimist ignores opportunity, Franklin extends faith to his new surroundings and ultimately profits. As noted by modern editors, the encounter with Mickle occurred shortly after Franklin established his printing business but also following a short-term depression and currency depreciation. Franklin, who was apparently lucky enough not to encounter Mickle when he first arrived in Philadelphia, managed to defer his need for instant gratification and keep his own doubts in check—despite the fact that the city was bolstered by unsecured credit and new buildings that for the moment housed nothing.[29]

While Franklin's constant emphasis on the necessity and rewards of start-up loans implies how that mind-set might be applied to public ventures, the story of Mickle illustrates explicitly the importance of *public* credit and carries particular weight as the reader moves to the more publicly oriented installments of the *Autobiography*. Franklin wrote the four parts of the *Autobiography* over the two decades from 1771 to 1790, and the maturation and independence chronicled in the text parallels America's own coming of age. Christopher Looby has observed that Franklin drew a figural relation between his own biography and that of the nation, rehearsing in the story of his own life "both the past and the (predicated) future of America."[30] To this thinking I would add that the text draws a specific analogy between Franklin's own rise on credit as a budding entrepreneur in the first half of the text and the enterprising use of public credit for community development in the second half. With this shift Franklin's role changes: in the first two installments of the memoir he relies on the willingness of patrons to grant him credit; in the third and fourth parts Franklin, having benefited from those who invested in him when he was young, lends his patronage to fledgling public projects. The very word *project,* forms of which appear more than thirty times in the *Autobiography,* reinforces the notion that Franklin's schemes can serve the public. Like Daniel Defoe's *Essay upon Projects* (which Franklin cites as a key influence on his own philanthropy), Franklin's *Autobiography* presents "projection" as a valuable and communally serviceable form of speculation.

That the *Autobiography* itself is such a public project is signaled in the opening of part 2, in which Franklin inserted personal letters from friends Abel James and Benjamin Vaughan. These letters highlight Franklin's narrative transition from familial letter (an epistle to his son, William) to a document "intended for the Public" (*ABF* 57). In particular, the letters emphasize that his memoir is itself a public project that could benefit the new nation. Vaughan's letter, for instance, predicts that Franklin's story will not only promote desirable qualities in young businessmen (industry, frugality, and the patience to await one's advancement) but also "tend to invite to [America] settlers of virtuous and manly minds." Vaughan adds, "And considering the eagerness with which such information is sought by them, and the extent of your reputation, I do not know of a more efficacious advertisement than your Biography would give." While Vaughan suggests that the *Autobiography* might be representative in the sense of being typical of—or "connected to"—the "*rising* people" of the United States, his very term *advertisement* suggests another process at work: the use of an extraordinary story to publicize America. Vaughan's letter identifies the memoir's potential to promote the new nation in the eyes of prospective immigrants (59). It serves as a fitting prelude to the more publicly oriented sections of the *Autobiography,* in which Franklin, as both protagonist within the narrative and author of the autobiographical advertisement, works to promote civic ventures.

Although the *Autobiography* emphasizes from the start Franklin's natural inclination for civic projects—at the age of ten, he boasts somewhat in jest, he showed "an early projecting public Spirit" by organizing the construction of a wharf so his playmates would have a place to sit while fishing for minnows (*ABF* 7)—it is not until part 3 that Franklin recalls assuming a position as spokesman for such projects. This moment in the narrative is crucial, for it marks a shift in the value of his public persona.

In the narrative of the first two sections, which cover Franklin's work before his retirement, Franklin recalls that he regularly submitted project proposals anonymously or under the auspices of a group so as not to arouse suspicions of his own interests: "The Objections, and Reluctances I met with in Soliciting the Subscriptions, made me soon feel the Impropriety of presenting oneself as the Proposer of any useful Project," he writes, explaining his decision to put himself "as much as [he] could out of sight" (*ABF* 64). About a third of the way into part 3, describing his anonymous proposals for an academy, Franklin performs a similar move: "I stated their Publication not as an Act of mine, but of some *public-spirited Gentleman,* avoiding as much as I could, according to my usual Rule, the presenting myself to the Public as the Author of any Scheme for their Benefit" (99). Five paragraphs later, however, Franklin recalls that his "usual rule" changed once he "disengag'd" himself from "private Business." He writes, the "Public now considering me as a Man of Leisure, laid hold of me for their Purposes; every Part of our Civil Government, and almost at the same time, imposing some Duty upon me" (100).

The strategic self-effacement before Franklin's retirement has exemplified, according to some critics, his use of depersonalized print media to construct a universal, archetypal life. Michael Warner has written that Franklin effaces the particularities of his own personality in order to achieve a "republican impartiality" that refutes his own personal authority and embodies, through writing, the legitimacy of a public statesman. Grantland S. Rice argues that Franklin, by producing and circulating written representations of himself, suppresses the idiosyncrasies of his personality in favor of a disembodied self constituted in print. This "objectified self," realized in letters, public proposals, treatises, newspaper articles, and the autobiography itself, takes its cues from a burgeoning capitalist economy in which the exchange of goods and money replaces interpersonal relationships. John William Ward argues that the indecipherability of Franklin's character is precisely what makes him characteristic of an age in which markers of social status were increasingly destabilized. He writes, "Franklin stands most clearly as an exemplary American because his life's story is a witness to the uncertainties about social status that have characterized our society."[31]

This criticism, however, has focused on Franklin's self-presentation in the narration of events before his retirement from his printing business in 1748, and these conclusions are simply not applicable to the latter part of the *Autobiography*. In the narration of events after his retirement, Franklin's service entails the public endorsement of projects, and his visible connection to such projects supposedly ensures their success. Indeed, after his retirement, there is no mention of the self-effacement strategies that he describes earlier. According to Franklin, when Dr. Thomas Bond tries to establish a hospital in Philadelphia, he discovers that Franklin's name has acquired new value: "At length he came to me, with the Compliment that he found there was no such thing as carrying a public-spirited Project through, without my being concern'd in it; 'for, says he, I am often ask'd by those to whom I propose Subscribing, Have you consulted Franklin upon this Business? and what does he think of it? And when I tell them that I have not, (supposing it rather out of your Line,) they do not subscribe, but say they will consider of it'" (102). Convinced that this project will benefit from his own signature, Franklin subscribes, enlists other subscriptions, petitions funds from the Pennsylvania Assembly, and even pens and publishes a signed article in its support. Because of this endorsement, according to Franklin, the plan is executed and the hospital soon erected.

While Franklin's retirement from private business may not, in fact, have satisfied those adversaries who accused him of harboring ulterior motives, the narrative nevertheless sets up the distinction between his life as a man of private interests and his life as a civic statesman. According to biographer Edmund S. Morgan, the elder Franklin would have recalled this moment as the beginning of his most meaningful public service. In the first few years after his retirement, Morgan writes, Franklin "developed a new commitment to using his talents in behalf of others." Taking inspiration from Richard Savage's poem "On Public Spirit in Regard to Public Works," Franklin wrote often of the importance of "living usefully" and came to value scientific discovery primarily for its public utility. In addition, after refusing to serve in the Pennsylvania Assembly years earlier, he finally accepted election to the legislature in 1751.[32] In the *Autobiography* Franklin claims that his retirement removed him from the business world, and, as a result, the public "laid hold" of him for its "purposes." The social prominence he attains later in life transforms his name from a liability to an asset that can be exploited for public ends.[33]

This alignment of visibility and public-spiritedness is evident in Franklin's relation of family history in the opening pages of the *Autobiography*. He recalls that his ancestor Peter Folger made a point of signing a treatise condemning religious persecution precisely because he was civic-minded. He writes, "His Censures proceeded from *Goodwill*, and therefore he would be known as the Author" (*ABF* 5). Rice finds this brand of authorship in striking contrast to Franklin's "various dependent, feminized, and masked personae," but such anonymous personae really constitute only a portion of Franklin's self-representations.[34] Folger's rhetorical strategy is in fact consistent with that of the *Autobiography*. Although the Franklinian protagonist strategically disguises his name as a young man, the *Autobiography* as a whole, composed by an elder statesman three and four decades after his retirement, does not suppress this name in the least. The *Autobiography* chronicles Franklin's creation of various personae, but the text as a whole posits itself as an unabashedly candid document.

In the *Autobiography* all of Franklin's endorsements eventually follow a model in which he uses his own prominence to vouch for a project. Notable among these projects are speculative issues of paper credit instruments. In the final passage of part 4, for example, Franklin recalls using his own personal credit to prevent a catastrophic repeal of 100,000 pounds of Pennsylvania currency. By cosigning a paper assuring the assembly that the proprietaries will not be hurt financially by the emission, he wins their confidence in the soundness of paper currency. Franklin, by the reputation of his name, safeguards its credit. "The Assembly look'd on my entering into the first Part of the Engagement as an essential Service to the Province," he writes, "since it secur'd the Credit of the Paper Money then spread over all the Country; and they gave me their Thanks in form when I return'd" (*ABF* 146). The *Autobiography* leaves off, then, with this dramatic illustration that public credit depends, in part, on the credit of Franklin himself.

Franklin also recalls serving as a spokesman for public credit during the French and Indian War and working to convince colonists to maintain their faith in the government's word. At a crucial juncture in the military campaign, according to the *Autobiography*, Franklin composes and prints a broadside advertisement soliciting military supplies and services in exchange for forthcoming metal specie. Franklin supplements the broadside with a more personal letter addressed to his "Friends and Countrymen," which encourages their support for the war and emphasizes that a lack of morale on the part of these creditors could jeopardize the financial underpinnings of the venture. One key paragraph of the attached letter attempts to entice the impoverished reader by spelling out the potentially lucrative consequences of patient investment: "The People of these back Countries have lately complained to the Assembly that a sufficient Currency was wanting; you have now an opportunity of receiving and dividing among you a very considerable Sum; for if the Service of this Expedition should continue (as it's more than probable it will) for 120 Days, the Hire of these Waggons and horses will amount to upwards of *Thirty thousand Pounds*, which will be paid you in Silver and Gold of the King's Money" (*ABF* 116). Franklin cannot say with certainty that victory is near (elsewhere he even admits that he harbored doubts about Braddock's campaign), but he articulates his own faith in the "more than probable" continuation of the expedition and, by example, encourages the support of his readers. Signed twice—"B. FRANKLIN" on the broadside and "your *Friend and Well-wisher*, B. FRANKLIN" on the letter that accompanies it—these documents attempt to secure the reader's support through a personal entreaty. Suspicions of Franklin's ulterior motives apparently still plague him, as he emphasizes at the end of his letter that he has "no particular Interest in this Affair" (*ABF* 117). Nevertheless, he likely recognizes that his name is still more apt to increase than diminish the credibility of the scheme.

Public paper money was probably enhanced by such personal credit. Even though technically issued by a government (in contrast to banknotes, which were issued directly from the president and directors of the bank itself), paper money nevertheless bore the signatures of reputable individuals in an attempt both to safeguard against counterfeiting and to increase their acceptability. Prominent citizens were likewise encouraged to accept paper money so as to boost its value in the eyes of buyers and sellers (and so Mather applauds William Phips for his exemplary willingness to accept Massachusetts paper money). While Thomas Paine might have correctly identified a democratic credo in the mechanisms of a credit system that invests so much power in popular opinion, a more elitist philosophy governed this reliance on distinguished citizens. Reflecting on the U.S. petition for French war loans during the Revolutionary War, Alexander Hamilton emphasized the role of visibly wealthy and reputable men in the support of public credit. "I venture to assert, that the Court of France will never give half the succours to this Country," he wrote in a letter to financier Robert Morris in 1781, "while Congress holds the reins of administration in their own hands, which they would grant, if these were intrusted to individuals of established reputation and conspicuous for probity, abilities, and fortune."[35] Morris, a wealthy merchant who was appointed superintendent of finance in 1781, was the best-known practitioner of this personal approach to public finance. The government's credit was debilitated, according to financial historian William G. Anderson, until Morris "placed his own reputation and credit behind his acts as superintendent."[36]

Franklin keenly understood that individuals could obtain credibility in concrete, personalized ways that an institution or government could not. Drawing from his own experience as financier, he depicts a public credibility that is bolstered by his own credibility: the more reputable his own name and success story, the more viable is the American life for which he is a spokesman. The financial mechanisms at work in this text, then, make irrelevant (at the rhetorical level, for it would hardly deter his detractors then or today) the common criticism that the *Autobiography* is thinly veiled self-promotion. He makes self-promotion and national promotion mutually beneficial, enacting, in essence, a Franklinian pragmatism by which one could do well and do good at the same time.[37]

Franklin's equation of personal authorization and public-spiritedness was shaped by his economic times, and his *Autobiography* uses the particulars of his name and experience to accredit the new nation and its financial risk taking. But how might Franklin's advocacy of credit undermine the rhetorical effectiveness of such a voucher? Given Franklin's emphasis on the importance of appearances, one may not be inclined to take his candor at face value. Is the undisguised Franklin, in other words, just another disguise? Franklin himself acknowledges the possibility that print belies another value or character, and his own lamentation of depreciated bills that present fraudulent "accounts" is itself a reminder that representations can lie (or at least lie until their realization at a future time). Arguing for provisions to curb rapid currency depreciation during the French and Indian War, he recognized that readers must be discriminating: "At present every Bill that I receive tells me a Lie, and would cheat me too if I was not too well acquainted with it. Thirty Shillings in our Bills, according to the Account they give of themselves should be worth *five* Dollars; and we find them worth but *four*."[38] Aimed at denouncing depreciation (though not paper currency itself), Franklin's rhetoric here is a departure from his other, more optimistic writings on paper money and an acknowledgment of the capacity of print to misrepresent. The passage, which depicts nominal value as a first-person account given by anthropomorphic bills, inevitably suggests that autobiographical representation can, like currency, be inflated. If Franklin is promoting a life that others *might* lead, his account is doubly speculative and therefore subject to doubt.

And yet, if the narrative's relish for credit inevitably raises doubts about the *Autobiography* itself, it also rhetorically defuses this challenge by presenting doubt as a self-fulfilling prophecy. In this memoir doubts lead to financial collapse, and enterprising reading, as Franklin's own life demonstrates, keeps expectations in circulation and defers those redemptions that cannot materialize at that moment. As illustrated by Franklin's stories of wartime despair and the croaking Samuel Mickle, financial panic can sabotage potential profits. According to this financial paradigm, printed currency values and Franklin's projections of success are provisional but may, with the reader's faith, be realized in the future.

In Franklin's world of provisional value, appearances and public perception are crucial, but it is important to emphasize that these appearances do not necessarily belie reality. Rather, appearances are the exhibit or performance that makes that reality convincing in the eyes of others. Franklin's famous advice, after all, is to be *both* "in *Reality* Industrious & frugal" *and* "avoid all *Appearances* of the Contrary" when working to pay off loans. In ways that will be relevant to Royall Tyler's concept of performance in *The Contrast*, Franklin suggests that substance must exist or be forthcoming—and yet also be displayed.

One of the most important "appearances" for Franklin is the exhibition of faith itself. In Vaughan's letter, the memoir's most striking allusion to a reality outside Franklin's rhetorical world, the friend's intimated concern with the veracity of Franklin's autobiography is immediately subverted by his written vote of confidence. Contemplating Franklin's prospective conduct manual, *The Art of Virtue*, Vaughan writes, "As I have not read any part of the life in question, but know only the character that lived it, I write somewhat at hazard. I am sure however, that the life, and the treatise I allude to (on the *Art of Virtue*), will necessarily fulfill the chief of my expectations" (*ABF* 62). At one level the "expectation" to which Vaughan refers is his anticipation of Franklin's forthcoming text, and its fulfillment might simply be the publication of a well-written or efficacious manual. Having just distinguished between a "read" life and a "lived" life, however, Vaughan also suggests that Franklin's conduct manual is speculative because its veracity—that is, its fidelity to Franklin's lived life—is uncertain. The very reference to expectations, in fact, reinforces the analogy between text and promise, between veracity and financial fulfillment, between reading and risky investment. What must have appealed to Franklin—and what may have motivated him to include the letter with his manuscript—is Vaughan's confession of doubt but eventual expression of confidence in future fulfillment. Willing to extend his credit despite "hazards," Vaughan is Franklin's ideal reader. His example demonstrates that faith in Franklin and his America, if only the articulation of faith, is itself a public virtue.

CHAPTER FOUR

Performing Redemption on the National Stage

Royall Tyler's play *The Contrast*, composed and staged in 1787, was perfectly poised to respond to the American postwar credit crisis. In this comedy Tyler's hero, Colonel Henry Manly, insists that national integrity will require the redemption of public debts. Of primary concern to this Revolutionary War veteran is the possibility that the new nation's reputation will suffer if the government cannot pay its soldiers as promised. Men's reputations operate similarly in the play. In contrast to the profligate Billy Dimple, Manly triumphs because he meets his obligations—and we are to admire him because he wants the new nation to do so as well. Like Georgian English comedies that made solvency a gauge of a man's character, *The Contrast* defines heroism as fiscal responsibility.

It would be wrong to assume, however, that Tyler's play in any way endorses an end to national or personal borrowing. In fact, Manly triumphs precisely because he borrows and borrows well: he is a "man of punctuality" who demonstrates his credibility in the very act of repayment. Read in the context of the national credit crises of the 1780s (and the play itself repeatedly encourages such a reading), *The Contrast* reveals the stresses that postwar finance placed on an already eroding republican ideology that saw public debts as debilitating. Far from lamenting the necessity of borrowing, the play endorses a compromise between full-scale redemption and utter recklessness, a mean between complete solvency and bankruptcy which paralleled the new monetary thinking of Federalists such as Alexander Hamilton and James Madison. Although aimed at curbing fiscal recklessness, such thinking did not stress the importance of a complete and immediate redemption of the national postwar debt; indeed, it even entertained the notion that a well-managed permanent public debt might best serve the new nation. This thinking, rather, valued fiscal solidity insofar as it made possible a demonstration, or "performance," of redemption which would, in turn, bolster confidence and economic growth. Like Franklin, who advised tradesmen to bolster the "reality" of their industry with a corresponding "appearance," this Federalist rhetoric emphasized that even financially solid institutions and persons, unless continually demonstrating their credibility by discharging debt, would risk losing the confidence of creditors.

Performance is also, of course, an ongoing concern of the play. Tyler's metatheatrical comments remind the audience that actors perform the roles the playwright has created, and, within the fictional world of the play, characters themselves assume roles and create spectacles of their own (the rake acts a part to seduce, the social upstart apes his superiors, and even the virtuous republican indulges in histrionics). But the play's denouement and Manly's victory add an additional layer of performance to this mix. In the contemporary parlance of performance studies, performance is not simply the "aesthetically marked and heightened mode of communication" one sees enacted on the stage or in prescribed social roles, for it is also the "actual execution of an action."[1] In the theatrical arts actors carry out this execution through their own rendition of the scripts provided them, but individuals on and off the stage can also perform by completing an undertaking. Manly "performs" in this additional sense as a saint might perform miracles or a sports car might perform well. While its visibility is crucial, this performance is not a charade but a deed with tangible results. This is the performance that earns him Maria's hand, and it is the same performance of which Madison and Hamilton spoke when they emphasized that worthiness, no matter how real, needs to be publicly demonstrated.

Revolutionary Figures

Just a few months before composing *The Contrast* in the spring of 1787, Royall Tyler, a major in the U.S. Army, helped quell Daniel Shays's rebellion in the hinterlands of western Massachusetts. He wrote his play while stationed in New York City to assist with negotiations between insurgents and the state government.[2] Although Tyler's military stint was brief, it is essential to understanding the play. As Richard Pressman has written, *The Contrast* was shaped by Tyler's firsthand knowledge of pressing political "concerns of the moment": a postwar deficit and economic depression, countryside struggles between debtor farmers and merchant creditors (the most notable of which was Shays's uprising), and the consequent move for a new centralized government invested with the powers to regulate the national economy.[3]

Underlying Shays's Rebellion was a contentious debate about the role of paper credit and the scope of federal powers in the new nation. On one side of the debate were those demanding that the public debt be eliminated. On the other were those who justified the continuation of paper credit on the basis of its role in American independence: "I spent my life, fortune and character for America," the persona of Paper Money declared in the 1786–1787 *Worcester Magazine* exchange, "and though I died, I died in their defence." Advocating the revival of such instruments for circulation in the nation's domestic economy, this writer added, I "will rise again to deliver them from their domestick [foes], rather than America should forever be enslaved by the lovers of yellow dust."[4]

This writer imagines that the Continental's resurrection will allow the new nation to thrive. In contrast, *M'Fingal*, John Trumbull's 1782 epic poem about the Revolutionary cause, proclaims that the Continental can only achieve honor through precisely this kind of martyrdom and death. Marching to his grave in the vision of the fourth canto, the specter of Continental money appears wan, propped up on crutches, draped in tattered robes, and bearing a breastplate that reads, "The faith of all th'United States." As the funeral procession makes its way, the speaker praises paper money as the "longsought Philos'pher's stone" that magically "proves the tale of Midas true" more than any famed financial scheme of Europe.[5] The magic, however, is finite:

> A patriot firm, while breath he draws,
> He'll perish in his country's cause;
> And when his magic labours cease,
> Lie buried in eternal peace.[6]

According to Trumbull, what will make the Continental bill magical and productive—and not simply duplicitous—is its *death*. Only with the retirement of the debt can the Continental become the legitimate and resourceful means that raised, fed, and clothed the soldiers. Trumbull anticipates the day when the Continental bill will lie buried in *eternal* peace, and he does not envision a permanent national paper currency. Five years later he would help write *The Anarchiad*, a satire urging the Constitutional Convention to outlaw paper money and create a powerful federal government to boost the nation's credibility at home and abroad.

Ironically, many merchants joined the call of *The Anarchiad* for the full-scale redemption of war debts. Having speculated in those debts by buying up devalued war bills during dire economic times, these merchants now hoped to redeem them at full face value and pocket the profit. It was an odd alliance between conservatives who insisted on solvency and merchants who played the market—and an alliance embodied in the marriage of Manly into the Van Rough family. In a controversial move in 1780 which clearly favored this merchant class, the Massachusetts legislature voted to redeem war currency at its full value despite the fact that it was severely devalued and worth in market value only a fraction of its original denomination. In order to procure the income to retire this currency, the government also imposed taxes that fell hardest on rural farmers, who lacked ready cash. Compounding the rural agitation over new taxes was the fact that many farmers were Revolutionary War veterans who had desperately sold their public bills at discounted rates to speculators for metal cash, and so they were now being taxed to fund the profits of those stockjobbers.

In response to this redemption plan, the farmers countered with an alternative, two-part debt-funding program, demanding, instead, that a speculator receive only the amount he had paid plus interest and that the remaining amount be turned over to the original holder. In addition, they demanded that the state government retire the public debt not by imposts but by using new paper money, rather than metal specie, to pay off public creditors—in essence, a loan to retire a loan.[7] In Massachusetts the call for a split between current and original bill holders generated some support outside the rural community, but the plan was eventually deemed impracticable and condemned as a breach of government contract.[8] The cry for paper money also went unheeded, and debtor distress continued to grow. In the summer of 1786 a group of armed citizens led by Daniel Shays gathered at a Northampton courthouse demanding a reprieve for debtors, and in January 1787 insurgents attempted to seize a federal arsenal at Springfield and clashed with local militia. The Shaysites were effectively put down, but the uprising did manage to convince the legislature to make drastic cuts in taxes.

Although it was actually the culmination of years of postwar distress, the rebellion proved a turning point in what historians have termed the "critical period" of the 1780s, confirming for Federalists the inability of state governments to manage their own debts and the need for a stronger national government invested with fiscal powers superseding those of the state. The incident also raised the dangerous specter of democracy gone awry. *The Anarchiad* condemns Shaysites as social radicals intent on cheating their creditors, using easy credit to buy up luxuries and pose as their social betters. In the poem allegorical figures such as Jack Tar (a generic label for a sailor, referring to the tarpaulin of his pants) and Blackleg (a name for a land swindler) suggest that paper money is the tool of an upstart class. With Chaos as their mouthpiece, cries for democracy, agrarian reform, and the "rights of man" all become objects of satiric attack.

That Shays and many of his followers were disgruntled Revolutionary War veterans was especially unsettling. Many observers felt that Shays represented a startling decay of republican values and that only those veterans helping to suppress the rebellion were holding true to the ideals of the war. Shays's cause, however, did garner sympathy among those who felt that the market could not be trusted to distribute its rewards fairly. Even those who opposed Shays's act of violence were initially scandalized that soldiers who had risked their lives for the country were now required to fill the pockets of stockjobbers. In the March 1790 issue of the *American Museum*, the year Hamilton's federal funding plan was passed, one sentimental writer used the "affecting and true story" of an impoverished veteran to lobby for reform. In the story the soldier, who is poor but "no common beggar," recalls being told "how it was honourable and proper for every man to fight for his country" and promised "a great deal of money and backlands, after the war was over." He clings to the hope "that congress will make good their promises."[9] In contrast to *The Anarchiad*, which portrays the veteran Shaysites as greedy and self-serving, this sentimental piece features a pitiable soldier who has not been sufficiently compensated for his service.

The first national paper money entered circulation through the hands of soldiers, and so at the center of these postwar debates stood the controversial figure of the veteran. He was characterized variously as a patriot who had been victimized by his country's monetary policies and a greedy proponent of easy credit. To those who had taken American Revolutionary aspirations seriously, the fate of these soldiers was deeply symbolic. If the new United States abandoned its veterans, how could it possibly be a virtuous republic? Or, alternatively, if soldiers who had come to represent Revolutionary ideals were themselves quickly corrupted after the war, surely this did not bode well for the nation as a whole. It is not coincidental, then, that Sally S.B.K. Wood's novel *Dorval; or, The Speculator* features a Revolutionary War veteran who speculates in soldier's certificates and falls victim to a duplicitous investment scheme. This cautionary tale about the dangers of land speculation is made more tragic by the fact that an honorable soldier and delegate to the Constitutional Convention comes to financial ruin.

In Tyler's play the inclusion of a Revolutionary hero and references to Shays's insurrection foreground this controversy. Manly has just helped put down a rebellion by backwoods farmers who were once fellow soldiers, but his feelings regarding the Shaysites seem somewhat mixed. He would not endorse their violence, and he finds it a "burning shame" that sons of liberty would rebel against the government they had "a hand in making"; he would likely sympathize, however, with soldiers who have been victimized by stockjobbers and lament the loss of fraternity with those against whom he must now fight.[10] That he is in New York City, after all, to petition Congress for soldier's pensions indicates that he is sensitive to those who have not been rightfully compensated for their service.

So, while Tyler modeled *The Contrast* after Richard Brinsley Sheridan's English comedy *The School for Scandal,* his play also registers the concerns of a specific post-Revolutionary moment in the new United States.[11] In these turbulent times Manly's desire to protect the nation's credibility is particularly heroic. Unwilling to sell his government securities to stockjobbers, Manly insists he will not commit an exchange that would debase the word of the Continental Congress that issued them: "I may be romantic, but I preserve them as a sacred deposit. Their full amount is justly due to me, but as embarrassments, the natural consequences of a long war, disable my country from supporting its credit, I shall wait with patience until it is rich enough to discharge them. If that is not in my day, they shall be transmitted as an honourable certificate to posterity, that I have humbly imitated our illustrious WASHINGTON, in having exposed my health and life in the service of my country, without reaping any other reward than the glory of conquering in so arduous a contest" (*C* 47). In contrast to the fops and coquettes who will gladly cash them at less than face value to buy baubles and trinkets, Manly feels a nostalgia for these "musty notes" (46) and refuses to acknowledge that they have succumbed to the ravages of time and market forces. He dreams that the government will someday live up to its promise and redeem them with metal specie at full face value. He would rather remove them from circulation and transform them into an emblem, a reminder of the Revolutionary past, than accept partial payment. He considers these views part of a larger republican outlook that condemns the "tribe of Mandevilles" who embrace luxury, dissipation, and unbridled self-interest (79).

In this sense Manly might seem hopelessly obsolete. While his good intentions are admirable, he has much in common with the quixotic Captain Farrago of Hugh Henry's Brackenridge's *Modern Chivalry*. Farrago also finds himself clinging to old notions in a swiftly changing world and shocked at the ease with which vows are discarded. Manly's denial of the market's inevitable dynamism is firmly rooted in his resistance to any kind of change. He is the antithesis of currency, or things current. A soldier who insists on wearing the outdated regimental coat that was once respectable during the war, Manly bucks fashion trends because he does not accept the changes brought by the postwar era. "In America," he laments, "the cry is, what is the fashion? and we follow it indiscriminately, because it is so" (*C* 51). To follow fashion blindly, he suggests, is to lack integrity and surrender to the dictates of public opinion.

In his denial of market forces Manly would seem to stand in stark contrast to those characters associated with New York society. Dimple, Charlotte, and Letitia embrace the coy and artificial language of "politeness." They speak in bifurcated dialogue, addressing other characters directly and then revealing their true feeling in "asides" to the audience. They do not concern themselves with whether tenor and vehicle match: words are what they want to make of them. As Charlotte herself admits, coquettes attend plays and "torture some harmless expression into a double meaning, which the poor author never dreamt of" (*C* 49). In the faux-aristocrat Billy Dimple, the reader finds the standard vices of a vilified paper credit advocate. A foppish slave to fashion, he cannot transcend the dictates of society. He relies on credit schemes to claim assets on paper and to maintain a chimera of wealth while he is, in fact, bankrupt. He plots to marry a wealthy woman and seduce others for sexual gratification. As Maria succinctly puts it, Dimple is a "wretch whose only virtue is a polished exterior" (38-39).

Any neat distinction between Manly and Dimple, however, is complicated by the fact that the war hero's values are often the object of gentle mockery by other characters and Tyler himself. Cathy Davidson calls the colonel a "prig," and Walter Meserve finds him "a stiff and sentimental bore." Pressman asks, "If Manly is the hero, carrying an indisputably patriotic message, then why should he, too, be the object of criticism?"[12] While the politeness of Dimple, Charlotte, or Letitia does not represent an ideal, many of Manly's views, presented initially as the mark of his integrity, reveal him to be obsolete, impractical, and alienated from social interactions. Manly favors a currency that may be, like his own principles, noble yet *without currency*. In a telling discussion of her brother's outdated coat, Charlotte claims that Manly fails to understand that people value things according to the times. "Now another kind of coat is fashionable, that is, respectable," she says to him, "And pray direct the taylor to make yours the height of the fashion" (*C* 51). Charlotte's equation of "respectability" with public perception is perhaps troublesome, but so is Manly's obsolescence. His heart, like an "old maiden lady's bandbox," is "too delicate, costly, and antiquated for common use" (42–43).

Manly is especially subject to mockery because, despite his celebration of candor, he is every bit as much of a performer as these other characters. In keeping with the tradition of Restoration comedy and later eighteenth-century English farces, this hero has no worth until he has demonstrated it in the final act. Manly draws his sword and protects his sister from the untoward advances of Dimple, proving both her sexual propriety and his own heroism. Shortly before this final scene, it has also been revealed that Dimple is seventeen thousand pounds in debt to a British merchant, the aptly named Mr. Hazard.

Ironically, Manly, who insists on absolute values that do not depend upon the estimation of others, is triumphant because he has publicly upstaged Dimple. Tyler prepares the reader for this final spectacle with Maria's soliloquy in the first act, which emphasizes that male honor depends upon these moments. While men league to destroy female honor, she proclaims, virtuous manhood requires that men protect this honor as well: "Reputation is the life of a woman; yet courage to protect it is masculine and disgusting; and the only safe asylum a woman of delicacy can find is in the arms of a man of honour" (*C* 33–34). Maria marvels at the inconsistency that a "man should be leagued to destroy that honour upon which solely rests his respect and esteem," but in this play the dual natures of man—part rakish, part virtuous—actually manifest themselves in the two separate characters of Manly and Dimple (33). If male virtue entails the protection of female virtue, Manly's manhood depends upon men like Dimple, for it is Dimple's rakishness that provides Manly with the opportunity to perform.

Punctuality and the Main Chance

The telling ways that Tyler revises the denouement of Sheridan's play reveal an even more complex notion of performance at work. In Sheridan's play Maria faces a choice between two brothers: Joseph, who masks a base interior with the careful management of his reputation, and Charles, who is tender and virtuous but hounded by scandal. Maria favors Charles, but her guardian approves the match only once he witnesses Charles's good-heartedness and Joseph is caught in a tryst with Lady Teazle. Similarly, in *The Contrast* Manly proves his character by defending his sister's honor, and simultaneously Dimple is exposed as a bankrupt rake. That Manly must prove himself to win Maria's hand would suggest that Tyler's play closely follows *School for Scandal* and other late-eighteenth-century comedies, in which the male lover triumphs by proving his virtue (and not by suddenly acquiring wealth through inheritance or some similarly convenient means, as is often the case with plays earlier in the century). But Tyler builds into Manly's victory one additional detail that speaks specifically to the new nation's concerns with credibility.

Immediately following Manly's triumph, Maria's father, Van Rough, reveals that prior knowledge of the colonel's character had already swayed him in his favor. What has won Van Rough over is not, in fact, Manly's willingness to fight for a woman's honor but, rather, an investigation into the colonel's character. Van Rough is obviously satisfied with his future son-in-law's reputation, yet, even more telling, what has sealed his approval is not the colonel's status as debt-free but, rather, the fact that he meets his financial obligations in a timely fashion: "And you talked very prudently, young man," Van Rough says to Manly. "I have inquired into your character, and find you to be a man of punctuality and mind the main chance" (*C* 113). The phrase *main chance*, which derived originally from the parlor game Hazard, refers to the primary risk made in a wager, and so Van Rough would seem to favor Manly because of the success with which he can manage risk and preserve capital when engaged in speculation.[13]

The most telling of Van Rough's words is *punctuality*, a common shorthand that conveyed a respect for payment deadlines on the part of an individual, government, or financial institution. This word was part of the vocabulary of everyone writing on financial affairs at this time: Benjamin Franklin urged punctual redemptions of Pennsylvania currency and wrote in the *Autobiography* that "Diligence and Punctuality" could "recommend" a man who had "no Stock"; in a 1785 sermon the minister Ezra Stiles predicted that American commercial success would be made possible, in part, by the nation's "ability and punctuality of Remittance"; in an annual message to Congress, George Washington lamented the "failure of punctuality" among some states with regards to congressional requisitions; and in Tyler's own novel, *The Algerine Captive* (1797), a pinched relation of Benjamin Franklin gives "promises of punctual payment" when he borrows from the old gentleman. In these and many other writings *punctuality* is consistently identified as the foundation of good credit. Indeed, it was essential to Pelatiah Webster's definition of credit itself: "Credit, in a commercial sense, *is the confidence which people place in a man's integrity and punctuality, in fulfilling his contracts, and performing his engagements.*"[14]

When used in reference to a woman or child, *punctuality* might connote orderliness, adherence to rules, attention to details, or respect for another's time: children should arrive punctually at school, and women should serve dinner in a punctual manner. While these connotations would also have been applicable to men, the phrase *man of punctuality,* when coupled with the phrase *mind the main chance,* would suggest a timeliness with respect to duties outside the home and seems unmistakably financial in nature. Van Rough is a merchant whose outlook is determined by the bottom line (he repeats the phrase *mind the main chance* no fewer than ten times in the play), and he would likely not have any other kind of punctuality in mind. Although Manly never refers to his own borrowings, Van Rough seems to have discovered that the colonel borrows and discharges those obligations on time.

For Van Rough what makes Manly manly is mercantile proficiency rather than a transcendence of credit relations. His concept of manliness contrasts markedly with a classical republican characterization of "economic man," in J.G.A. Pocock's words, as "a feminised, even an effeminate being, still wrestling with his own passions and hysterias and with interior and exterior forces let loose by his fantasies and appetites."[15] This characterization was premised on the notion that landownership afforded financial independence and disinterestedness befitting a man, while mercantile activities, which necessarily entailed credit use and involvement in complex webs of market relations, rendered one dependent and subject to the dictates of the marketplace. Van Rough, however, distinguishes not between the effeminate dependence of moneyed men and the masculine independence of landowners but, rather, between effeminate and reckless forms of speculation and a more manly, prudent speculation. Van Rough is dismayed that Dimple, who "always appeared so prudent," lost his money at the gaming table (he will reprise this language later when he praises Manly for talking "very prudently"). He says frankly that he could have accepted Dimple's loss if it had occurred through trade, for "the best men may have ill-luck," but gaming is to him a reckless form of speculation which is unacceptable for any man who truly "minds the main chance" (*C* 96).[16]

This attention to the "main chance" is similar to what Joyce Appleby describes as the hallmark of the liberal modern citizen: "a man's capacity to look out for himself and his dependents."[17] Carroll Smith-Rosenberg writes that, while "classical republicanism had rooted virtue in the independence created by unalienable land," the new commercial men in the early United States "had transposed the gentry's landed independence into the independence of productive industry."[18] In their study of the English middle class in the late eighteenth and early nineteenth centuries Leonore Davidoff and Catherine Hall draw a similar conclusion about the way such gender typing served the middle class's challenge to aristocratic notions of virtue: "The valuation of actions and materials in monetary terms was regarded as a quintessentially masculine skill and prerogative. Such expertise was an essential part of the middle-class challenge to the aristocratic male whose skills lay with gambling, dueling, sporting and sexual prowess. The accomplishments of middle-class men were primarily sedentary and literate, the manipulation of the pen and the ruler rather than the sword and gun. They implied a cerebral control of the world but [were] no less effective in yielding economic rewards which could lead to wealth and power."[19] Here mercantile activity does not mark the merchant as impetuous and dependent. The merchant is empowered by his ability to manipulate and control, and it is the aristocratic rake, or the faux-aristocratic rake in Dimple's case, who suffers dissipation and effeminacy.

Manly's own triumph, based in part on a demonstrated punctuality, indicates that borrowing itself is an opportunity to perform fiscally: indeed, Pelatiah Webster defined credit as confidence in a man's "punctuality, in fulfilling his contracts, and *performing* his engagements."[20] In 1787, the year Tyler composed and staged *The Contrast,* one anonymous writer on public credit also concluded that confidence would rest on performance: "Public faith, once pledged, should be observed with sacred punctuality. The creditor of government should be able to view the note or promise which he receives, as competent security, and to rely on the performance, unless he, in some way or other, makes a release or remission."[21] Writers like this one did not call for a one-to-one correspondence between metal reserves and circulating bills but, rather, insisted that metal specie be used as a display to gain confidence. A 1780 essay by James Madison, simply entitled "Money," indicates that this view of metal specie was the product of new ways of thinking about currency depreciation. In this essay, according to Janet Riesman, Madison refutes the classical "quantity theory" that credit instruments depreciate (and prices rise) when they are admitted in abundance, and he argues, instead, that instruments depreciate when too much time elapses between their issue and redemption. Both theories propose that weakened confidence drives down values, but Madison insists that quantity alone will not weaken confidence so long as buyers and sellers regularly see some indication that their instruments are convertible. A financial institution must continually remind buyers and sellers of its ability to perform.

While Madison decried the abuse of credit, his essay indicates a nuanced understanding that a complete redemption of all paper bills, even if possible, would concentrate specie in the hands of speculators, reduce the amount of currency in circulation, and create a stagnant economy. The goal of a national economy, he argued, should be to redeem just enough bills to instill confidence in buyers and sellers that their bills were, in fact, redeemable. Such confidence would bolster their value and convince buyers and sellers not to cash them in. Crucial to Madison's "revolutionary departure from old ways of thinking about paper money," Riesman observes, is a reconsideration of the importance of metal specie. Whereas traditionally hard money was the "real" value behind the representative paper, Madison values it for its performative power. Its material value becomes irrelevant except to the extent that it instills confidence. Deploying a fitting idiom that equates theatricality with the demonstration of moral character, Riesman writes, "Redemptions were, in effect, only for show—to reassure people of the integrity of the bank."[22]

Madison's monetary ideas inspired proposals by Alexander Hamilton, Robert Morris, Thomas Paine, and others for a government-chartered bank founded on specie for the purposes of funding the public debt. The very language with which these thinkers described their plans for redeeming governmental debt indicates the importance of an ongoing spectacle of regular redemption. Paine, writing in 1786 under his standard pseudonym of "Common Sense," observed that a nation's credit fails "by non-performance" and that "people will not put confidence in the paper promises or paper emissions of those who can neither perform the engagement within the time their own power exists, nor compel the performance after that time is past." Hamilton, in a lengthy, well-known letter to Robert Morris outlining his plans for a bank, called for banknotes "payable at sight" because this visibility would "inspire the greater confidence and give them a readier currency." William Barton, in his "Observations on the Nature and Use of Paper-credit," maintained that "punctuality" and the "honorable redemption of the bills of credit" would "evince the determination of government to redeem the paper currency, at it's full and original value." His very word *evince* suggests that the appearance of such determination must accompany the determination itself. In a like manner one anonymous writer on the Pennsylvania debt insisted that the contract between the government and citizens is "sacred" and "must be performed" because payment would "be considered as an extraordinary and incredible circumstance by those who reflect on it."[23] John Trumbull's depiction of the Continental in *M'Fingal* also advances this monetary theory in the fourth canto, when nonperformance leads to the collapse of credit and the end of the Midas touch:

> O'er heaps of rags, he waves his wand,
> All turn to gold at his command,
> Provide for present wants and future,
> Raise armies, victual, clothe, accoutre,
> Adjourn our conquests by essoign,
> Check Howe's advance and take Burgoyne,
> Then makes all days of payment vain,
> And turns all back to rags again.[24]

The several dates inscribed on Continental's breastplate indicate that redemption dates have come and gone. Without some spectacle of redemption Continental dollars quickly depreciate, becoming only as valuable as the rag paper on which they are printed.

Although financiers proposed different forms of a government-chartered bank and methods to call in public securities and exchange them for new interest-bearing bonds, most agreed that the regular payment of interest and the backing of reputable, wealthy private subscribers would be crucial in confirming in the public eye that the government had every intention to pay off its debts.[25] Whether the government would eventually pay off the principal of its debts (in addition to the interest that came due immediately) became increasingly a matter of indifference to people like Morris and Hamilton. Whereas Madison insisted loans eventually be retired, these more commercially minded men were quite comfortable with the idea of a permanently circulating currency. (Hamilton, in fact, argued specifically that branch banks be located in the country's interior not only for security's sake but also because their "distance from the capital trading points" would "make applications for the payment of bank-notes less convenient.")[26] Regardless of their long-term plans for retirement, however, all stressed the importance of the government's public performance.

The confirmation of Manly's credibility through a performance witnessed by Van Rough reinforces this understanding of credibility. The confirmation of Maria's virtue, which comes only once she has been *tested* by a rake, also parallels Federalist thinking on credit. Acknowledging that the best credit ratings would be reserved for institutions that undertook large financial obligations and proved they could meet them, Federalist writers saw the public debt as an opportunity to demonstrate that the government could withstand the challenge of large loans. Federalist finance programs were designed not to put an end to the public debt but, rather, to bolster national credibility both domestically and abroad so that the nation could continue to borrow money in the future. The aim, in other words, was not to develop an economy that would not need to borrow but an economy that would borrow and, like Manly, prove itself in the process.

Unlike Dimple, who is condemned for a heart that is "insensible to the emotions of patriotism" (*C* 39), Manly is ennobled by his concerns over national credit. That this play takes place in the aftermath of Shays's Rebellion also underscores how pressing those concerns were. The rebellion, which revealed the inefficacy of state governments to handle fiduciary matters, was the single most important catalyst for the move for a new constitution that would create a federal government strong enough to regulate the economy itself. A strengthened federal government would also potentially restore governmental credit in general and, in turn, help bolster both the value of public securities and the credibility of the new United States abroad.[27] While Pressman and other scholars have argued that this play was shaped by nationalist concerns provoked, in large part, by Shays's Rebellion and the call for a constitutional convention, I would add that foremost among these concerns was the restoration of public credit under the aegis of a centralized government. As Cathy Matson has written, the convention was an attempt to create "the political authority necessary for establishing America's commercial reputation among nations." It was to be a performance that would hopefully restore the nation's standing.[28]

In light of these national concerns we might rethink Manly as a performer. When Charlotte characterizes Manly's speech on credit bills as the "well said heroics" of a man whose head is "filled with old scraps of tragedy," her point is well taken (*C* 47).[29] The colonel is repeatedly compared to an actor, and his language is, as Roger B. Stein writes, "as far gone in its pretentiousness and pomposity as Dimple and Jessamy's." A number of scholars have accounted for Manly's staginess by pointing to the commonly perceived distinction between negative and positive forms of theatricality in early American culture. Before theater was institutionalized in the new nation, Jeffrey Richards writes, religious and patriotic rhetoric often deployed metaphors of the world stage, or *theatrum mundi*, to describe the arena in which Americans carried out momentous actions. Jay Fliegelman describes a prevalent early American notion of a republican "natural theatricality" that was mimetic but nevertheless *realized* the natural. This theatricality, according to Fliegelman, would also have been validated as "rhetorical communication and pedagogical instruction" distinct from bourgeois self-representation.[30] Accounting for the play's references to the nation's financial crisis, however, I would emphasize that Tyler's work also presents a slightly different, though still related, positive form of performance which drew from economic experience. While Dimple's performance masks an empty interior—his *only* virtue, according to Maria, is his "polished exterior"—Manly's performance confirms in the eyes of others a value that already exists but must be demonstrated through action. When in the last lines of the play Van Rough cuts off what is sure to be more of Manly's histrionics, he makes clear that he is looking for this latter kind of performance: "Come, come, no fine speeches; mind the main chance, young man, and you and I shall always agree" (113).

This is not the kind of performance that has been the focus of Jean-Christophe Agnew's *Worlds Apart* and other important studies of theatricality and market relations. Agnew has argued that on the early modern stage theatricality takes it cues from the "crisis of representation" in the Renaissance marketplace and becomes "the calculated *mis*representation of private meanings in the negotiated relations among men and women." This theatricality assumes the "social world to be so thoroughly 'staged' as to make its truths accessible not so much by what those performances claimed to display as by what they unwittingly betrayed."[31] In *The Contrast* the play's low plot introduces, but ultimately provides an alternative to, this notion of theatricality as calculated misrepresentation. The comic interactions between the two servants, Jessamy and Jonathan, draw a clear distinction between performance as misrepresentation and nonperformance as truth telling. The self-fashioning Jessamy takes advice from Chesterfield's letters and finds the Mall a "fine place for a young fellow to display his person to advantage" (*C* 53). Jonathan, in contrast, thinks a theatrical stage is a neighbor's house and mistakes a production of Sheridan's *School for Scandal* for real life. Although the precursor to a later Yankee type known for his savvy, Tyler's Jonathan takes spectacle at face value, voices a New Englander's distrust of theater, and is incapable of detecting and creating artifice. Ultimately, however, the play complicates this dichotomy with a third value: performance as truth telling. Certainly, Dimple and Jessamy's notion that you discredit others to acquire credit yourself is itself discredited at the play's end, when Charlotte admirably repents for her attacks on the characters of others. But Jonathan's insistence on face value, expressed most obviously in his desire not to circulate the clipped coin that symbolizes his affection for Tabitha, simply cannot account for the importance of spectacle in commercial life. What Jonathan does not understand, but what the play ultimately demonstrates, is that some kinds of public performance can make manifest, rather than belie, a truth.[32]

Finally, given Manly's performance, we might reconsider what kind of union is achieved by his marriage into the Van Rough family. Pressman argues that the marriage represents a pragmatic alliance of Manly's landed class with Van Rough's mercantile interest at the moment the new Constitution was taking shape.[33] But farmers borrowed as much as anyone, and so this marriage may represent, more specifically, a modification of agrarian views of credit itself. The agrarian sector of early national society, though certainly imbued with commercial sensibilities, viewed indebtedness as something to be avoided. While credit could provide start-up loans or necessary advances in the interim before receiving payment for a crop, agrarians (including the Shaysites) undertook debt with every hope of eventually being debt-free. For the commercially minded, economic historian Donald R. Stabile writes, debt was instead "just another tool of business, another way to keep goods circulating."[34] Although debt needed to be managed, it carried no stigma and was viewed simply as a necessary line of credit, paid off only when required and often through additional debt.

If Manly's attitudes toward debt are in keeping with this portrait of agrarian borrowing, then he would see borrowing as a short-term risk that might debilitate credit. Van Rough, on the other hand, would see managed indebtedness as a desirable and permanent condition through which one attains additional credibility. Van Rough, whose name aligns him with the commercial culture of Dutch New York, is crass and abrasive, but he also understands how debt might be used profitably. Manly's marriage into the Van Rough family might well represent an American future based on managed borrowing. Habits of *reckless* borrowing, in fact, are displaced onto the Anglicized Billy Dimple, and therefore the Manly–Van Rough alliance projects a future of sound American credit which stands in stark contrast to the fiscal recklessness of Britain. According to popular nationalist rhetoric, the new United States—by virtue of its land supply, labor opportunities, and, most important, regular payment of interest on the debt—would maintain the confidence of the public and avoid the mounting national debt that had long plagued Britain. While such distinction between American and British public credit was overwrought, the condemnation of British insolvency—particularly its failure to perform regular redemptions and pay out interest—was central to patriotic rhetoric on the U.S. economy. "The bad policy of Britain has been in multiplying their paper, almost without any limitation," William Barton wrote, "thereby creating an amazing quantity of *imaginary* wealth, unsupported by a necessary proportion of real; the nation having long since, abandoned the hope of being ever able to pay off their debt."[35] Although Barton did not call for a one-to-one ratio between paper and metal, he claimed that Britain had suffered for having not maintained—and demonstrated—*at least some* ratio of real to imaginary money.

The ending of *The Contrast* proposes with sentimental patriotism an American fiscal solidity imbued with a speculative spirit and the conviction that national vitality will rest not upon the elimination of debt and dependence but upon the performances of credibility through ongoing borrowing. Although this particular performance is an action rather than illusion, it needs an audience in order to be effective. Charlotte ultimately is correct when she insists early in the play that social perception matters and that Manly is hopelessly naive in his proclaimed indifference to public opinion. Manly cannot triumph until he has been witnessed, just as the success of the new nation's performance will depend on a national and international audience.

Part Three / Bonds of the New Nation

If the Federal debt, which is 42 million of dollars, be equally divided between the 13 states: What will be the share of each?
    ALICE ARNOLD HOLMES, ARITHMETIC BOOK, 1795

Hamilton was indeed a singular character. Of acute understanding, disinterested, honest, and honorable in all private transactions, amiable in society and duly valuing virtue in private life, yet so bewitched & perverted by the British example, as to be under thoro' conviction that corruption was essential to the government of a nation.
    THOMAS JEFFERSON, *THE ANAS, 1791–1806*

You're thinking of this place all wrong, as if I had the money back in a safe. The money's not here. Well, your money's in Joe's house—that's right next to yours—and in the Kenny house and in Mrs. Macklin's house and a hundred others. You're lending them the money to build and then they're going to pay it back to you as best they can. What are you going to do—foreclose on them?
    GEORGE BAILEY PREVENTING A BANK RUN, *IT'S A WONDERFUL LIFE*

Reporting to the U.S. Senate in 1795, Alexander Hamilton used an organic metaphor to describe the nation's credit system. "Credit is an *entire* thing," he wrote. "Every part of it has the nicest sympathy with every other part; wound one limb, and the whole tree shrinks and decays." The sympathy Hamilton describes is not a moral sensibility or emotional response but, rather, a state of interdependence through which any ailment has far-reaching effects for the national body politic. Banking networks, according to Hamilton's metaphor, create a national sympathetic nervous system. In *Federalist* 35 Hamilton had previously written that this form of sympathy was also the basis of representative government. Legislators would identify with those they represented if they stood to gain or lose as their constituents did: "common interest may always be reckoned upon as the surest bond of sympathy."[1]

In Hamilton's sense one has sympathy with, rather than sympathy for, another. In the first U.S. novels, however, sympathy *for* another is commonly the fortuitous byproduct of financial dependence. As Mrs. Holmes explains to Myra in William Hill Brown's 1789 novel, *The Power of Sympathy*, those who pride themselves on the virtues of affluence and independence "make but an indifferent figure."[2] Disinterested characters are apathetic bystanders who refuse to involve themselves in the affairs of others, while admirable characters exhibit a fellow feeling grounded in their own vulnerabilities. Using the examples of Charles Brockden Brown and Judith Sargent Murray, these final chapters investigate how early national literature made morally consequential this concept of credit-based sympathy.[3]

What Brown and Murray had in common with Hamilton was a sense that vulnerability, and even corruption, could hold the nation together. Hamilton understood that the erosion of autonomy made sympathetic relations possible, and he credited Britain for opening his eyes to the virtues of corruption. Modeled on the older Bank of England, his national bank was designed to corrupt wealthy and influential subscribers, turning them into speculators whose assets would motivate them to care about the nation's future success. National banknotes would be less susceptible to over-emission because they would be issued by individuals whose own assets would be affected by depreciation—unlike government-issued paper money, which was legislated by politicians whose personal assets were not as directly involved in the outcome. Hamilton's plan for the federal government to assume the Revolutionary debts of individual states was governed by a similar belief. If the federal government assumed state debts, then state creditors would become federal creditors, and Hamilton hoped this transfer of securities would realign their allegiances as well.

Hamilton's thinking, as well as Brown's and Murray's, should be understood as part of a general effort by Americans to imagine means by which private and public interests might reinforce each other. Much of the elite class of American Revolutionaries, as J.G.A. Pocock, Bernard Bailyn, and Gordon S. Wood have detailed, took inspiration from the Country tradition in English politics, which grounded civic personality in property ownership and an idealized transcendence of market involvement. Through the financial independence of land ownership the virtuous man did not depend on persons or events for his well-being, and so he could act disinterestedly on behalf of the state. People whose fortunes resulted from market transactions, no matter how large their fortunes, were assumed dependent on the creditors from whom they must await payment

Figure 5. This Continental bill equates unity with interdependence. The motto, WE ARE ONE, is accompanied by the image of thirteen interlocking rings, suggesting that the fates of all states are intertwined by the political and economic venture of rebellion. In the postwar years Alexander Hamilton hoped pragmatically that financial interdependence among states as well as individuals could continue to bind the new nation. Courtesy of Special Collections, University of Notre Dame.

and on the larger economy on which their personal assets rode. Public paper credit, which amplified these webs of obligation and touted the nation itself as an investment opportunity, constituted an extreme form of corruption in the republican paradigm. But, as Wood also writes, it was this particular brand of corruption which emerged in the wake of the Revolution as the cement to bind the union in the absence of disinterested leadership.[4]

Figure 6. The detail from the 1800 masthead of the *Forlorn Hope*, a New York newspaper advocating the reform of debtor punishment, draws an analogy between a black slave and an imprisoned debtor. While the masthead calls for liberation, the dependence of these figures on the "Humane Society" has also made possible a positive form of communal bonding. Courtesy of the American Antiquarian Society.

While earlier colonial and Revolutionary public credit schemes were also understood to render individuals dependent on the market, their rhetoric had tended to emphasize the power of a collective action that could sustain currency values. Post-Revolutionary rhetoric often emphasized, instead, the potential of credit structures to exploit individual needs and interests for national benefit. This rhetoric also questioned the Revolutionary generation's enshrinement of disinterestedness as a moral matter.[5] Although compassion had traditionally been an important facet of the republican personality, the post-Revolutionary generations felt increasingly that its philosophy was morally limited and devoid of emotion. As a result, according to Andrew Burstein, they brought to politics a new language of feeling that even "provided a decisive vocabulary by which political leaders could claim true representation" of others.[6] Therefore, *direct* legislative representation, through which a statesman identified intimately with his constituents, was not conducted with republican disinterest, but nor was it the result simply of unemotional Hamiltonian sympathies.

Fictional plots of Charles Brockden Brown and Judith Sargent Murray use financial scenarios to stress the impossibility of disinterest and, more important, its tendency to promote apathy where the suffering of others is concerned.

In their narratives financial vulnerability promotes a character's fellow feeling. In one sense this sentimentalizing impulse would persist in Jacksonian and antebellum literature. Joseph Fichtelberg has recently detailed how the popular fiction of these eras often conceived "commercial relations in sentimental terms," featuring heroines, for example, who reestablish stable homes in the midst of economic crisis. These works, however, are more interested in coming to terms with the "challenges to autonomy" that economic distress had forced on Americans than they are in imagining collectivity. There is, moreover, a strain of antebellum writing which decidedly resists the hope that social relations might be solidified in the marketplace. The narrator of Herman Melville's *Confidence-Man* mocks as illusion any notion that credit structures might make the world a more humane one. Only with sarcasm does he identify the joint-stock company as a hallmark of modern cordiality: "In former and less humanitarian ages—the ages of amphitheatres and gladiators—geniality was mostly confined to the fireside and table. But in our age—the age of joint-stock companies and free-and-easies—it is with this precious quality as with precious gold in old Peru, which Pizarro found making up the scullion's sauce-pot as the Inca's crown. Yes, we golden boys, the moderns, have geniality everywhere—a bounty broadcast like noonlight." Geniality—itself a dubious quality that can belie base intentions—abounds like Peruvian gold and midday sun. Just as the gold is used to cast a sauce pot, geniality is pressed into mundane services. It is ubiquitous as daylight. "Geniality has invaded each department and profession," his friend replies, and "the next thing we shall have genial hangmen."[7]

When, in a more optimistic moment in *Moby-Dick*, Ishmael observes that the monkey rope binding him to Queequeg merges his own individuality into a fraternal "joint stock company of two" through which "another's mistake or misfortune" might plunge him into disaster, the financial metaphor remains metaphor.[8] Ishmael conceives of his situation "metaphysically," and Melville does not suggest that financial entanglements might literally foster fraternity. While the metaphor of a joint-stock company aptly illustrates the binding of the friends' fates, the analogy is poignant because it is so ironic—because Melville simply did not see commercial relationships themselves as fundamentally fraternal. When reading the literary works of the new nation, however, one need not assume such conceits are strained. What often gives their financial plots power, in fact, is the promise that credit structures might actually be the means by which one person's interests could become another's.

CHAPTER FIVE

Arthur Mervyn and the Reader's Investments

Mathew Carey's famous chronicle of the 1793 yellow fever epidemic opens with a telling indictment of the city's financial overreaching. Like the croaking Samuel Mickle of Franklin's *Autobiography,* Carey describes a Philadelphia that is suspiciously marked by new houses and rising rents. On the eve of the plague, he recalls in his *Short Account of the Malignant Fever* (1793), prices were exceeding the "real value" of property, men were "regulating their expenses by prospects formed in sanguine hours," and extravagance was "gradually eradicating the plain and wholesome habits of the city." Carey wonders, hesitantly, if the plague was not, in fact, divine punishment for the city's bloated economy: "And although it were presumption to attempt to scan the decrees of heaven, yet few, I believe, will pretend to deny, that something was wanting to humble the pride of a city, which was running on in full canter, to the goal of prodigality and dissipation." Philadelphia is a bubble about to be pricked. Elsewhere Cary considers the prevailing medical theories about the plague's origins, but here he cannot resist assigning providential significance to the fact that credit-based expansion was leveled by catastrophe.[1]

Charles Brockden Brown's *Arthur Mervyn; or Memoirs of the Year 1793* draws its own connections between the 1793 fever and a credit economy. Although it is very much about the horrors of the disease, the novel nevertheless uses illness as a fictional device to make a dramatic statement about the potentially toxic effects of burgeoning commerce on the city's moral fiber. As Brown himself knew, the actual 1793 fever affected, and was affected by, economic practice, but the coincidence of disease and commerce in this novel is unmistakably and aesthetically heightened.[2] Illness spreads symbolically in tandem with commercial transaction, targeting the merchant class and especially those indebted persons who lack independence of the marketplace.[3] As many of the novel's characters are driven by their own financial concerns, disease and corruption set in as well, causing physical and moral constitutions to crumble simultaneously.

I read this moral corruption according to the specific terms of classical republicanism: as the erosion of disinterest which comes when one is enmeshed in commercial relations.[4] While this interpretation is probably familiar to readers of this novel, I propose that we view the consequences of this corruption differently.[5] Specifically, this brand of corruption figures in the novel as a force capable of strengthening, rather than destroying, social bonds. In *Arthur Mervyn* the corruption that comes with indebtedness and economic insecurity promotes communal union precisely because it encourages a process by which readers and auditors of narratives come to sympathize with others. In the fictional world Brown creates, the men most susceptible to disease and financial distress are also easily enticed by narratives. With their personal and financial well-being at stake, they clamor for news of the disease's progress and succumb to curiosity at the same time that they succumb to the ravages of disease. Although characters are seduced by their own needs, suspicions, and curiosity, these impulses draw them together into a nexus of readers and auditors linked by financial obligations. These characters ultimately come to sympathize with others only once they care about—or are invested in—another's narrative by virtue of their own economic concerns. *Arthur Mervyn* does not glorify the unchecked self-interest of a character such as Welbeck, but it does suggest that disinterestedness carries a price because it hinders the vital process by which one is drawn to investigate and identify with another's fortunes.

The novel's Philadelphian setting and the prominence of banking mechanisms in its plot are particularly suited to Brown's project, for some of the most important public statements on self-interest and civic welfare arose from debates on national banking in this city. A notorious debate in 1786, which Gordon S. Wood has described as "one of the crucial moments in the history of

American politics," concerned the rechartering of the Bank of North America, a precursor to the two Banks of the United States. During this debate one Pennsylvania backcountry legislator, William Findley, a defender of debtors and paper money advocates, insisted that even the affluent and elite stockholders of the bank had no claim to disinterested status in arbitrating the dispute; nor should they, Findley added, since the promotion of one's own interests was not only inevitable but politically legitimate. According to Wood, Findley anticipated the openly competitive, interest-driven government that would prevail in the United States. Equally important, however, his fellow anti-Federalists claimed repeatedly that the disinterest of political representatives, even if possible, would hinder their ability to feel sympathy for constituents and speak on behalf of their interests and concerns.[6]

In Brown's novel Arthur Mervyn's discovery of a contested $20,000 banknote sewn into a literary manuscript dramatizes how such theories of self-interest and sympathy could carry consequences for a national reading community. We are never told which bank has issued the note, but in 1793 the likely source would be the Bank of the United States, the new Bank of Pennsylvania (established in the year of the fever itself), or any number of government-chartered banks of neighboring states. Regardless of its source, the banknote represents a mechanism by which the "security of each creditor" becomes, in Alexander Hamilton's words, "inseparable from the security of all creditors."[7] Like reading and auditing, this mechanism forges sympathy by rendering one's gains and losses palpable to others. It is not so much that Brown champions economic liberalism over civic republicanism in this novel as it is that he dramatizes what he perceives to be the realities of a credit-dependent national economic community.

Although my analysis of *Arthur Mervyn* will concern characters' sympathetic identification with others through both oral and written narratives, I am ultimately interested in Brown's treatment of readers because it illuminates his concept of the novel and its social function. In *Arthur Mervyn* readers are driven by economic needs, but, more important, their economic vulnerability nurtures a mind-set that responds to the novel's form—even in those moments when economic need is not immediately at stake for readers. The reader's response entails for Brown a sympathetic identification that invests the novel with a specifically social dimension. Like many novels of the new republic, this one belies the common characterization of the genre as privately oriented. Even though it replicates a psychic interiority, focuses on the personal desires of characters, and is intended to be enjoyed by readers in solitude, it nevertheless addresses the pressing question of how the new nation would hold together. In *Arthur Mervyn* and some of his shorter prose pieces, Brown envisions a reading process that would serve private and public needs simultaneously. This process is brought to bear on narratives within the text but may well suggest how Brown's own readers are to approach his novel. This vision, moreover, was specifically shaped by a notion that one's own material concerns might foster sympathy for others in an insecure economy.

Speculation and the Romance

"The Man at Home," a series of fictional sketches Brown published in the *Weekly Magazine* in 1798, suggests how the speculative individual might respond to the "romance" (a term he used interchangeably with *novel*).[8] This series, which features a protagonist-narrator who has fallen into debt by endorsing the credit note of an unreliable acquaintance, might seem at first glance only a meditation on the ethics of debtor punishment.[9] It is equally concerned, however, with delineating the qualities of the commercial mind and explaining how that mind responds to specific narrative techniques.

This mercantile mind, according to Brown's narrator, boasts a facility with language, a knack for abstractions, and the ability to calculate the likelihood of future events. Such a mind is also likely to be governed by self-protectiveness, and the fictional series draws clear distinctions between characters who look after their own interests and those who do not. Although the landlady feels concern for the welfare of others, she is not driven by economic self-interest to investigate carefully the possibility of future outcomes that might affect her financial standing. She knows nothing, in fact, of the "art of trafficking" and is "incapable of foreseeing or estimating" evils. The mark of her provincial nature is that she had not the "curiosity or interest" to investigate the "new world" beyond the two rivers that bound her abode.[10] In contrast, the narrator, whose only wealth is tied up in public securities, must possess foresight and scrutinize carefully the world around him in order to protect his assets. He must be a good judge of character because, in an exchange of credit, the integrity or reliability of a business partner or financial institution is crucial. *Curiosity* emerges from this comparison between narrator and landlady as a key term for understanding Brown's presentation of the speculative mind-set. Appearing repeatedly in Brown's oeuvre, the term connotes care and precision but also inquisitiveness and even nosiness (all are included in the *OED*'s definition as well). When

Brown writes that the landlady has neither "curiosity" nor "interest," we should understand that the two qualities are inseparable: an individual is careful, inquisitive, and even nosey when he or she has economic interests at stake. According to the narrator, the cerebrations activated by this curiosity are worthwhile: to "speculate on the possible and the future, is no ineligible occupation. The invention is active to create, and the judgment busy in weighing and shaping its creations."[11]

Although the connection is not explicit, one can begin to imagine how Brown might draw a parallel between the scrutiny necessitated by financial vulnerability and the scrutiny that the engaged reader or writer brings to fictional works in order to penetrate the mysteries of character and events. The narrator's discovery of a trunk left behind by a victim of the fever suggests more deliberately that the speculator is attuned to the operations of a suspenseful plot. In ways that parallel Mervyn's discovery of a banknote in Lodi's manuscript, this discovery excites conjecture and anxiety. At the pivotal moment when he awaits the attendant with the key, the narrator recalls: "If my conjecture be just, what a strange coincidence of events will be unfolded in this part of my life. To supply me with the means of discharging my debt, and restoring to a greater height than ever my fallen fortunes, my creditor had only to doom me to a prison, and compel me to seek a refuge in this obscure retreat. Here am I on the verge of poverty, and in danger of a gaol, yet thousands are within my reach. I confess I have some eagerness to ascertain this point. I wish my attendant would hasten her return."[12] Acknowledging the unpredictable vicissitude that can accompany any speculation, the narrator marvels at the possibility that a man living in danger and obscurity could enjoy a complete reversal of fortune and discover riches. But, with so much at stake, he also admits his nervousness and impatience to know the contents of the chest. Fearing his "curiosity would not suffer [him] to wait till the key is furnished," he attempts to lift the trunk and surmise its contents, only to discover it is nailed to the floor. This narrator's anxiety is heightened by a deferral of disclosure.[13]

For Brown this tendency to suspicion and conjecture is the hallmark of the commercial mind. In *Arthur Mervyn* this impulse is exacerbated by the fact that commercial schemes take time to mature and bear fruit. When, out of financial desperation, Welbeck undertakes a carefully calculated shipping scheme, the interval of unknowing which precedes the anticipated outcome is an "interval, not devoid of suspense and anxiety." He admits that his own "mercantile inexperience" and utter dependence on the scheme's success have made him distrustful and apprehensive (*AM* 317), but, like the narrator of "The Man at Home," he grows more fearful with delay. "Time added to my distrust and apprehensions," he recalls, when for months at a time "intelligence was still withheld" (317–318).

In "The Man at Home" the locked trunk is similar to the stalled plot in its ability to elicit scrutiny, hypothesis, and a desire for exposition and revelation. That the experiences of opening the trunk and watching a plot unfold are similar becomes even clearer when Brown puts his own reader in a situation similar to that of the narrator. As if to defer the reader's gratification and heighten interest in the episode, Brown plots the scene so that the narrator first discovers an empty trunk and then finds a manuscript hidden in a secret compartment. The contents of the narrative, like the contents of the trunk, are withheld from the reader for a measure of time. Like Welbeck and Mervyn, whose own plans to publish Lodi's memoirs are tinged by their desire for profit, the narrator is clearly roused by the possibility of attaining financial independence through the publication of this "precious" tale, and the delay only heightens the excitement for someone in need. The manuscript is a history of the American Revolution but one that has all the "circumstantial and picturesque minuteness of a romance." Its "grand and forcible" depiction of human nature especially demands a reader who can analyze and assess character.[14] The narrator is drawn to the manuscript out of economic necessity, but that necessity has also fostered a mind that will respond to its very narrative techniques.

Brown's most elaborate explanation of the compatibility of speculation and novel reading appeared in an 1800 essay entitled "The Difference between History and Romance." A tale of what *might* have happened, Brown writes, the romance is fictional yet must also be plausible and bound by the limits of probability. History, on the other hand, is a tale of what *has* happened and, though truthful, may be implausible (*Arthur Mervyn* also claims repeatedly that the truth often does not necessarily fit with expectations of the probable). Whereas the historian and the reader of history can limit their knowledge to recorded human actions, according to Brown, the romancer and reader of romance must constantly interrogate the probability of actions as they are depicted in fiction: "Curiosity is not content with noting and recording the *actions* of men. It likewise seeks to know the *motives* by which the agent is impelled to the performance of these actions; but motives are modifications of thought which cannot be subjected to the senses. They cannot be certainly known. They are merely topics of conjecture. Conjecture is the weighing of probabilities; the classification of probable events, according to the measure of probability possessed by each."[15] In this passage the interrogation of human probability compelled by curiosity is the same procedure required by commercial exchange and financial speculation in a text such as "The Man at Home." Because the romance purports to take the probable as its subject matter, it is the genre most likely to activate curious speculations.

"The Man at Home" and "The Difference between History and Romance" indicate that Brown perceived an intimate relation between a kind of reading practice and the reader's economic standing and outlook. In an essay entitled "Thoughts on American Newspapers," Brown makes the case that this kind of reading also fosters sociality. Defending the American penchant for newspapers, Brown claims that curiosity and character scrutiny motivate self-governing citizens to examine their government. He writes that the "curiosity" of the American nation of readers "that is attentive to the character and conduct of our rulers, so far from being merely harmless, or only moderately useful, seems to be the grand and indispensible duty of every citizen." He adds, "Since it is our privilege to choose, it is our duty to choose wisely; and, for that end, to be vigilant in scanning the practices and principles of public men, to employ all practicable means of forming a true decision ourselves, and to recommend that true decision to our neighbors."[16] One result of the reader's curious speculations, then, is the kind of vigilance Jürgen Habermas attributes to a bourgeois public sphere intent on keeping the abuses of the state in check: specifically, curiosity sharpens an observer's understanding of the "public men" running the state.[17] But this scrutiny and understanding, I would add, are not directed exclusively at those in office. Defending the American newspaper against attacks that it is too laden with financial news, Brown also insists that newspaper reading, even if motivated by a self-interested search for information, can enlarge the reader's understanding of the country and the way other people live.

When a newspaper combines "mercantile intelligence" with more "general speculations," Brown writes, "the trader is prompted to extend his view beyond his professional concerns by the vicinity of other topics." Brown adds, "instead of censuring the connection that is thus formed between literature, and lucre, and politics, [the friend of mankind] should give honour to his countrymen for permitting the alliance, and ardently approve of such effectual means for introducing the teacher of virtue, and the preceptor in useful arts, to the counters, desks and tea-table of every rank and profession in society." This newspaper, distributed as many as one hundred miles away, introduces one class of

Americans to another in the absence of personal interaction. The non-merchant acquires mercantile intelligence, and the trader is prompted to open his mind to other topics. For promoting such "useful ends," the editor should receive the approbation of "every lover of his country."[18]

Readers today might be tempted to see similarities between Brown's description of the newspaper and Benedict Anderson's claims about print capitalism and the conception of the modern nation-state, particularly because Anderson sees the interaction at work initially in the Creole Americas. Anderson argues that newspapers were one condition for imagining the nation because they created a sense of simultaneously shared experiences among disparate readers who would not otherwise have face-to-face encounters.[19] But, although Brown certainly applauds the newspaper for its ability to foster understanding among otherwise nonaffiliated Americans, he is primarily interested in the affiliation between the merchant and non-merchant. In Brown's estimation the newspaper creates national affiliations in its particular appeal to individual interests. Because "intelligence of what is to be bought and sold" is of interest to everyone, the newspaper is the most effective means of fostering understanding.[20] The connection Brown draws "between literature, and lucre, and politics" in the American newspaper is also consistently forged in the plot of *Arthur Mervyn*, in which economic necessity drives a reading process that ultimately binds individuals.

Corruption and Sympathy

Arthur Mervyn looks different once approached in light of these shorter prose pieces. This novel is the story of a young man's journey from innocence to experience, but, more specifically, Arthur's coming-of-age dramatizes exactly what these pieces theorize: namely, that curiosity and speculation are socially beneficial byproducts of economic self-interest. The young Arthur is born in the countryside, corrupted upon his entrance into the city, and by novel's end ostensibly able to counter corruption through the acquisition of a liberal education (the second volume, published more than a year after the first, often bears little resemblance to the first except in the continuation of Mervyn's quest for liberality). Arthur's maturation provides the structural framework for an otherwise dizzying plot, but it also makes possible Brown's exploration of the social and political consequences of self-interest with respect to the novel form.

The rather straightforward plot of Arthur's maturation is complicated by numerous subplots as well as by the nonlinear fashion in which it unfolds for the reader in tales related by various characters. In the end the novel is as much about storytelling as anything, and the complex structure foregrounds Brown's ongoing concern with narrative itself. When the novel opens, as Mervyn is recovering from fever at the home of Doctor Stevens, the doctor tells of how he rescued the young man, and then Mervyn tells of how he came to the city and, finally, to the street outside Stevens's house. Interspersed throughout Mervyn's narrative are both the tales he has told to others and the tales told by those he has encountered in his journeys, such as Welbeck, a forger and seducer, and Watson, a young man from the country who surrenders to the city's plague. Stevens's narration also contains the accounts of others, including one woman who accuses Mervyn of wrongdoing, and, to complicate things further, Brown presents as many as three layers of narration at a time: in chapter 3 of part 2, for example, Stevens tells a tale of Wortley telling a tale of Williams telling a tale of Watson. The alliterative names only add to the confusion, making the reader feel trapped inextricably in a web of narration.

Mervyn's loss of innocence occurs on several fronts, most notably perhaps through his introduction to forms of wealth not based on land or real property. Having grown up on a farm, where the rent of houses and lands was the only "perfectly intelligible" species of property, Mervyn is at first "unhabituated to ideas of floating or transferable wealth."[21] Although Mervyn's books have taught him "the dignity and safety of the middle path" and rural life, a bizarre encounter in an opulent private home—in which he is led into a closet and overhears an incriminating conversation about Welbeck's financial scheming—whets his appetite for finer things and shows him that Welbeck's wealth, and wealth in general, need not consist of inherited land (*AM* 272). Initially baffled by Welbeck's commercial wealth, Mervyn wonders at first if his new acquaintance is a French or Italian fugitive who has transported his inheritance overseas. Soon, however, he embraces the concept of commercially generated wealth and ruminates on how he might cultivate a sophisticated deportment that can help him advance economically. Tellingly, this exposure to new forms of wealth nurtures an impulse to analyze conditions that might affect his own financial status. Immediately following this encounter, he recalls that his "curiosity was awake," and he took to the streets to observe city life (282). Because the commercial man is always bound to the marketplace, he must be its keenest observer.

According to the logic of the novel, once Mervyn has been initiated into the ways of commercial wealth, it follows that he will be vulnerable to a disease that targets and marks as corrupt the commercial community in Philadelphia. The debtor's prison is filled with men of delicate physical constitutions. The agrarian utopia of the Hadwins, on the other hand, is removed from urban commercial life and hence remains impervious to pestilence. In fact, it is only when the once innocent Wallace chooses to remain in the city out of indebtedness to his employer that he falls ill. A closer look at Wallace's contraction of the disease reveals just how marked is the coincidence of fiscal and physical corruption among the merchant class in the novel.[22] Wallace's demise begins once he ignores advice to return to the country and instead remains in the city in the hopes of making enough money to marry Eliza. Persuaded by Thetford's "powerful arguments" that his "interests depended upon the favour of his present employer" and a promise of doubled salary if he stays, Wallace reasons to himself, "By going, I should alienate the affections of Thetford . . . and blast all the schemes I had formed for rising into wealth" (*AM* 384, 348, 385). As Mervyn narrates Wallace's eventual flight from the city, he describes a weakness in character as well as body:

> Wallace had now enjoyed a few hours rest, and was persuaded to begin the journey. It was now noon-day, and the sun darted insupportable rays. Wallace was more sensible than I of their unwholesome influence. We had not reached the suburbs, when his strength was wholly exhausted, and had I not supported him, he would have sunk upon the pavement.
>
> My limbs were scarcely less weak, but my resolutions were much more strenuous than his. I made light of his indisposition, and endeavoured to persuade him that his vigour would return in proportion to his distance from the city. The moment we should reach a shade, a short respite would restore us to health and cheerfulness. (390)

The use of *influence* to describe the sun's heat indicates that a republican vocabulary is in place here. Mervyn, whose complete assurance that he remains unaffected is suspect, clearly aims at drawing a distinction between Wallace and himself. Although Mervyn's limbs are also weak, he possesses the "resolution" to leave the city. "Vigour" will replace effeminate weakness, he reasons, once they have escaped the toxicity of Philadelphia.

The plague thrives in the city, where economic self-interest blinds people to its dangers, but the plague also compounds self-interest by putting private assets in jeopardy. The pestilence, in other words, is not simply a marker of commercial corruption but also a phenomenon that generates very tangible economic consequences. When people die before they have paid off their bills, assets become susceptible to the "rage of the creditors" wanting to recoup their losses (*AM* 395). Portable property, already insecure, is made more vulnerable in a disease-ridden environment in which death brings quick demise to property owners before they can settle accounts or transfer ownership. Speaking of a house that symbolizes the proprietary confusion wrought by the plague, Eastwick tells Mervyn, "This house has no one to defend it" because the whole family was killed in a single week. "Perhaps no one in America," he adds, "can claim the property" (368).

When money belonging to Lodi's sister inadvertently falls into Mervyn's hands, one can see just how the plague has made the "precincts of private property" doubly "perilous" (*AM* 270). Although he is not sick at this time, Mervyn worries over his own precipitous death and rationalizes that it would be "prudent to dispose, in some useful way, of the money which would otherwise be left to the sport of chance" (392). Tellingly, however, Mervyn begins to feel the onset of fever shortly after this money comes into his possession. Just as Wallace's bodily ailments begin at the moment he seeks to maximize his own profits, Mervyn's physical deterioration begins once he is in a position to exercise his self-interest. Although he fancies himself its guardian, Mervyn actually endangers this property, as he cannot help but wonder how he might keep it for himself. As with other characters, his illness signals metaphorically the corruption of his virtue, but the plague has also created the very circumstances on which he might capitalize. A catalyst for corruption as well as a sign of its onset, the pestilence compounds the acquisitiveness first ignited by the spectacle of Welbeck's wealth. In the city afflicted by fever, Mervyn notes, "No one's attention could be found disengaged from his own concerns" (381).

This is particularly true of those whose financial fate is tied to Welbeck. When Welbeck disappears mysteriously, his abandoned house "naturally [gives] birth to curiosity and suspicion" among the creditors who wished to lay "claims to the property remaining in the house" (*AM* 339). As Brown wrote of the plague in "The Man at Home," "the motives to plunder, and the insecurity of property, arising from the pressure of new wants on the poor and the flight or disease of the rich" unleashed conjecture among the populace.[23] In another episode Mervyn "contract[s] a suspicion" about Welbeck's behavior precisely because he lacks a candid deportment and a "sufficient firmness to propose the cool and systematic observation" of the man's character. Whereas Welbeck's behavior would present to a different observer "no food for his suspicion or his wonder," it excites in Meryvn "vague and tumultuous ideas" (296–297). Like Welbeck's creditors, Mervyn stands to gain or lose according to Welbeck's actions, and his impulse to scrutinize the man arises from his own precarious economic position.

Although Mervyn laments his own suspicions and curiosity, his "propensity to look into other people's concerns, and to make their sorrows and their joys" his own is, in fact, a form of compassion (*AM* 530). The episode in which Mervyn discovers Welbeck hiding in his house illustrates how the novel aligns curiosity with compassion. Ensconced in this house with the newly discovered banknotes, Mervyn is particularly vulnerable: he feels his own sickness coming on, he fears he will be attacked by plunderers, and he is fighting his own base desires to keep the money for himself. That he must weigh "with scrupulous attention, every circumstance that might influence" his decision regarding the banknotes indicates his susceptibility and weakened constitution at this particular moment (396). Fittingly, Mervyn reacts to the sounds of Welbeck's intrusion with endless questions, speculations, and a "curiosity and compassion" that impel him to call out (399). It is his own weakened position that allows him to speculate or imagine the motives that might have led a similarly vulnerable fugitive to the house: "Perhaps the motives which led me to this house, suggested the suspicion, which, presently succeeded to my doubts, that the person within was disabled by sickness.... Why might not another be induced like me to hide himself in this desolate retreat? ... The person was a brother in calamity, whom it was my duty to succour and cherish to the utmost of my power" (398). Mervyn sympathizes with the fugitive precisely because he can identify with someone whose experiences have been similar to his own—someone who has been induced like he has been to hide. He makes *projections* in both senses of the term, speculating on outcomes that might affect his own well-being but also attributing to the unnamed victim his own feelings and motives.

Like Francis Hutcheson, David Hume, Adam Smith, and other eighteenth-century moral philosophers, Brown is interested here in analyzing the response of the spectator or auditor to scenes of distress.[24] That Mervyn pronounces the fugitive a "brother in calamity" immediately after pondering the similarities of their motives and positions implies a concept of compassion similar to that made famous in Smith's *Theory of Moral Sentiments*. According to Smith's postulation, we sympathize with someone when "by the imagination we place ourselves in his situation ... and thence form some idea of his sensations, and even feel something which, though weaker in degree, is not altogether unlike them."[25] But, although there are striking similarities between Smith's and Brown's depiction of sympathetic observation, Brown's use of the banknote to foreground the novel's concerns with emotional and financial investment also asks that we read the novel in relation to early U.S. debates over federal banking in which disinterestedness was criticized for hindering the sympathy necessary for representative government and social bonding.

In her study of sympathy in the American novels of the 1790s, Julia Stern has identified a related form of disenchantment with traditionally valued forms of disinterest. She finds in certain novels a "feminized zone of imagination" which criticized republican philosophy as cold, dispassionate, "unmoored from fellow feeling," and predicated on a privileged and exclusive notion of white, male civic-mindedness. Such criticism, she adds, was motivated by an "alternative vision of democratic community" and gave expression to disenfranchised Americans who stood outside the republican collective.[26] Stern finds an implicit critique of republican ideology, for example, in *The Coquette*, a story of a young woman abandoned by her friends when their dispassionate deportment is expected to "supercede the claims of any possible 'interest' in Eliza."[27] In *Arthur Mervyn*, however, the disenchantment with disinterest neither emanates from a feminized and disenfranchised imagination nor upholds selfless benevolence as the cohesive force in American society. Instead, it remains grounded in a pragmatic insistence that one of the greatest bonds between individuals is commercial and that credit systems will ensure that individual concerns necessarily take into account the concerns of others.

Jane Tompkins's analysis of this novel does examine its representation of commercial bonds, but Tompkins claims they produce selfless, benevolent commitments to the larger economic community and never examines how such commitment might be driven by self-concerns.[28] Those self-concerns must be accounted for, especially because the novel goes to great lengths to depict the corruptive, if ultimately socially redeeming, effects of commerce.

Tompkins and other scholars have tended to conclude that communality and corruption would have been understood as mutually exclusive. In her study of the early American novel Cathy N. Davidson observes that many critics, including Tompkins, Leslie Fiedler, and Emory Elliott, have read Mervyn as *either* benevolent or corrupt: "Take your pick," she writes, "America the corrupt or America the beautiful. There is ample evidence for either reading." Refusing to choose one herself, Davidson argues that the paradox of Mervyn's character is a design on Brown's part to deny, among other things, the "interpretive propensities" of the "individual committed to a rationalist model of mind."[29] I would propose, instead, that one reading need not exclude or undermine the other because, in Mervyn's case, benevolence and corruption are more intertwined than these critics have allowed. Corruption for Brown was not synonymous with criminality or dishonorable intentions. Corruption mitigates disinterestedness, and it is when Mervyn is most susceptible to the influence of his own interests that he is also most capable of imagining the distresses of a "brother in calamity." For this reason the commercial-minded are uniquely positioned to investigate and identify with the misfortunes of others, and this positioning governs how they process narratives as well.

Investing in Narratives

In the climate of paranoia and suspicion created by the fever, narratives assume added importance for the commercial class vulnerable to disease. A tale of the plague's progress might be "distorted and diversified a thousand ways" but also invested with life-or-death significance (*AM* 346). As the disease gives rise to rumors, those in the most immediate danger—fugitives "whom curiosity had led to the road"—are compelled by instincts of self-preservation to seek out such narratives (355). Plunderers and profiteers also clamor for tales of death and flight from the city. According to Mervyn, people are "differently affected" by such rumors. Hearing tales of the disease's progress, one vulnerable Philadelphian grows pale, "his breath . . . stifled by inquietudes, his blood . . . chilled, and his stomach . . . bereaved of its usual energies." In contrast, Mervyn, who still occupies a position of security when the outbreak occurs, can enjoy the "sublimity" connected to the plague's danger because his "own person was exposed to no hazard." He stresses that he has the "leisure to conjure up terrific images, and to personate the witnesses and sufferers of this calamity" because he does not pursue these stories out of "necessity." At the far end of this spectrum stands Hadwin. A farmer of "placid mien and plain garb" and model of republican candor and disinterestedness, he remains "superior to groundless apprehensions" generated by rumors and listens to Mervyn's own tale of the city "with complacency" (347, 340).[30]

Surely Brown's attention to rumor was shaped by what he knew of the fevers in Philadelphia and New York as well as by narratives such as Carey's *Short Account*, which emphasized the rampant and destructive nature of gossip during the epidemic.³¹ But I would argue that Brown also uses rumors in his plot to posit a theory about the way economic standing can shape one's response to narrative. Most notable among those anxious auditors and readers is the creditor whose debt remains unsettled at the time of his debtor's death. When Welbeck stages his own demise, Mervyn notes that his "property was swallowed up, and his creditors left to wonder at his disappearance" (*AM* 335). Among Mervyn's auditors as he tells his tale at Stevens's house are a number of Welbeck's creditors. Mervyn's prefatory remarks suggest that these creditors will process Mervyn's narrative according to their own financial exigencies: "My own fate is connected with the fate of Welbeck, and that connection, together with the interest you are pleased to take in my concerns because they are mine, will render a tale, worthy of attention which will not be recommended by variety of facts or skill in the display of them" (243). Readers' "interests," rather than literary merits, will make this tale worthy of his audience's attention. These auditors will, by virtue of their financial investment, take an interest in the tale of a man whose own fate is intimately connected to the fate of Welbeck. Only Dr. Stevens, a member of the learned professions and supposedly above financial entanglements, listens with candor. What distinguishes the "interested" from the "candid" listener is an irresistible need on the part of the former to speculate about others' motives.

The interested reader (as opposed to auditor) appears most vividly in the scene in which Mervyn reads Lodi's tale of hidden treasure. This episode illustrates just how financial vulnerability gives rise to a curiosity that is heightened by suspenseful novelistic plotting. Mervyn recalls:

> Having arrived near the last pages, I was able to pursue, with little interruption, the thread of an eloquent narration [about the Milanese count's discovery of hidden treasure]....
>
> My tumultuous curiosity was suddenly checked by the following leaves being glewed together at the edges. To dissever them without injury to the written spaces, was by no means easy. I proceeded to the task, not without precipitation. The edges were torn away, and the leaves parted.
>
> It may be thought that I took up the thread where it had been broken; but no. The object that my eyes encountered, and which the cemented leaves had so long concealed, was beyond the power of the most capricious or lawless fancy to have prefigured; yet it bore a shadowy resemblance to the images with which my imagination was previously occupied. I opened, and beheld—*a bank-note!* (*AM* 343–344)

Both financial and narrative uncertainty are at work here: the tumultuous curiosity generated by Lodi's tale coincides with another curiosity about the undisclosed banknote between the glued pages. Mervyn draws a parallel between his discovery of the banknote and the count's discovery of treasure in Lodi's tale (later he refers to the banknotes as a "treasure" unfolded), and the analogy between fiction and banknotes suggests how narrative tension is built on a deferral of disclosure. The reader's interval of unknowing, generated both by plotting as well as by the glued pages, is similar to an interval of financial uncertainty. In other words, financial deferral has a narrative counterpart—an interval of withheld information which heightens curiosity. Once again, the economically interested reader is most easily drawn in by suspense.

Brown's "Walstein's School of History," a fictitious review essay of several nonexistent books, offers a remarkable explanation of how this kind of curious and speculative reader is also uniquely positioned to sympathize with others. One of the reviewed texts, "Olivo Ronsica" by an author named Engel, is a thinly veiled version of *Arthur Mervyn* itself (the young, rustic Olivo journeys from country to city, where he is corrupted by the influence of a schemer, almost killed by a pestilential disease, and rescued by a benevolent doctor to whom he tells his tale), and so the description of Engel's literary methods might also be read as a description of Brown's rhetorical strategies in *Arthur Mervyn*. According to the review, Engel hopes the story will operate didactically and provide the reader with an imitable model of right conduct. He worries, however, that the book's lesson will be of limited influence, given that "the forms of human society allow few individuals to gain the station of generals and statesmen" and the civic-mindedness necessary to appreciate his tale. Pragmatically reasoning that "men, unendowed with political authority," relate to one another through their possessions, Engel decides that no topic could "engage the attention of man" as well as property itself. And so the story of Olivo, who succeeds "in spite of ignorance" and "in spite of poverty," is designed to attract the attention of the commercial-minded and "forcibly suggest to the reader the parallel between his state and that described." Although Engel appeals to the reader's proprietary aspirations, the moral benefits conferred by this tale ultimately outweigh the selfish concerns that drive the reader. It is a book, according to the reviewer, "from which, it is not possible for any one to rise without some degree of moral benefit, and much of that pleasure which always attends the emotions of curiosity and sympathy."[32]

Here Brown pragmatically acknowledges that "generals and statesmen" imbued with republican disinterest are few compared with the commercial-minded who make up the bulk of novel readers. Many political thinkers of the 1790s reasoned that the bonds of necessity might replace the bonds of republican virtue, and, in a similar vein, Engel and Brown both create protagonists who are oriented to others through market relations and appeal to a readership that is similarly oriented as well. Readers of novels do not, like readers of newspapers, stand to gain financially from what they discover on the page, but they can be drawn in by a similar impulse to investigate and identify with another's fortunes. The curiosity that arises from self-interest provides the foundation for "sympathy."

Although the novel has been traditionally associated with a solitary reading experience, the novel in early America, Michael T. Gilmore writes, was "as intent upon collective as individualistic ends . . . a form in transition and at odds with itself, as much a partisan of post-revolutionary republican culture as a harbinger of nineteenth-century liberal society."[33] Michael Warner discovers that, "even in the novel, American writers consistently regard their writing as belonging to the civic arena," creating works they believe to be consistent with its virtues and aimed at readers assumed to be participants in public discourse and not private consumers of books.[34] In this novel Brown suggests that individuals supplement their private consumption of narrative with civic concerns precisely because they submit to mercantile impulses of curiosity and speculation. The most engaging plots, according to the logic of this novel, are built around financial uncertainty: Arthur's own stories (both as told to his listeners and as conveyed to the novel's readers), Lodi's manuscript, and Ascha's account of her early life all create suspense through the narration of deferred economic outcomes. Mervyn himself is drawn to Ascha precisely because she is a Jewish woman who has always been deprived of fixed property and so knows the "hardship, danger and privation" that Eliza Hadwin will never know (AM 495). He considers these vagaries essential to human growth, and Brown likely would have considered them essential to a coming-of-age story. The merchant himself is not necessarily in a position to read novels—Mervyn mentions in the book's first chapter that becoming a clerk would leave him no time for pleasure reading—but a man similarly enmeshed in the market and similar in mindset would be a responsive reader.

Fittingly, Mervyn forms his most important social bond in response to Ascha's narration of her economic vicissitude. Her account of her reversal of fortune, indebtedness, and risky scheme to immigrate to America all appeal to him because they are experiences with which he can identify. Listening to her account is a pleasurable process by which he vicariously experiences and identifies with her misfortune, partaking "of all her grief" and hailing, "with equal delight, those omens of felicity which now, at length, seemed to play in her fancy" (*AM* 619). Reading and auditing, though emotionally charged, are pleasurable now that Arthur and Ascha have attained more financial stability. One fortunate outcome of the resolution of Ascha's problems is that she now has "a mind enough at ease, to read with advantage" and "find pleasure" in books (617). The same is likely true of Mervyn, whose new financial stability will mean he does not have to clerk for a living. But, though they have achieved comfort and marital happiness, they do not obtain complete financial independence. His financial security depends upon her fortune, which, in turn, is commercially vested and embedded in the marketplace. He has also taken up professional writing, an unreliable and usually nonlucrative vocation that is always subject to the whims of the book trade. Their ongoing dependence is manifest in the very ways they carry on literary exchange: "Obsequious to [his] curiosity," she manipulates her stories to please Mervyn as if he is a consumer who craves her tales. "Partly selfish," Mervyn writes, "I have said my motives were, but not wholly so, as long as I saw that my friend derived pleasure, in her turn, from my company" (619). Their financial and emotional interdependence is both the mark of their marital happiness and the vulnerability that enriches their reading experience.

Banking structures may have created sympathetic national structures that made each individual vulnerable to ailments elsewhere in the body politic, but the intended effect was not an emotional one. In Brown's novel, however, the sympathetic structures of finance foster vulnerable constitutions capable of compassion. Like other novels in early America which dramatized in various ways the tension between classical republican values and economic liberalism, *Arthur Mervyn* depicts a privatized reading process that parallels economic privatization. But, whereas Brown imagines a reading process driven by personal concerns, his novel posits a communal reading process driven by the very speculative curiosity that he believed would drive all social and commercial interaction in the new nation.

CHAPTER SIX

The Medium between Calculation and Feeling

Judith Sargent Murray, the new nation's most prominent women's advocate as well as a novelist, playwright, and essayist, did not advance or oppose public debt or paper currency. She accepted them as inescapable facts and worked to imagine the impact of a volatile economy on American society. To this task she brought her own financial experiences directly to bear. Although she was born into a family of successful merchants, Murray struggled with debt for most of her adult life, first as the wife of John Stevens, a merchant who died in exile trying to escape debtor's prison after his fortunes were devastated by a trade embargo, and later as the wife of John Murray, a minister whose scant earnings did little to alleviate her sense of deprivation. In essay after essay in *The Gleaner*, the miscellany of one hundred installments which Murray published in 1797, the fictional narrator offers advice to the reader on how to weather such financial vicissitude. In her novel and plays the object of sympathy is not a sexually seduced and abandoned woman—as in the novels of William Hill Brown, Susanna Rowson, and Hannah Foster—but a woman whose husband is the victim of a financial downturn. Personal and biographical as they are, however, these stories also aim to envision an ideal republican society. Murray's writings, both her published work and her extensive, largely unpublished correspondence, repeatedly suggest that a new credit-based economy, if combined with the right kind of education, could produce a more astute population and foster national solidarity. Murray makes women central to this vision of a new society.

An ardent advocate of women's intellectual equality, Murray argues that women, if trained to think like entrepreneurs regardless of whether they actually engage in economic ventures, will become better thinkers, capable of calculating, reasoning, and assessing the probability of future outcomes. She celebrates financial speculation as a supremely rational and intellectual activity, insisting that properly trained women will be better equipped to deal with economic vicissitude but also better prepared to choose compatible husbands, educate their own children, and even evaluate their own government. At stake in Murray's discussions is not simply the material condition of women but also the fate of their intellect and their potential contributions to the new republic as wives, mothers, and citizens. When the intellect of half the nation's population is neglected, Murray argues, families and the nation suffer.

Yet this is only the first step in Murray's argument, for even the most reasoned calculations can fail, and, when the speculator has suffered for reasons beyond his or her control, compassion must be the rule. In such instances Murray sentimentalizes, rather than refutes, the conventional notion that women are dependent. Dependence, Murray emphasizes, is not simply a feminine state but a *human* state, particularly in a credit-based economy in which individual fortunes are increasingly intertwined. As Elizabeth Barnes has observed, sentimental plots in the early republic frequently cast sociopolitical issues as family dramas, and Murray's are no exception.[1] *The Story of Margaretta, The Traveller Returned, The Medium* (later renamed *Virtue Triumphant*), and her miscellaneous tales in the *Gleaner* all identify compassion as a byproduct of financial dependence. *The Medium* in particular links credit relations among small social circles to larger networks of public credit, situating familial sympathy in the context of a national economy. The heroine of this play, Matronia Aimwell, knows from her own investments in public securities that no one is truly independent, and she is well poised, as a result, to intervene compassionately on behalf of her indebted nephew. Although many of Murray's writings concern personal, rather than public, credit relations, the two were inseparable for her. From personal financial experience women might learn to balance calculation and compassion and hence become exemplary investors in the future of the nation—as mothers, as participants in political life, and even as public securities holders. Because she is endowed with both business acumen and sympathy, Matronia does not have to withdraw her investment in a public bank in order to help her nephew, allowing her to support family and nation simultaneously.

Murray's depiction of credit relations also allows her to make claims about the exemplary status of women in the new republic. Her financial plots posit a mind-set particularly suited to women but one that men might emulate as well: one that strikes a medium between the extremes of cool rationality and intemperate passion, one that squares and calculates but can also discern the limits of human reason. Murray tells a woman's story, using financial plots to urge her readers to reconsider the capacities of women and their role in the new republic, but she believes this story is one that can benefit men as well. Sympathy is an affective response that comes easily to women, who often live at the mercy of an unpredictable marriage market and, once married, at the mercy of their husband's fortunes. It is also, however, available to men and a virtue that might help sustain the republic.

Rational Prospects

To grasp how Murray positions women in relation to credit structures, it is necessary first to grasp how early national writers understood the cerebral nature of speculative economic practices. Consider, for example, these prefatory remarks to the anonymous poem "The Glass; or Speculation": "Speculation now employs the heads and hearts of all the monied characters in the state—so immense are their profits, that they bid fair to be the richest citizens in the world. The arts and sciences are entirely neglected—the genius of the times is engaged in pursuits that, philosophically considered, hinder all improvements; that, in a moral view, corrupt the heart by the most diabolical intrigues, and render it callous to every thing but self; that, in a political sense, sap the foundation of republicanism, and pave the way for aristocracy and despotism."[2] The poem, which condemns stockjobbers, catalogs the standard vices attributed to speculative practices. Such behaviors, the author warns, will corrupt morals, unleash economic self-interest, and undermine the civic duty that is the basis of republican government. In this passage, however, speculation will exact an additional price: the wane of intellectual pursuits as economic ventures enlist the collective brainpower of the new nation. If speculation employs "the heads" as well as the hearts, and if the "genius of the times" is devoted to financial pursuits, who will attend to the arts and sciences?

What is unclear in the preface is whether or not speculation constitutes for the writer a legitimate intellectual activity. Is the danger that such ventures require valued skills and will, therefore, misdirect talents that might otherwise be devoted to learning and inquiry? Or is it that such ventures do *not* require valued skills and so will cause the community's intellect to atrophy over time? Ultimately, this poem indicates the latter, drawing a conventional equation between speculative impulses and the capricious dreams of a feverish brain, but the initial ambiguity also reflects the contradictory ways that speculation was understood as a mental procedure. As I discussed in chapter 4, although speculation was commonly characterized as womanly and fanciful, forms of so-called prudent speculation were also admired as manly intellectual maneuvers.

The eighteenth-century "economic man" whom J.G.A. Pocock describes is emasculated, insubstantial, and governed by dreams of wealth. He too closely resembles the woman who craves luxury and whose supposedly natural inclinations for romance have been fueled by excessive novel reading.[3] Pocock locates the origins of eighteenth-century republicanism in the Florentine republicanism of Machiavelli, and this gendering likewise has roots in Machiavellian thought. As Hanna Pitkin has written, Machiavelli appropriated the figure of the Roman goddess Fortuna and transformed it into a trope of female capriciousness and dependence. Men who trusted in and depended on others subjected themselves—economically, morally, and politically—to the whims of chance and so sacrificed their own autonomy and manliness. While it was standard in Roman mythology for feminine goddesses to embody qualities not specifically feminine, Machiavelli emphatically associated this figure with feminized behaviors. In short, he wrote, "Fortune is a woman."[4]

In eighteenth-century English responses to commercialization this equation often appeared in depictions of female consumers of luxuries, emasculated male merchants, and allegorical figures such as Daniel Defoe's Lady Credit.[5] The association of credit use with the feminine was also reinforced by the fact that women were beginning to number prominently among speculators and invest in schemes like that of the infamous South Seas Company. In Alexander Pope's "To a Lady: Of the Character of Women" women play the lottery and gamble at the card table, and their seductively protean nature makes them comparable to the very Dutch flowers that sparked the notorious ill-fated speculations of the 1630s: "Ladies, like variegated tulips, show; / 'Tis to their changes half their charmes we owe."[6]

In both England and the new United States the association of financial volatility with women themselves—in addition to emasculated men—was not simply a reaction to their increasing participation in the marketplace but also an attempt by a predominantly male merchant class to distance itself from reckless forms of speculation by aligning *prudent* speculation with masculinity. The celebration of a man's skills in borrowing and speculation challenged the characterization of economic man as effeminate. The virtue bestowed by unalienable land was replaced by the virtue of productivity—at the very moment, Caroll Smith-Rosenberg observes, when the bourgeois woman was increasingly required to be "both elegant and nonproductive"—and well-calculated speculations were characterized as cerebral manipulations of the pen distinct from reckless forms of gambling. Karen Weyler finds in many works of early American fiction a distinction between "virtuous trades," which were legitimated forms of industry involving moderate forms of speculation and credit use, and more corrupt trades that had no basis in industry at all, such as opportunistic speculation, gambling, or even inheritance.[7]

Such prudent speculation was aligned not simply with cerebral skills but, more specifically, with the rational processes celebrated by Enlightenment science. The term *reason* was variously defined by Enlightenment thinkers: it could refer to an order imposed on nature; the "common sense" that made one a "reasonable" person; a logically valid argument; or the process of induction based on empirical evidence. Although these meanings were used interchangeably without much concern over their distinctions, the last definition bears most significantly on the concept of financial speculation as a rational process. That is, to speculate on future economic performance one needed first to assess the empirical evidence of past performances and make predictions accordingly.[8]

Enlightenment thinking emphasized the use of induction drawn from empirical observation rather than deduction based on a priori arguments, and the goal of such empirical observation was to infer laws that could predict future natural occurrences.[9] If one could use, as Isaac Newton had, records of the earth's motions to predict the motions of all other planets in the solar system, or if one could use a theory of gravity to predict the next appearance of Halley's comet, could one not also use empirical evidence of past market behaviors to speculate on future economic performances? Subject to empirical observation, then, were not only the motions of planets, pendulums, and collision balls but also the roll of the die and the fluctuations of the market itself. Not coincidentally, "probability science," one of many scientific fields that arose during the long eighteenth century, began as a theoretical inquiry into everyday practices of gaming and gambling. Fittingly, Hume's *Enquiry Concerning Human Understanding* looks to the gambling table when defining the probable: if a die has one marking on four sides and another marking on two sides, Hume writes, the probability of the former turning up is higher and our "belief or expectation of the event more steady and secure."[10]

As Murray would likely have understood, the term *probability* always contains the suggestion that such conclusions risk error. Probability, Locke wrote in his *Essay Concerning Human Understanding*, is a *likeliness* of something being true, which humans accept "without certain knowledge that it is so."[11] Inquiries into probability were based on the precept that humans, fallible and limited in their access to knowledge, could only infer this likelihood from the calculation of odds, the testimony of others, or the use of evidence conforming to past experience. Inquiries into gambling stakes, while often conducted scientifically, defied the application of standard scientific methods.[12] The prediction of human emotions, such as confidence and despair, was also acknowledged as an equally tricky enterprise. Newton, who lost twenty thousand pounds when the South Sea Bubble burst, allegedly declared, "I can measure the motions of bodies, but I cannot measure human folly."[13] As a result, Adam Smith's attempt to construct a science of economics necessarily depends upon his conception of humans as *predictably* self-interested creatures who act consistently according to their own needs.

In diaries and correspondence early American women display uneasiness with this kind of commercial analysis. Mary Beth Norton records that women frequently lamented an "inability to reason properly" or arrange their thoughts, and the Revolutionary experience in particular revealed their inability to cope with family finances when husbands left for war.[14] Even Eliza Pinckney, the daughter of a South Carolina planter, whose experiments with plant hybridization made her one of the most successful female entrepreneurs of the eighteenth century, cannot comfortably assume the role of rational speculator.[15] Corresponding in 1742 with Mary Bartlett, the niece of her future husband, she writes:

> I have planted a large figg orchard with design to dry and export them. I have reckoned my expence and the prophets to arise from these figgs, but was I to tell you how great an Estate I am to make this way, and how 'tis to be laid out you would think me far gone in romance. Your good Uncle I know has long thought I have a fertile brain at schemeing. I only confirm him in his opinion; but I own I love the vegitable world extremely. I think it an innocent and useful amusement.

Pray tell him, if he laughs much at my project, I never intend to have my hand in a silver mine and he will understand as well as you what I mean.[16]

It is not entirely clear here whether Pinckney is being sarcastic or betraying ambivalence about her own commercial endeavors. Regardless, one can infer from her letter the kind of criticism to which the female entrepreneur was often subjected. She details the careful way in which she has "reckoned" her expenses and profits in order to make sure the project will be worthwhile, and there is no apparent reason to doubt her calculations except that the final numbers are dramatic. While the project shows no signs of haste or impracticability, she expresses concern that she will be deemed "far gone" in the kind of romance found in novels. She agrees, perhaps with pride, that her own imagination is "fertile" like the land she cultivates, but, in order to counter the potential perception that her head brims with fantasies, she immediately assures Mary and her uncle that she has no intentions of pursuing get-rich-quick schemes.

Pinckney, though of a different region and slightly earlier era, was similar to Murray in that she considered herself of an enlightened age and believed that rationality and self-restraint could find expression in commercial activities. Yet her discussion of economic ventures, despite their deployment of careful calculation, always simultaneously acknowledges that women's speculations risk being perceived as excessively imaginative. In a letter to Mary a month later she writes: "Wont you laugh at me if I tell you I am so busey in providing for Posterity I hardly allow my self time to Eat or sleep and can but just snatch a minnet to write to you and a friend or two now. I am making a large plantation of Oaks which I look upon as my own property, whether my father gives me the land or not; and therefore I design many years hence when oaks are more valuable than they are now—which you know they will be when we come to build fleets."[17] As this passage illustrates, Pinckney saw everywhere in the "vegetable world" opportunities for long-term investment. With minimal initial cost she might plant oak seeds and hope to reap a handsome profit once colonial shipbuilding increased and the demand for hardwood rose. In describing her well-laid plans for the future, she can be confident, claiming the trees regardless of whether or not her father bequeaths the land to her down the road. She cannot, however, help worrying that she will be mocked and deemed a "little Visionary." Undoubtedly, Pinckney's plan entails risk. For it to come to fruition, the colonial economy must continue to thrive, and, as any landowner's letter-book would attest, agricultural pursuits were always subject to hazard (proprietors sold products to a market that was itself often in flux, and inclement weather, crop diseases, pests, and other damaging circumstances were beyond human control). But, these obvious risks aside, what most dramatically upsets Pinckney's picture of rational calculation is a concern that, as a woman, she is more likely to be dismissed as whimsical.

Murray's refusal to apologize for her entrepreneurial activities seems exceptional for her time. Her second marriage, to John Murray, a minister who was unskilled with finances and eventually entrusted his wife with the family's money, was proof for her that commercial rationality could transcend gender difference. In one letter to her husband, written in 1791, Murray warns that, though he is "sufficiently economical," he seems "to have no fixed plan" regarding his financial future.[18] Seven years later she is resigned to the fact that her husband simply does not relish the accountant's mental maneuvers as she does: "Mr. Murray, willing to divest himself of embarrassing attentions, consigned to me the care of our little property, and the pleasure I derived, upon every revolving week, from appropriating the stated stipend in a manner which should answer of our various exigencies, none but those who are attached to order will conceive."[19] Murray was aware that her attempts to engage in enterprise might raise eyebrows, and she may even have kept some of her investing schemes a secret from her second husband.[20] Never, however, does she qualify her insistence that women are capable of becoming "attached to order" and responding to life's contingencies.

In other writings Murray insists that when a woman does suffer capriciousness it is often a function of the generally unstable life she is forced to lead. The female sex, she writes in number 88 of *The Gleaner*, plays "the sport of contingencies" and is "unnaturally subjected to extremes"; thus, she asks rhetorically, "Is it wonderful, then, that they evince so little stability of character?"[21] The reasons for this vulnerability should come as no surprise to the modern reader: women have very few means of achieving financial security outside of marriage—sewing, teaching, caring for children, and possibly writing are among the few options—and husband seeking is no more secure an enterprise. The marriage market, in fact, is as unpredictable as the market in which the merchant or banker operates. The crucial difference, however, is that most women do not have the mental wherewithal to cope with its unpredictability. In number 17, an essay arguing that children be outfitted with skills for financial security, Murray stresses that girls are the least equipped of all: "But if the male part of our American world are, in the morning of their lives, too much neglected in this respect, females have abundantly more reason to complain. Our girls, in general, are bred up with one particular view, with one monopolizing consideration, which seems to absorb every other plan that reason might point out as worthy their attention: An establishment by marriage; this is the goal to which they are constantly pointed, the great ultimatum of every arrangement."[22] That young girls are trained to bank on marriage indicates for Murray the deplorable state of female education. The problem is not simply that girls are not taught to value self-respect and independence but also that they are taught to neglect their rational faculties.

Like the reckless speculator who invests all assets in one scheme without assessing the probability of its success, women rely too heavily on the uncertain prospect of marriage. In number 91 she writes: "The chance of a matrimonial coadjutor, is no more than a probable contingency; and if [girls] were early accustomed to regard this *uncertain* event with suitable *indifference,* they would make elections with that deliberation, which would be calculated to give a more rational prospect of tranquility. . . . To neglect polishing a gem, or obstinately to refuse bringing into action a treasure in our possession, when we might thus accumulate a handsome interest, is surely egregiously absurd, and the height of folly."[23] Talents should be cultivated, Murray emphasizes, and so to focus one's time exclusively on the search for a husband risks missing out on the "handsome interest" garnered through other skills. Here and elsewhere Murray invokes the very terms used by others to feminize reckless speculation ("height of folly") and masculinize its more prudent form ("deliberation," "calculation"). In number 17 Murray emphasizes that "contingent events" such as marriage should not be "made an absolute part of [a girl's] expectations," and her training should encourage "deliberation" and discourage "precipitation." A girl must be occupied by "schemes" that would "involve a greater probability of fruition," and she must rise "superior to the caprices of those about her."[24] When she does meet a potential husband, she must be able to calculate the probability of his being suitable. Cautioning one young woman about the importance of analyzing character, Murray wrote in 1804, "I am free to own that the false calculations which I have, through life, been in the habit of making have constituted one of my principal sources of suffering."[25]

The skills needed to weather the caprices of marriage market and commercial market alike were also the very skills increasingly called for in female education. At the time Murray wrote, educators were evaluating girls' curricula and insisting they be trained to cope with the vicissitudes of life in the fledgling republic. Norton writes that "Americans' wartime experiences convinced them that women needed broader training to prepare them for unforeseen contingencies," and Linda Kerber concludes that this reevaluation of girls' education represented the "common sense of a revolutionary era in which the unexpected was very likely to happen; in which large numbers of people had lived through reversals of fortune, encounters with strangers, physical dislocation."[26] Aside from Murray, the most significant voice for improved female education was the prominent Philadelphia doctor Benjamin Rush, who in 1787 declared that female education should accommodate the "state of society, manners, and government" of the new nation and that some "knowledge of figures and bookkeeping" was "absolutely necessary to qualify a young lady for the duties which await her in this country."[27]

Rush's reform efforts had limited effect. For one thing, other educators, such as Samuel Magaw, did not agree with Rush and advocated a traditional distinction between a girl's education that aimed to produce sensible women and a boy's education that stressed the "higher exercise of mind" and the development of speculative and rational powers. Also, progressive though it was, Rush's plan still emphasized only a shift from ornamental accomplishments to practical skills. What was still missing was an emphasis on inference and problem solving. The new American woman might learn the computations needed to calculate her family's gains and losses, but she remained unequipped to estimate the "probability of fruition" of a given scheme. Women might learn arithmetic, but, as Patricia Cline Cohen writes in her study of numeracy in early America, these basic arithmetical computations would only have been associated with commercial transaction and not considered intellectual exercises like the problem solving of geometry, trigonometry, or calculus. Although women were not considered deficient in the basic computations, according to Cohen, these higher forms of mathematics were considered inappropriate for female students. (When, in the early nineteenth century and antebellum era, schools would increasingly teach arithmetic as a way of instilling reasoning skills, the teaching of arithmetic would quickly become sex typed and focused on boys.)[28]

In her well-known piece "On the Equality of the Sexes" Murray identifies precisely this blind spot in female curricula. This work, part poem and part essay, divides knowledge into four categories—imagination, reason, memory, and judgment—and assesses women's capacities in each. While the average woman boasts a remarkably "fertile brain" and memory, Murray writes, her reason and judgment are hindered by limited education. To advance the cause of female educational reform, Murray invokes both a Lockean concept of the mind's malleability and the Cartesian belief that the mind is genderless (even if bodily form is sexually distinct). "I have conceived that the distinction male, and female, does not exist in *Mind*," she wrote in 1801, "and it appears to me that my opinion is sanctioned by the imposing authorities of nature, reason, and scripture."[29] With proper education, then, woman might forsake baubles, gossip, and social calls for more worthwhile pursuits:

> Fashions, in their variety, would then give place to conjectures, which might perhaps conduce to the improvement of the literary world, and there would be no leisure for slander or detraction. Reputation would not then be blasted, but serious speculations would occupy the lively imaginations of the sex. Unnecessary visits would be precluded, and that custom would only be indulged by way of relaxation, or to answer the demands of consanguinity and friendship. Females would become discreet, their judgments would be invigorated, and their partners for life being circumspectly chosen, an unhappy Hymen would then be as rare, as is now the reverse.[30]

Learned speculations about stellar constellations, far-off lands, the natural sciences, and the workings of providence—all phenomena subject to conjecture—could fill the mind of the educated girl or woman. Her "judgment" would be invigorated, and, as a result, she would choose a husband based on lifelong prospects rather than the flimsy romantic notions promoted in sentimental novels. After reason, judgment was the skill most closely aligned by educators and scientists with successful speculation. It was, as Locke wrote, the faculty that compensated for our "want of clear and certain knowledge" and allowed humans to decide the truth or falseness of a proposition "without perceiving a demonstrative evidence in the proofs."[31]

To provide a model of female circumspection, the *Gleaner* narrator offers number 18, the story of sisters Helen and Penelope. Orphaned and separated at birth, the two follow dramatically different paths as they mature. Helen leads a dissipated life filled with card playing, shopping, and novel reading; meanwhile, her guardian, Aunt M——, offers no guidance whatsoever and feels these activities "are quite sufficient for a person in [her] line of life." The clearest indication that Helen is headed for unhappiness is that she thinks nothing of her future. Dismissing such thoughts as foolish soothsaying, she writes to her sister, "for calculations of every kind, and all peeps into futurity, as I pretend not to the least skill in astrology, I leave all these occult matters to the wise penetration of my sister Pen."[32] Helen, who has mistaken the reasoned speculations of astronomy for the fortune-telling of astrology, mocks the fact that her sister lives "systematically" and embraces an "economical disposition," and she claims that her own prospects of marriage will put her ahead in the end.

It is easy to see where this story is headed. The sober and methodical Penelope has had the advantage of good training, and her virtues will be rewarded in the end. Her Aunt Dorothy has encouraged her to cultivate her sewing skills in the event that she will have to rely on them for future income. Guided by this training, Penelope has made a crucial calculation based on her assessment of past events, and she hopes to impart this insight to her sister. She warns, "agreeably to the course of nature the probability is, that those nearest to you in consanguinity, will be removed; and will you be content to remain the dependant upon the caprice, or even bounty, of more distant relations?" Her parents' death has taught Penelope the ease with which life can be taken away, and so she is determined to acquire a "mental fund" that will enable her "to encounter with due equanimity the ills of life, thereby avoiding that hurricane of the passions."[33]

Reiterating the claims of other essays, Penelope announces that marriage simply does not figure in her plans for financial security: "With regard to my matrimonial expectations, upon which you are so ludicrously playful, I have to say, that the idea of marriage makes no part of my *present* plans; this, my dear, is a *calculation, at which you seem to be abundantly* more expert than myself; it is a contingence which, being within the chapter of possibilities, may, or may not happen; if it should, my arrangements must, in some respects, be different; if it should not, I am contented; at any rate, I esteem it an error; to reckon upon an event, which is at best but uncertain." In the end marriage does happen for Penelope. Her virtues are "soon distinguished by an amiable man," and a happy marriage follows. Meanwhile, the "dissipated manners of Helen" deter "the sensible part of the male world," and, with the death of her aunt and uncle, she is forced to become dependent on distant relatives.[34]

Girls and young women, the story emphasizes, must be taught to think differently. They need to acquire the skills of the prudent speculator in order to cope with a topsy-turvy world. To solidify this connection between speculative processes and rational thinking, the narrator offers one telling detail. Each sister was given one hundred pounds by an uncle to do with as she wished. Recollecting this one "*capital transaction,* in which [her] *judgment*" was "called into action," Helen boasts that she advantageously disposed of her money on an elegant suit of clothes. In contrast, Penelope utilized the "handsome dividend" of hand-me-down clothes (improving upon them, not surprisingly, with her sewing skills) and used her sum, instead, to make a low-risk investment that will earn "legal compound interest"![35]

Ironically, the only way Murray can make this lesson compelling is to reward Penelope with a husband. While the celibate life of a seamstress may be preferable to marital misery or poverty, it still does not provide the most appealing or conventional image with which to end the story. But it is also worth emphasizing that rationality is not a means of acquiring a husband, and it is not dispensable once a woman marries. The speculative and calculative skills Murray celebrates are to assume an important role in married life as well as in single life. Obviously recalling her own efforts to help John Stevens, she writes in number 91, "*The united efforts of male and female* might rescue many a family from destruction, which, notwithstanding the efforts of its *individual* head, is now involved in all the calamities attendant on a dissipated fortune and augmenting debts." The efforts of one man are sometimes not enough, and families need the help of a "husbandwoman," as Murray calls her, in times of distress. Drawing a direct link between the husbandwoman's education and the greater commonwealth, Murray adds, "the more we multiply aids to a family, the greater will be the security, that its individuals will not be thrown a burden on the public."[36] Stable familial economies make for a stable republic overall.

Murray's story of Penelope ends well because she has undertaken a financial risk that is well managed; in fact, this investment is not even depicted as a risk but, rather, as a cautious procedure to hedge against future contingencies. In this and other *Gleaner* installments Murray seems to obscure the risk of speculative acts in her attempt to celebrate the careful, circumspect manner in which they have been carried out. In number 3, for example, her depiction of a prudent accountant, Ernestus, seems completely detached from the realities of the postwar economy:

> The close of every week states exactly the accounts of Ernestus; the posting of his books was, from the first, the work of every day; as often as possible he passeth receipts; and when this desideratum cannot be obtained, so precisely is debt and credit announced, that the foot of every page presents the most unerring information; the whole amount of his *possessions* he knows; every farthing for which he is indebted is in legible characters expressed, and in a very short space of time, he can estimate to a penny, what he is *really* worth; no person demands of Ernestus a second time his dues, for he never *hazards larger sums, than his capital can at any*

time command; this enableth him to wear the wreath of punctuality, and he supports, unimpeached, even by the tongue of slander, the character of an honest man.[37]

This depiction is a fantasy of economic stability, fueled perhaps by Murray's own economic hardship. Murray, herself a speculator in public securities, knew that the key to economic expansion was, in fact, hazarding larger sums than what one commands at a given moment, for it is borrowing and credit use that enable the entrepreneur to break through the limitations of his or her current capital. So, while Ernestus plays it safe, he may also ensure his own economic stagnation. Moreover, the absolute fiscal certainty depicted here is impracticable. No matter how scrupulously Ernestus tabulates what he is "*really* worth," the realization of that worth will depend upon circumstances beyond his control. If debtors renege on their obligations, he cannot realize the entirety of his assets. If the economy takes a downturn, any assets that exist on paper will shift on a moment's notice.

Complete independence of these circumstances is never feasible. The rational calculations that square all accounts in a given moment, in other words, imply an unqualified self-determination that Murray herself knew was impossible. While she celebrates financial independence and methodical foresight, she must ultimately account for the fact that there are no guarantees against vicissitude. As she wrote in response to her first husband's bankruptcy, "Mercantile interest must ever be fluctuating and he who confides his property to a treacherous element must always consider his circumstances precarious."[38] Murray considered speculation and risk an inevitable component of money-making, and so the question for her was not whether one should invest but how one should do it so as to minimize the risk. When misfortune could not be avoided, Murray's antidote was always compassion.

The Happy Mean

Murray's understanding of benevolence was formed in the days when, as the wife of a debtor, she had to hide from her husband's creditors beyond the closed blinds of her house. In her personal correspondence Murray continually draws a crucial distinction between insolvency as the result of negligence and insolvency as the result of circumstances, such as trade embargoes, currency fluctuations, and the default of debtors, which are beyond one's control. Letters by Murray defending her first husband's bankruptcy echo the carefully drawn distinction between defeat and dishonor which historian Toby L. Ditz perceives in many of the mercantile narratives of business failure at this time. "The integrity of his heart acquits him of <u>intentional error</u>," she explained to her brother in 1786, "his every step hath been paved by misfortune and one sad event hath unavoidably produced another!" A few months later she assured one of her husband's creditors, "he had a rational prospect of retrieving his affairs, but, alas! His vessels returned with very little fish, and the loss of cables, and anchors, the consequences are such, as might be expected, his possessions are wrested from him."[39] Her husband's losses, in other words, were not only unintentional but beyond the purview of rational speculations.

Murray "condemned anyone whose troubles were the result of idleness or extravagance" and insisted that "debtors should make every effort to reimburse their creditors," according to biographer Sheila Skemp, but she also "heaped praise on creditors who exhibited compassion toward deserving supplicants."[40] Murray's play *The Traveller Returned* uses two characters to illustrate this double-sided attitude toward indebtedness: the bankrupt Dutch merchant Vansittart is despicable because he is an upstart who gives his "creditors the slip" and absconds with Rambleton's hard-earned cash and personal belongings without making any efforts to pull himself out of debt; the orphaned Emily Lovegrove, on the other hand, is an object of sympathy precisely because her patrimony has—beyond her control—been "reduced by the ruinous paper currency almost to nothing."[41] Murray's personal letters also recount anecdotes of women like Emily, who are saved by the leniency of a "humane creditor" and ultimately repay the loan and profit themselves.[42]

Given Murray's own struggles with debt, her vindications of the virtuous debtor are in many ways projections. Nina Baym suggests that, when Murray "urges women to surmount life's trials and find happiness in their own virtue, she is in a sense writing to herself."[43] But these tales are also responses to common concerns that debtors were being unfairly imprisoned, and Murray's treatment of debt is also a function of her understanding of human experience: one might master one's own impulses, but mastering one's circumstances was a far different matter. Dependence was inherent to mercantile activity, Murray continually reminds her readers, but humans were generally subject to unforeseen "contingencies" of all kinds. Consider, for example, the extended metaphor of the sea venture she uses to describe the vagaries of a literary career: "In consequence of the repeated mortifications, and rebuffs, which I have encountered in my literary career, it is my present determination, never again to venture upon so fluctuating an ocean as publick opinion, except my invitation to embark, should be both publick, and unequivocal. Urged by the illusive gales of private friendship, or adulation, I embarked on a troublous sea, and if I have not been wrecked, my shattered bark has barely escaped, and now, laid up in the harbour of discretion, we are terrified even at the idea of again braving the storms which are abroad."[44] Murray did, in fact, assume the position of debtor when soliciting advanced subscriptions for her *Gleaner* collection, and she understood that "publick opinion" could determine the financial outcome of her literary endeavors, but this passage emphasizes the emotional, as well as financial, vulnerability of a life in print. Women were particularly attuned to such vagaries, and their brand of compassion could alleviate these strains. In this passage an "I" embarks on the troublous sea, but it is finally a "we"—presumably Murray buttressed by the biased but well-intentioned "private friendship"—who look with terror at the prospect of another venture.

Although Murray insists the intellect is genderless, she simultaneously takes the more traditional position that sympathy is an essential part of woman. In "On the Equality of the Sexes," in fact, she claims that men and women are endowed with unequal measures of tenderness, adding that "sensibility, soft compassion, and gentle commiseration, are inmates in the female bosom."[45] In her study of the changing definition of the term *virtue* in the early republic, Ruth H. Bloch observes that, as a man's virtue was increasingly defined as rational self-interest, a woman's virtue came to be understood as the moral rectitude that accompanies emotional sensitivity. Murray, however, seems to claim both attributes for the properly trained woman.[46]

In Murray's 1795 drama *The Medium* the female investor Matronia Aimwell admirably combines both types of virtue. This heroine is a medium in that she negotiates between debtor and creditor, but she also occupies the very middle ground between calculation and feeling which Murray calls for throughout her essays. Matronia is compassionate because, as a woman, she belongs to the "unhappy sex" whose "ways are environed with peril."[47] But she also understands vulnerability through her investments in public securities. Far from lamenting her interdependence, Murray sentimentalizes those credit relations and makes them the basis for a necessary compassion.

Matronia is an accomplished businesswoman—surely a version of what Murray aspired to be—and "punctual" with repayment, earning the respect from Maitland which Tyler's Van Rough grants to male business partners. And yet, when her niece's husband, George Bloomville, falls into dire financial straits over cargo that is delayed or possibly lost at sea, she intercedes on his behalf and goes into debt to lend him aid. She borrows the necessary funds from Maitland so that she will not have to withdraw her own bank stock, and, when the play builds to a denouement, in which George stands on the brink of a devastating exposure of his insolvency, it is she who steps in to help. Because of this benevolent "matron" (a female "patron" who brings a maternal compassion to the role of creditor), George is granted a temporary reprieve, and by the last act his ship has, literally, come in. Significantly, she has accomplished this without withdrawing her investment in the "public repositories."[48]

The credit instrument is precisely the medium through which Matronia strikes her balance. Financial entanglements draw her into social interaction, and the negotiation of outstanding debts is an opportunity for benevolent behavior on the part of the creditor to whom debts are outstanding. Matronia's concern for those who fall victim to vicissitude is distinct from the rational self-interest she otherwise displays. Murray is not interested here in commerce's ability to foster politeness, and she does not suggest, as other writers in her time did, that social relations themselves could be an economic resource for those pursuing their own profits.[49] Matronia's investment in her friends is emotional and not rationalized by economic payoff.

The play's marriage plot proposes a similar medium between calculation and feeling: "friendship" between a man and woman represents the happy mean between a prudent but cold marriage for money and a passionate but dangerously all-consuming love. Maitland, who compares marriage to gambling and investments, beseeches his son Charles to follow "prudent calculations" and marry for money. He opposes his son's marriage to Eliza, a virtuous but penniless woman, because he assumes that an orphan is the embodiment of "fortune," but Eliza's "unexampled prudence" and "calm equality of disposition" win him over by play's end. The elder Maitland, who is given to platitudes about the "happy *Medium*" between passion and rationality—or, in his words, "the torrid and the frigid zone"—comes to realize that his own opposition to the marriage would "constitute the extreme of obstinacy."[50] He has mistakenly believed that dependence precludes moderation, when, in fact, it fosters moderation by bringing feeling to calculation.

Eliza also must strike a balance. She refuses to consider a union to a wealthy man like Charles for fear that it would make her a dependent and cast suspicious light on her character. A "step so reprehensible," she says of marriage to Charles, "would indeed evince [her] unwarrantably interested." Even though

Eliza only agrees to marry Charles once her long lost uncle conveniently appears and hands over an inheritance, the marriage represents a softening of her insistence that she maintain independence. Indeed, while the uncle's sudden appearance may fulfill her (and, vicariously, Murray's) desire for financial security, she is dependent for that security on the "matron" of her mother, who "carefully improved" her "patrimony" to pass on to her daughter after death.[51] Moreover, Eliza only receives her inheritance because her uncle accidentally discovers she is still alive, making her good fortune as much a function of vicissitude as another's misfortune.

That Eliza's own happy ending depends upon this patrimony indicates the far-reaching effect of these webs of interdependence. Although she has insisted that she wants no patron, Matronia and Eliza's mother represent a positive version of patronage which comes naturally to women but might be adopted by men as well. Both the younger Charles and Mellfont, in fact, are "men of sensibility" who are humane creditors and approach their business affairs with exemplary compassion. Murray's *Story of Margaretta* also emphasizes that men and women alike acknowledge their dependence on others and act compassionately as a result: in this novel Margaretta's husband is condemned for his refusal to accept financial assistance from friends, and the heroine's own maturation is complete only when she has assumed the role of philanthropist.

In *The Medium* domestic and commercial interactions are not exclusive of each other, and a character might express fellow feeling through an involvement in a "multiplicity of affairs." The most damning trait of Dorinda Scornwell, in fact, is her unapologetic contempt for all forms of business. Speaking to Captain Flashet in the fourth act, she proclaims, "the word *business* admits various significations—there are domestic affairs, there are commercial affairs, and a multiplicity of affairs—all of which come under the description of business, and all of which, I do assure, Captain Flashet, I most truly detest."[52] Dorinda mistakenly assumes that her removal from such business is the mark of a gentlewoman, when, in fact, it reveals an inability to share others' concerns.

In Murray's view, benevolence, like speculative intelligence, is specifically grounded in economic experiences and sensibilities. Like Harriet Beecher Stowe and other Victorian American writers, Murray wrote of a uniquely feminine, and even morally superior, sphere in which women are naturally endowed with benevolent impulses that can counter the harsh realities of economic transactions. But, while Murray's vision of female sympathy has much in common with later ideals, she decidedly locates such benevolence within, rather than separate from, the marketplace. It is because of her business acumen that Murray's exemplary woman—who is, in turn, an example for all Americans—can both investigate a situation rationally and feel compassion in the face of human limitations. The entanglement of creditors and debtors is not degenerative but, rather, an opportunity for the formation of sympathetic relationships that are not limited to women but are certainly gendered as female.

That Murray believed speculation fostered both rationality and compassion is indicated in a letter she penned in December 1808 to a man whose name is now lost to us. Referring to him only as "Sir" in her letterbook, she writes in search of financial advice after discovering that nine hundred dollars' worth of her husband's public securities are depreciating rapidly. She worries that the notes they once "called property" are diminishing and "that nominal thousands" will "presently crumble to nothing!": "The idea I entertain of your benevolence induces me to believe, that you will pardon the intrusion of a stranger, who wishes your advice in the line of your commission. Mr. Murray, unacquainted with the nature of publick stocks, generally oppressed by ill health, and much engrossed by professional duties, has neither inclination nor leisure to investigate the value of the various currency of our Country."[53] Fearing her husband's declining health and her own limited means of employment, Murray seeks the stranger's help in rendering the currency "permanent and productive." In one sense her assumption that she can take over and potentially resuscitate her husband's failing finances reveals remarkable confidence in her own business acumen. She believes her application of calculative skill can potentially put those public securities to work for her family. Yet in another sense she is utterly dependent on the stranger's willingness to explain to her the workings of these securities. She seeks benevolence as much as know-how, and the letter presents a mixture of self-reliance and dependence, distance and intimacy. Murray is a "stranger" but, as the reference to "our Country" emphasizes, a fellow American in need of help. Murray clearly hopes the particular circumstances will engender a fellow feeling.

Although Murray emphasized that the husbandwoman's contribution to the stability of home and family was itself a boon to the nation, the happy medium could also be the basis for a woman's participation in civic life outside the home. In this way her heroines embody the combination of qualities many political thinkers would have considered vital in an experimental new republic: namely, the talent for speculation as well as an understanding of speculation's shortcomings. In *The Federalist*, one of the era's greatest feats of speculation, political theory yet to be put into practice is often justified both because it is the result of the author's careful speculations *but also* because it safeguards against the failings of those speculations. Alexander Hamilton considered scientific modes of thought to be of limited use for political theorists because "objects of geometrical inquiry are so entirely abstracted from those pursuits which stir up and put in motion the unruly passions of the human heart." Anticipating the new nation's fiscal needs in *Federalist* 30, for example, he tallies the "present and future exigencies of the Union," only to concede that its "future necessities admit not of calculation or limitation," and, in number 31 he argues that superintending the national defense involves "a provision for casualties and dangers to which no possible limits can be assigned."[54] Here, as elsewhere, Hamilton calls for a central government of extended powers precisely so it can make provisions for the unforeseen contingencies of the future.

Murray shared Hamilton's sense that contingency was unquantifiable, but she looked to feminized benevolence rather than governing structures to mitigate the shortcomings of analytical thinking. Arguing that women were fitted for politics, she wrote to the novelist Sally Wood that women could balance a theoretical skill with affective responses to suffering. A woman will be equally concerned with men in the public weal, she argues, because she is "outraged at the wrongs, which a tyrant may inflict," has "eyes to weep for the misfortunes, that a ruinous administration may create," and "hands to be manacled, organs, dimensions, senses, affections, passions, all of which will keenly suffer from the rod of the oppressor." We might expect this much, but Murray also emphasizes that the woman's response to wrongdoing does not end with her emotional reactions. "If you would not confine us to a state of idiotism," she writes a few sentences later, "we shall assuredly enquire into the *causes* of *effects,* and our researches will furnish us with a knowledge of the resources of national respectability, or they will unveil to our view, the origin of those calamities, which despoil and enslave us."[55]

Here Murray states explicitly that a woman's combination of speculative intelligence and compassion can foster her public contributions. Her skilled but sympathetic inquiry into causes and effects, which Murray repeatedly traces to financial experience, can prepare her to raise children but also enhance her participation in the life of the nation. This balance is essential when public credit structures bring financial volatility and equally so when individuals invest financially in the nation itself. Women, once properly educated, are Murray's exemplary investors.

EPILOGUE

Headwork, Literary Vocation

> I cannot easily buy a blank-book to write thoughts in; they are commonly ruled for dollars and cents.
> HENRY DAVID THOREAU, "LIFE WITHOUT PRINCIPLE"

As eighteenth-century Americans contrived new ways to carry on exchange and to finance enterprise, the period's literature identified public benefits in communal debts. Writers imagined that borrowing, speculation, and risk taking could be a means of coping with a lack of capital and expanding economically, but, just as important, they hoped these measures might initiate cultural improvements, enhance the community's reputability, strengthen social ties, and invest people in their communities.

These writers did not consider writing their vocation. Each carried out his or her literary endeavors in conjunction with other kinds of work—as a minister, statesman, farmer, printer, merchant, lawyer, wife, mother, educator, political radical. The point is worth emphasizing because an emerging concept of authorship, which celebrated the writer as writer, placed aesthetics above public serviceability, and stressed the personal rewards of writing (be they artistic or monetary), would bring new meaning to the act of financial speculation. This concept of authorship would find its fullest expression in the Romantic writing of the antebellum era, but its beginnings are evident in Hector St. John de Crèvecoeur's *Letters from an American Farmer* and, especially, Washington

Irving's tales. In these works financial speculation is analogous in many ways to writing and intellectual enterprise. It is a positive form of castle building—a cerebral maneuver that need not be limited by the realities of the present moment—but one that is individual rather than collective.

In these texts the writer's "head-work," to use Irving's phrase, has much in common with the speculator's. Both are radically creative—capable of making much of nothing and building castles in the absence of earthly foundations—and both locate that creativity in the mind itself. Writers and speculators alike had to answer the charge that theirs was an unproductive form of labor. This writer was to be a writer exclusively, and, as a result, was often, like the speculator, dismissed as a dabbler, dreamer, and even parasite. Crèvecoeur and Irving place a high value on the opportunity to write full-time, liberated of practical concerns, and therefore are much more capable of appreciating the speculator's impulse to dream. Even Irving, who looked to writing as a moneymaking venture, valued headwork in its unremunerative form. There is an obvious irony to the analogy between speculator and writer, for the Romantic culture to follow would consistently proclaim that the rewards of writing—creativity, expression, self-actualization, the discovery of wonder in the familiar—were not to be monetary: hence, Thoreau's conclusion that a book ruled for accounting is not conducive to writing. The analogy obtains, however, because the speculator defined *creativity, labor,* and *productivity* in ways that nicely complemented how these writers wanted to think about their own literary efforts.

Jacksonian and antebellum writing responded variously to economic conditions, and Irving's portrayal of speculation cannot wholly represent the literature of the next century. In that era, in fact, one finds many instances of enterprise that damage individuals and communities alike. Jotham Riddel's silver-mining scheme is a capricious folly that divides the frontier community in James Fenimore Cooper's novel *The Pioneers;* the "projector" of Herman Melville's sketch "The Happy Failure," who is obsessed with perfecting a swamp-draining apparatus that can make land instantly valuable, is a miserable man; and Topsy's innocent claim that she was not born of parents but, rather, "raised by a speculator" provides some of the most powerful proof of slavery's inhumanity in all of *Uncle Tom's Cabin*.[1] But, even if it is not entirely representative, Irving's portrayal of speculation tells us much about the changing conception of literature in his time and brings into relief the claims of this book.

Irving's tales underscore, by comparison, the way in which the writers I have examined understood the social dimension of their writing through their promotion of economic welfare. Irving celebrates America by celebrating enterprising individuals, such as Ichabod Crane and Rip Van Winkle. But, unlike works that use entrepreneurial figures to solicit faith in public credibility or to portray a community bolstered by reputability or sympathy, his tales display little or no awareness of their capacity to intervene in the larger economy. In Cooke's *Sotweed Redivivus* headwork produces the public "project" in the planter's pate, but in Irving's fiction it is a source of personal reward.

Crèvecoeur's Farmer James offers an early and telling example of a writer whose literary aspirations are likened to the speculator's headwork. In this collection of letters about immigration and settlement, one of the riskiest acts is James's decision to become a writer. In the first letter James tells the reader that the text came about when an English friend requested that James provide an epistolary account of life in America. For the unschooled farmer to grant this request would risk the ridicule of his readers in England, but his wife has other risks in mind:

> I would not have thee, James, pass for what the world calleth a writer; no, not for a peck of gold, as the saying is. Thy father before thee was a plain-dealing, honest man, punctual in all things; he was one of *yea* and *nay,* of few words; all he minded was his farm and his work. I wonder from whence thee hast got this love of the pen? Had he spent his time in sending epistles to and fro, he never would have left thee this goodly plantation, free from debt. All I say is in good meaning; great people over sea may write to our townsfolks because they have nothing else to do. These Englishmen are strange people; because they can live upon what they call bank notes, without working, they think that all the world can do the same. This goodly country never would have been tilled and cleared with these notes.[2]

James's wife distrusts writing because she finds it insubstantial and unproductive. She is not surprised that Englishmen would rather write than work, for in her mind they also invest pieces of paper with value and live off them without putting in hard labor. Belletristic writing and credit instruments are similar contrivances, or "schemes" (a word she uses just a few sentences later), recklessly built upon nothing tangible.

Many readers have found—erroneously—that the wife's complaints reveal an uneasiness with professional letters which implicates literary vocation as a whole. Larzer Ziff writes that the wife suspects "her husband's commitment to writing—to his represented rather than his immanent self—somehow shadows the operation of commercial paper." And Grantland S. Rice writes that by the end of *Letters* James shares his wife's concern that writing undermines individualism, fearing "the growth in—and uses of—print because it linked the American farmer to a distinctly European, capitalistic, and legalistic 'paper culture.'" *Letters* does indeed betray fears that exploitative capitalism and legal systems have already encroached, and will continue to encroach, on American agrarian life, but these fears are not present in this particular passage. Readers are in fact cautioned *not* to take the wife's advice as seriously as they have. Her assumption that notes impede community building is one we should question, especially given how much literature of the period celebrates the productive and hardworking qualities of paper credit. But, more so, in expressing her skepticism about paper credit, the wife voices an opposition to individual intellectual pursuit, which is ultimately suspect in this text.[3]

What the wife fears most is that her husband's profits will dwindle if he spends too much of his time at the writing desk rather than in the fields. As she continues with her warning, it is never entirely clear whether she has problems with "paper culture" *in principle* or whether she simply believes such schemes will yield no economic reward in the agrarian economy of America:

> I am sure when Mr. F. B. was here, he saw thee sweat and take abundance of pains; he often told me how the Americans worked a great deal harder than the home Englishmen; for there, he told us, that they have no trees to cut down, no fences to make, no Negroes to buy and to clothe. And now I think on it, when wilt thee send him those trees he bespoke? But if they have no trees to cut down, they have gold in abundance, they say; for they rake it and scrape it from all parts far and near. I have often heard my grandfather tell how they live there by writing. By writing they send this cargo unto us, that to the West, and the other to the East Indies. But, James, thee knowest that it is not by writing that we shall pay the blacksmith, the minister, the weaver, the tailor, and the English shop. But as thee art an early man, follow thine own inclinations; thee wantest some rest, I am sure, and why should'st thee not employ it as it may seem meet unto thee. However, let it be a great secret; how would'st thee bear to be called at our country meetings the man of the pen? If this scheme of thine was once known, travellers as they go along would point out to our house, saying, "Here liveth the scribbling farmer."[4]

The tone is certainly condescending toward mercantile ways, but the warning strikes me as far more concerned with the bottom line than with the possible correspondence between imaginative accounting and her husband's epistolary endeavors. She suspects he has already fallen behind in his work (apparently he was supposed to send Mr. F. B. timber and has, instead, been contemplating writing), and she fears they will be unable to meet their obligations and that the townspeople will laugh at his "scheme" to write. There is no paper culture in America, and so she fears a writer will simply have no respectable or profitable role to fill in this society.

Although the banknote and epistle are the products of cerebral, rather than physical, labors, writing is not necessarily aligned with the menacing economy found elsewhere in *Letters*. In fact, here it figures as a dematerialized form of speculation, for it is financially unprofitable and stands directly *opposed* to the practical economic concerns of the wife. It is an act of individual daring but one with rewards that will not be monetary. The wife's concerns are not unfounded, but she advocates a conformity and risk aversion that itself risks loss. Indeed, the book would not have been written if James had heeded her advice.

One might argue that this is precisely the point and that the book that results from James's efforts represents all that the wife and Crèvecoeur fear in writing. A parallel incident in letter 11, however, suggests that the book does not necessarily endorse the wife's opinion. In this fictionalized account of John Bartram (Crèvecoeur spells the character's name *Bertram*) the celebrated botanist recalls tellingly how his wife warned him against undertaking a similar venture. Upon plowing a field one day, Bertram recalls, he felt compelled to stop and examine a single daisy; when this "seeming inspiration suddenly awakened [his] curiosity," however, his wife grew concerned that botanical pursuits would diminish his farming profits: "I mentioned it to my wife, who greatly discouraged me from prosecuting my new scheme, as she called it; I was not opulent enough, she said, to dedicate much of my time to studies and labours which might rob me of that portion of it which is the only wealth of the American farmer. However, her prudent caution did not discourage me."[5] Bertram ignores his wife's advice, learning Latin and Linnaeus and, over time, becoming an esteemed botanist who educates the "old countries" about flora in the New World. Bertram, whose wall is adorned with an Aeolian harp—a popular subject for poetry at this time—is also an aesthete.[6] Like James's wife, Mrs. Bertram believes there is no place for intellectual and artistic pursuits in America, particularly for a man who is not of leisurely and aristocratic status.

Once again, credit schemes and risk taking are not associated with the fanciful and capricious behavior of women but with acts of masculine daring. The feminine impulse in these passages is one of conformity and risk aversion that stifles any potential for learning and letters in the New World. Consider, in particular, that James's wife and Bertram's wife are the only women who speak in all of *Letters,* and when they do speak they do so to dissuade their husbands from undertaking intellectual pursuits. These wives are less shrill versions of the famously termagant Dame Van Winkle, whose husband, Rip, is only free to dream once he has escaped her and headed off to the Catskills. If these women are set up to be dismissed—which they seem to be—then *Letters* applauds a man who is free to devote himself to intellectual pursuits that may not be deemed profitable or legitimate by others. His pursuits are not simply cerebral rather than physical (for, by that definition, the work of the doctor, lawyer, or minister would also qualify) but the product of creative mental faculties. Reverie, the tool of artist and financial speculator alike, is doubtless something these wives would denigrate as childlike, fanciful, and wasteful.

In Irving's tales this type of cerebral labor is also misunderstood and unappreciated by others. While they are positioned as throwbacks to earlier times, Rip Van Winkle and Ichabod Crane must each struggle to find a place in a community that has yet to accept the distinctly modern concept of headwork. Even in those moments when Irving laments rampant commercialization, his fiction celebrates the general enterprise of castle building. After returning home, Rip finds his place as a storyteller because his wife, who could only carp about the bottom line, has conveniently died. The story may well be Irving's fantasy of a writer unencumbered by practical concerns, but it also reflects a new way of thinking about the storyteller's productivity. Indeed, Herman Melville would make "poor good-for-nothing Rip" the Romantic artist whose productivity cannot—should not—be measured in dollars and cents. In "Rip Van Winkle's Lilac," Melville's posthumously published retelling of Irving's tale, Rip returns home to find that, although his house has crumbled to the ground, a lilac slip he planted twenty years earlier has filled the entire valley with flowers. This flower, which, like Whitman's lilac, represents artistic profusion, has been made possible by a man previously deemed feckless. "Where man finds in man no use," Melville writes, nature finds a boon.[7]

Yet Irving's presentation of the writer is complex because other artistic figures are unabashedly profit-driven. Irving's fiction, in fact, presents two competing visions of the author, both of which are aligned with individual enhancement: on the one hand, he is an artist whose aesthetic concerns and desire for expression—detached from practical considerations or social obligations—mark him as Romantic; on the other, his author is an entrepreneur, aggressively marketing his wares to a growing audience of consumers for monetary profit. (Although Rip is indifferent to financial concerns, the popularity of his tales points the way to a literary vocation that could be profitable.) The two visions are not, as they might first seem, entirely opposed. As Michael T. Gilmore has written, they work in tandem with each other and reflect a new literary specialization in Irving's time by which writers—whether as entrepreneurs or artists—might devote themselves full-time to letters. Even though Irving could not always rely financially on his book sales, his fiction, in Gilmore's words, "legitimated the writer as writer."[8]

Ichabod Crane provides a compelling example of this double-sided artist. Ichabod's "appetite for the marvellous" fuels his ridiculous fantasies of western land speculation and spectacular wealth, but it also sets him apart as imaginative. His scholarly pursuits are questionable, but he is the closest thing Sleepy Hollow has to an aesthete or intellectual. He is a dreamer who only comes to his senses when the brawny and commonsensical Brom Bones, disguised as a phantom horseman, hurls a pumpkin head at the schoolteacher's dream-filled cranium (after his disappearance from Sleepy Hollow, rumor has it that Ichabod settles down to a respectable career in law and politics). Gilmore finds that Brom's expulsion of Ichabod preserves the "domain of art" from Ichabod's Yankee "predatory materialism," but I find that the schoolteacher's flights of fancy are *both* artistic and acquisitive. When Irving writes that the schoolteacher "was thought, by all who understood nothing of the labour of headwork, to have a wonderfully easy life of it," he expresses sympathy for a character whose cerebral pursuits, like Irving's own literary endeavors, are inevitably misunderstood by others.[9]

"Wolfert Webber, or Golden Dreams," one of four stories in the cycle *The Money-Diggers* (in turn, part of the fictitious Diedrich Knickerbocker's *Tales of a Traveller*), stands at the center of Irving's most elaborate exploration of authorship and enterprise. Webber is pure businessman and does not, like Ichabod, combine artistic and entrepreneurial sensibilities. Yet, when read in relation to the cycle of stories in which it was published, the tale of Webber's good fortune suggests that financial speculation and storytelling are intimately related operations. Set on the isle of Manhattan in the year "one thousand seven hundred and—blank [the narrator cannot recall the precise date]," the tale chronicles Wolfert Webber's struggle to adapt to the "growing prosperity of the city" and, most crucially, to a dramatic alteration in the ways Americans conceived and measured economic value.[10]

Webber, a cabbage farmer from a long line of Dutch landholders, finds himself squeezed out of an expanding agricultural market in the city and concerned for his own economic survival. Determined that new profits will forever elude him, he turns to "golden dreams," or schemes that might "make one's self rich in a twinkling." He dreams that the rumored buried treasure of the notorious pirate Captain Kidd might perhaps lie beneath his cabbage patch. His head "in an uproar with this whirl of new ideas," Webber ravages his garden in the hopes of overturning treasure and fruitlessly follows a lead to search haunted burial vaults off the island. Defeated, Webber ultimately resigns himself to poverty and death, only to discover that the city plans to build a road through his cabbage patch, which will make his family lands skyrocket in value. Webber, who decides to subdivide, develop, and rent his land, quickly brings himself up to speed in this new economy: "His golden dream was accomplished; he did indeed find an unlooked-for source of wealth; for, when his paternal lands were distributed into building lots, and rented out to safe tenants, instead of producing a paltry crop of cabbages, they returned him an abundant crop of rent; insomuch that on quarter-day it was a goodly sight to see his tenants knocking at the door, from morning till night, each with a little round-bellied bag of money, a golden produce of the soil." Webber is finally successful because he grasps what James Henretta describes as a key feature of the capitalist economy that developed in the eighteenth century: the increasing perception that land (as well as labor) was not the source of livelihood but a commodity that "could be bought and sold in the pursuit of wealth and status." The work of imagining his land as building lots proves far more profitable than the manual labor of coaxing fruit from its soil. By story's end the image of a cabbage on the crest adorning Webber's house comes to stand not for agrarian produce but the human brain. Its newly minted motto ALL HEAD signifies that Webber rose by "sheer head-work." Like the portrait of King George in "Rip Van Winkle," which is simply touched up to look like George Washington, this modified crest signifies that an earlier outlook has been adapted for new times.[11]

In one sense this story, and *The Money-Diggers* as a whole, criticizes forms of unearned wealth: the paper money, usury, and stock-jobbing that appear throughout these stories, particularly "The Devil and Tom Walker," are suspect modes of "making sudden fortunes from nothing."[12] The means by which Webber commodifies and profits off the land are similar to the means by which land speculators bought up cheap western lands and sold them off at high prices when frontier settlement increased their value. Webber is surely touched by the same speculative fever that gripped the aggressively upwardly mobile both in the American past and in Irving's own day. But in *The Money-Diggers* financial enterprise also stirs reverie and fosters a kind of storytelling which elicits the pleasure of narrators and their listeners.

As the convoluted story structure of *The Money-Diggers* indicates, golden dreams nurture the telling and auditing of stories, and entire literary productions arise from speculations about the whereabouts of hidden fortunes. In "Hell Gate," the first of the cycle's stories, Diedrich Knickerbocker tells of numerous sea disasters at the Hell Gate crossing off Manhattan Island; these perilous straits, Knickerbocker discovers, have given rise to an incredible number of fables of shipwrecked treasures, and one of these "unearthed" fables is the cycle's second story, "Kidd the Pirate." In this second story Knickerbocker recounts the history of Kidd and reports that this history has, in turn, "given birth to innumerable progeny of traditions" about his buried treasure and "set the brains of all good people along the coast in a ferment."[13] Fishing one day off the sound, Knickerbocker pulls a pistol from the waters, and, when one of his companions speculates that it may have belonged to Kidd, another companion is prompted to relate his own legend of exhumed treasure, the cycle's third story, "The Devil and Tom Walker." After this third story is told, the fishing companions discover a mysterious hidden family vault off the island, which prompts yet another member of the company to recollect yet another story of money digging: that of Wolfert Webber.

Irving's trope is a familiar one by now: Mather's *Life of Phips* uses the treasure-hunting sea voyage as a figure of collective risk taking, and Lodi's captivation at discovering a treasure tale in *Arthur Mervyn* dramatizes how a speculative mind-set is easily invested in others' narratives. But Irving's tales of discovered wealth comment not on communal interaction but on professional authorship. In *The Money-Diggers* stories are themselves personal treasures that could even, in the right literary marketplace, bring monetary reward.

With the first U.S. copyright law, in 1790, professional writers could actually earn a living off their intellectual property, but the prospect always entailed risk. As Michael Davitt Bell writes, authors tended to provide much of the financial backing for their own publications, and it was not until the emergence of a literary marketplace in the 1830s that publishers began to absorb a much larger percentage of the author's profits or losses. In the forty or so years between the first copyright law and the emergence of a publishing industry, book publication was for the author an act of market speculation. When Irving turned to the less reputable genre of fiction to write his *Tales of a Traveller,* the risk was particularly acute. Irving did revel in the notion that he could, like a money digger, unearth folklore and use headwork to accrue profits, but he was always keenly aware of the risks of intellectual enterprise. As Charles Neider writes, Irving "depended on writing for his livelihood," and when *Tales of a Traveller* failed commercially "he was forced to believe that the products of his imagination and art would fail to provide him with bread."[14] Following the failure of *Tales of a Traveller,* Davitt Bell notes, Irving quickly turned to the commercially safer genre of historiography and never again devoted an entire volume to fiction.

Washington Irving explicitly likened the headwork of literary pursuits to the headwork of credit schemes because he hoped that both could bear financial fruit. The epistolary endeavors of Crèvecoeur's James, however, are never intended to be remunerative, so they are similar only in the speculative spirit in which they are undertaken. In this way Crèvecoeur shares more with those American Romantic writers who would define the artist's compensation in immaterial terms—as a boon to the heart and spirit rather than to the pocketbook. Henry David Thoreau offers one final example of how the projecting impulse survives even when stripped of any explicit relation to economic transaction. As the opening chapter of *Walden* uses ledger book accounting to define values outside the marketplace, the book's conclusion uses an old analogy between airy castles and fanciful dreams of wealth to celebrate the mind's powers. "If you have built castles in the air, your work need not be lost," he writes in the final pages, "that is where they should be. Now put the foundations under them."[15] Castle building is the means by which the foundations are *later* realized. As with paper credit schemes and speculation in general, a risky projection can make possible a windfall, which then, in turn, provides the hoped-for collateral, or foundation.

Mather, Cooke, Franklin, Tyler, Murray, and Brown did not view speculation as frivolous fancy so much as vital mental processes that might be the basis for establishing and strengthening communities. Thoreau, too, rejects this negative characterization of speculative castle building, but he celebrates it, instead, as the Romantic mind's creation of the world, making more palpable the tendency of these writers to emphasize the social consequences of speculation. When Thoreau proclaims that castles *should be* in the air, one senses a defiant defense of otherworldliness and a defiant indifference to the practical concerns that often motivated his eighteenth-century counterparts.

I have stressed these differences to generate one final impression of the writers studied here, but the continuity is meaningful as well. Thoreau's formulation is indebted to the more explicitly economic concept of speculation, for these earlier writers also insisted that the castle builder's "work need not be lost"—that it was work that mattered. Although Thoreau imagines that his own castle building transcends practical concerns and economic necessity, the earlier American experience has shown how speculation might be a tool for projecting and realizing a future.

Notes

INTRODUCTION: Castle Building

Epigraph: This quotation derives from a short essay on paper currency which was originally part of Franklin's *Busy-Body,* number 8, but was withdrawn by the publisher, according to J. A. Leo Lemay, because it criticized the proprietors and their appointed governor. A few early editions containing the piece were published, and the Library of Congress owns the only extant copy today. See Franklin, *Writings,* 116–118, 1524.

1. For scholarship on the literary response to the financial revolution in Britain, see Nicholson, *Writing and the Rise of Finance;* Sherman, *Finance and Fictionality;* Thompson, *Models of Value;* and Brantlinger, *Fictions of State.* For a history of eighteenth-century public credit in Britain, see Dickson, *Financial Revolution in England.*
2. Ziff, *Writing in the New Nation,* 17, 58.
3. Marx, *Capital I,* 919.
4. Social, intellectual, and economic historians began analyzing these intricate workings of colonial and early national public finance in the late nineteenth century. This historiography, in fact, has a history of its own because, since the 1940s, revisionist historians have sought to reverse what they consider an anti-paper bias on the part of earlier scholars. For histories of early American paper currency, see especially Nettels, *Money Supply of the American Colonies;* Ferguson, *Power of the Purse;* McCusker, *Money and Exchange in Europe and America;* Perkins, *American Public Finance;* and Newman, *Studies on Money in Early America.* See also Newman, *Early Paper Money of America,* for graphic reproductions of the bills themselves; and Davis, *Colonial Currency Reprints,* for reprints of much of the pamphlet literature of the seventeenth and eighteenth centuries. For an example of revisionist scholarship aimed at correcting the perceived anti-paper bias in earlier historiography, see Ferguson, "Currency Finance."
5. Wise, *Word of Comfort,* 209.
6. Steele, *Spectator,* 158.
7. As John McCusker writes in his introduction to *Money and Exchange in Europe and America, 1600-1775,* moneys of account, or "imaginary money," were essentially abstract notational devices for keeping accounts between parties in the act of exchange (most commonly for those engaged in transatlantic trade because the shipment of metal specie to settle debts with London merchants was expensive, cumbersome, and time-consuming). Such moneys of account borrowed from the denominations of metallic, or "real," money (say, the pound) but did not in any way adhere to the original denotation of weight; hence, the pound became an imaginary unit of bookkeeping, equal to approximately twenty shillings and not equal to an actual pound's worth of sterling.
8. Witherspoon, *Essay on Money,* 7–8, 21; Madison to Thomas Jefferson, 106; Webster, "Remarks on the Manners," 110; Adams to F. A. Vanderkemp, 610.

9. See Appleby, *Economic Thought and Ideology;* and the chapter "Exchanging" in Foucault, *Order of Things.*

10. Metallists and cartalists tended to agree that precious metals were valued not for any intrinsic qualities but for their labor cost—the cost, that is, of extracting them from the earth. They also agreed that a coin's value would fluctuate according to interest rates, trade volume, and monetary supply and demand; unlike cartalists, however, metallists usually insisted that metal's labor cost was the necessary means of stabilizing a coin's value and making it acceptable.

11. Shell, *Money, Language, and Thought,* 1.

12. As Mark Osteen and Martha Woodmansee write in *The New Economic Criticism,* work on literature and economics has largely focused on parallels between money and language: "analogies" or resemblances between comparable artifacts and "homologies" deriving from a shared anthropogenic root. My work more closely resembles recent scholarship that is "more specifically historicist and more attentive to contextual discursive formations ... as they impinge upon literary texts" (19). For examples of post-structuralist approaches to money's linguistic nature, see Heinzelman, *Economics of the Imagination;* and Goux, *Coiners of Language.*

13. Emerson, *Nature,* 15–16.

14. See Gilmore, *American Romanticism and the Marketplace,* for a discussion of Emerson's changing economic views. See also Bell, "Hard Currency of Words." Bell argues that Emerson's urgency was amplified by a fear that the geographically expanding marketplace, made possible in large part by credit mechanisms that facilitated long-distance settlements of debts, would reduce all social interaction to faceless, abstract exchange. Beseeching a return to an "original language," Emerson called for linguistic integrity as well as economic reforms in the United States.

15. See Wilson, *Power "To Coin" Money.* Under the U.S. Constitution Congress was granted the "power to coin money," and records of the debates indicate that the framers intended that Congress *not* be invested with the power to emit paper money. During the Civil War, however, Congress assumed this authority again and issued federal greenbacks for deficit financing. After the war these powers were sanctioned as constitutional by the Supreme Court.

16. Emerson, *Nature,* 16.

17. Humphreys et al., *Anarchiad,* 15–16. According to the introduction, the poem is a collection of ancient manuscripts found in an archaeological site in "the West" of the American continent. The satiric editor, who intersperses his own commentary throughout the poetry and adds three appendices, claims to have only restored and made available the ancient manuscripts for publication. In keeping with this premise, the cataclysmic events depicted in the poem belong to an ancient American past and only foreshadow the possible disaster that could result in eighteenth-century New England.

18. Humphreys et al., *Anarchiad,* 36, 6–7.

19. The lines from Alexander Pope's *Dunciad* read,

> Lo! they dread Empire, CHAOS is restored;
> Light dies before thy uncreating word:
> Thy hand, great Anarch! lets the curtain fall;
> And Universal Darkness buries All.

In keeping with the comic premise of *The Anarchiad*, the fictional editor claims that Pope's lines were borrowed from the American poem. He does not, however, mention *Paradise Lost*. Pope, *Dunciad*, 2296.

20. This poem contains the kind of paradox that Patrick Brantlinger identifies in the Augustan satires of public credit in England. He argues that the British Empire was founded and flourished on such indebtedness, and this paradox was central to Augustan satires that were themselves built upon a foundation of indebtedness to classical literary models. In *The Anarchiad* the narrator's jocular claim that Pope's *Dunciad* is a mere plagiarism of the ancient American manuscript only emphasizes that the American writer owes an additional debt to the English model as well.

21. Smith, *Wealth of Nations*, 341.
22. Franklin, *Nature and Necessity*, 348.
23. Eric Roll writes that Ricardo, like Smith, "regarded the use of a substitute for the money metal as an important corollary of economic progress and he urged the complete withdrawal of gold from active circulation." He advocated a gold bullion standard but not circulating gold coins; banknotes would be convertible at a fixed rate, but they would only be convertible in large amounts and into gold bars. Roll, *History of Economic Thought*, 173.
24. Franklin, "Poor Richard Improved, 1758," 1300.
25. "Common Sense, in Dishabille," 150.
26. Hamilton to Robert Morris, 635. See also Gordon, *Hamilton's Blessing*, for a discussion of Hamilton's understanding of the benefits of a public debt.
27. Witherspoon, *Essay on Money*, 8.
28. See also Garson, "Counting Money," for an explanation of how coins, bills, and notes were instruments for promoting "affinity to the nation" after the Revolutionary War. "If money performed its proper function by encouraging trade and investment," Garson writes, "it would endear the population to the authority that was responsible for its issue." Garson adds that the images and words on both metal and paper currency were "visual reminders of the connection between finance, stability and national authority" (22).
29. Hamilton to Robert Morris, 635.
30. The committee made this announcement in the February 28, 1776, issue of the *Pennsylvania Gazette*. The two men, probably Quakers, defended their actions by stating that "scruples of conscience" prevented them from accepting "money emitted for the purpose of war," but the committee alleged that they had been known to accept similar bills in neighboring provinces and so rejected the defense.

PART ONE: New World Ventures

Epigraphs: Green, "The *Dying Speech* of Old Tenor"; Smith, *Description of New England*, 208; Maryland bill of credit (two shillings six pence), 1733.
1. *New News from* Robinson Cruso's *Island*, 128.
2. Hammond, *Banks and Politics in America*, 23.
3. Hammond, *Banks and Politics in America*, 4.
4. The South Sea Company was a private joint-stock company that assumed a great portion of the English national debt by allowing public creditors to trade their gov-

ernment securities for shares in the company. After months of speculative mania the value of these shares rose to record heights before the bubble burst in 1720.

5. Defoe, *Robinson Crusoe*, 43.
6. Vespucci, *First Four Voyages*, 107.
7. More, *Utopia*, 46.
8. See McIntyre, *Debts Hopeful and Desperate*.
9. Crèvecoeur, *Letters from an American Farmer*, 83.
10. Crèvecoeur, *Letters from an American Farmer*, 82–83.
11. Crèvecoeur, *Letters from an American Farmer*, 83.
12. Henretta, *Evolution of American Society*, 99.
13. Smith, *Narrative of the Life*, 374.
14. Smith, *Narrative of the Life*, 369. In his analysis of Venture Smith's narrative Philip Gould argues that the "persona of the venturesome capitalist" allows Smith to claim an "individuated identity from the anonymity of slavery." According to Gould, Smith also "masters the symbolic economy of slave society" through performance, such as when he schemes with Hempsted Miner to appear unruly and thereby lower his own market value. Robert A. Ferguson, on the other hand, does not see Smith as mastering this economy so much as rejecting "his own success as a cultural identification." Gould, "Free Carpenter, Venture Capitalist," 674, 678. Ferguson, "American Enlightenment," 521.
15. Equiano, *Interesting Narrative*, 49, 125.
16. William Byrd provides a striking example of this slaveholding mentality. Describing his Westover plantation in 1726, he takes care to emphasize that, while his "bond-men" and "bond-women" carry on every kind of work before him, a half-crown might "rest undisturbed" in his pocket for "many Moons together." Byrd's fantasy presumes that inherent obligation rather than coercion drives his slaves' labor. Quoted in Isaac, *Transformation of Virginia*, 39.

ONE: Crisis and Faith in the Puritan Society

1. Mather, *Book I: Antiquities, Magnalia Christi Americana*, 143.
2. Mather, *Theopolis Americana*, 12, 17.
3. Mather, *Lex Mercatoria*, 11.
4. Mather, *Man of His Word*, 14; Mather, *Fair Dealing*, 7; Winthrop, "Model of Christian Charity." Biographer Kenneth Silverman observes that Mather would have had personal reasons for advocating humane creditor-debtor negotiation, for he was himself financially entangled. As the administrator of the estate of Nathan Howell, Mather sued debtors who had owed money to Howell, but he was also sued by the estate's creditors. For an account of these financial entanglements, see chap. 11, "*Tria Carcinomata*," in Silverman, *Life and Times*.
5. Dunn, "'Grasping at the Shadow,'" 56.
6. In his study of early American money Curtis Nettels argues that initially the value of these bills was maintained not by governmental authority or a change in mind-set with regards to monetary value but, rather, simply by their limited quantity; not until the quantity increased during Queen Anne's War, he writes, did the bills of credit depreciate noticeably and become an issue of contention in Massachusetts. I would emphasize that, regardless of how the value was actually sustained, the existence of legal tender forced writers to contend, if only theoretically, with the concept of a demateri-

alized medium. Nettels, *Money Supply of the American Colonies*, 268–269.

7. In 1720, for example, Mather supported a private bank out of political allegiances, despite, according to Silverman, his own acknowledgment that a government scheme would probably better serve the public. Later, due to a different set of allegiances, he switched his position and opposed the private banking scheme. For an account of this episode, see chap. 11, "*Tria Carcinomata*," in Silverman, *Life and Times*.

8. Mather, *Christian Philosopher*, 127.

9. Mather, *Some Considerations*, 190.

10. Mather, *Some Considerations*, 191.

11. *New News from* Robinson Cruso*'s Island*, 131. While this writer's monetary views are consistent with those of Mather's *Some Considerations*, the pamphlet may ironically have been written in opposition to Mather. *New News from* Robinson Cruso*'s Island* was a response to *News from* Robinson Cruso*'s Island*, an earlier pamphlet that had criticized the supporters of a private bank. Silverman surmises that Mather penned the earlier pamphlet in an attempt to support the government. It is worth noting, however, that this pamphlet focuses on condemning factionalism and never touches on the economic issues themselves.

12. Mather, *Some Considerations*, 190.

13. Wise, *Word of Comfort*, 203.

14. *Second Part of South-Sea Stock*, 311. Debates in Massachusetts turned particularly heated when, in the 1720s and again in the 1740s, a group of merchants proposed an alternative to government bills of credit: private banks with a Crown charter that were secured by land mortgages instead of metal specie. These debates renewed original concerns over paper credit but also initiated new debates over whether credit should be privatized. Land bank proponents claimed that public bills violated the colony's charter, and their opponents argued that private land bills would only enrich wealthy bankers at the expense of the community.

15. See especially the chapter "A Medium of Trade" in Miller, *New England Mind*.

16. "The cause of our present Straits," the minister Thomas Paine wrote in 1721, is the arrogant insistence on being "*fine, ample and sumptuous in all Appearance*" and the refusal to "*employ our selves in making of our own Finery.*" The allocation of local resources through husbandry and housewifery, Paine argued, was what the colony needed to keep the flow of trade contained domestically. Paine, *Discourse Shewing*, 284–285.

17. Wise, *Word of Comfort*, 210.

18. Paine, *Discourse Shewing*, 285, 294–295.

19. In *The Protestant Ethic and the Spirit of Capitalism*, first published a century ago, Max Weber argued that a causal relationship existed between Calvinist Protestantism and the rise of modern capitalism: Calvinist predestinarians, in spite of *and as a result of* their belief that spiritual fate was predetermined and immutable, were driven to make manifest their election through a godly life that included *both* asceticism and the industrious pursuit of a calling. This Puritan double injunction against idleness and conspicuous wealth, moreover, resulted in a mind-set preoccupied with the reinvestment, rather than accumulation, of capital. The scholarly controversy generated by Weber's thesis has been, in the words of Gordon Marshall, "one of the longest running and most vociferous in the social sciences." Critics have charged Weber with, among other things, oversimplifying Calvinist doctrine, distorting empirical evidence, and placing undue emphasis on the role of the Reformation in the rise of capitalism. Acknowledging these

criticisms, I nevertheless recognize in certain writings by New England Puritans an undeniable relationship between predestinarian anxiety and commercial energy. Marshall, *In Search of the Spirit of Capitalism*, 9.

20. In his study of New England economic culture Stephen Innes emphasizes that this relationship between material and divine blessing is strictly a negative one. That is, the religious establishment agreed that only the *lack* of industry, not industry itself, could be taken as evidence of an individual's spiritual status. "While it was not possible to prove one's election by exhibiting diligence, conscientiousness, and moral seriousness," Innes writes, "the failure to display these qualities, all agreed, signified reprobation." Mather, for instance, finds moral significance in the ledger book, but he seems most preoccupied with the providential significance of debt. Irresponsible debtors bring "themselves into ill Terms with Heaven." Innes's qualification—one Mather would have been careful to make in order to avoid implying a covenant of works—is crucial to a complete understanding of Puritan capitalism because the absence of any exact correspondence between prosperity and election explains why not even the most materially blessed could ever cease laboring. Innes, *Creating the Commonwealth*, 131; Mather, *Fair Dealing*, 18.

21. Philip Gura writes that Mather's account lends official sanction to the secularization of the colony's political system in the 1690s; he speculates, in fact, that *Phips* was Mather's attempt to justify his family's role in that secularization. Silverman believes Mather probably celebrated Phips both out of a pragmatic acceptance that he "represented for better or worse the future of New England" and out of a self-serving desire to have "renewed access to government circles." Breitwieser takes a slightly different approach, arguing instead that *Phips* is not an anomaly so much as the clearest manifestation of the tension between piety and modernity with which Mather struggled throughout his life. Gura, "Cotton Mather's Life of Phips"; Silverman, *Life and Times*, 162; Breitwieser, *Cotton Mather and Benjamin Franklin*.

22. Bercovitch, "'Delightful Examples,'" 41.

23. Mather, *Life of William Phips*, 162; hereafter cited parenthetically as *LP*.

24. For a discussion of Mather's use of the exemplum, see Bercovitch, *Puritan Origins of the American Self*. Bercovitch argues that Mather's Lives represent a "transitional mode" between the allegorical exemplum and the modern biography of an individual. This "exemplary biography," Bercovitch writes, follows from Mather's "belief that the discrete fact and the moral generality could complement one another" (4).

25. Mather, *Ecclesia Monilia*, title page.

26. In one sermonic attempt to find meaning in the "impoverishing" natural disasters that had struck New England, Mather, invoking Matthew 6.19, used this image of rust to remind listeners that they not lose sight of the temporality of earthly treasure: "Let our losses by *Moth* and *Rust*, and *Thief*, make us more sedulous than ever we were, in securing of that *Heavenly Treasure*, which never can be prey'd upon." *Durable Riches*, 27–28.

27. Taylor, *Poems* (numbers refer to series, meditation, and line[s]), 1.19.23–24, 2.105.27, 2.69.39, 2.34.35–36; 2.60b.27. Taylor's image of a Communion wine that bears no price clearly borrows from the language of Isaiah's messianic prophecy that God would show his mercy through the gift of wine and milk that cost nothing (Isaiah 55.1).

28. In one meditation, for example, the healing hand of grace purges the "poison" and "ill Humors" breeding in the soul and clears the "liquor from the musty dregs" in

which the soul is trapped. Taylor, *Poems*, 2.67a.25, 30, 26. In "The Reflexion" the golden spade of grace taps the spring of tears that will cleanse the filth blocking the soul's conduit.

    29. Taylor, *Poems*, 2.106.34. Here Taylor draws from a numismatic idiom, for the "angel" was a British shilling that was minted from 1465 to 1643 and remained in circulation through Taylor's day. According to the *Oxford English Dictionary*, the angel was an "English gold coin, called more fully at first the angel-noble, being originally a new issue of the Noble, having as its device the archangel Michael standing upon and piercing the dragon." First minted in 1465 by Edward IV, this coin was often used to "touch," or bless, ill patients, and, "when it ceased to be coined, small medals having the same device were substituted for it, and were hence called touch-pieces." In the poem the fact that God's impression of grace is figured as a superscription on the coin's edge also situates the poem in relation to monetary crisis, for lettering on the circumference of a coin was an innovation introduced in the 1660s to prevent clipping or counterfeiting. Davies, *History of Money*, 242.

    30. Taylor, *Poems*, 1.6.1–6.

    31. Silverman, *Life and Times*, 247.

    32. Gura, "Cotton Mather's *Life of Phips*," 74.

    33. Edwards, "Faithful Narrative," 73.

    34. Mather, *Voice of God*, 4.

    35. A number of historians have tried to find cause-effect relationships that might explain the parallels between debates over money and debates over the revivals (in particular, they have searched for a pattern of monetary thinking among those involved in the revivals). Following a "linguistic turn" in intellectual history, T. H. Breen and Timothy Hall choose, instead, to examine the way shared categories structured a New England Puritan interpretation of experience. "Structuring Provincial Imagination."

    36. Mather, *Pascentius*, 11–12, 7.

    37. Mather, *Pascentius*, 18. It also seems possible that in the biography a tension exists between Phips, who, writing in his own conversion narrative, simplistically wonders what he "should do to be saved" (187), and Mather, who clearly struggled with the complexities of Puritan theology.

    38. Breitwieser, *Cotton Mather and Benjamin Franklin*, 156. Although it might seem surprising that Mather, who defended the witchcraft trials to his death, would celebrate this decision by Phips, it is actually quite consistent with his insistence that only credible confession be grounds for conviction. Kenneth Silverman writes that Mather maintained that "spectral evidence"—that is, alleged evidence of wrongdoing committed by an apparition of the accused—was inconclusive. Mather also cautioned that any confession procured through torture or possibly the product of duress or delirium be dismissed. Silverman, *Life and Times*, 98–99.

    39. According to the *Oxford English Dictionary*, the "main chance" (originally a term in the dice game of Hazard) refers to, among other things, "something which is of principal importance in life."

    40. Breitwieser, *Cotton Mather and Benjamin Franklin*, 157, 158; my emphasis. Scholars have concluded that antinomianism, in its rejection of a moral law (as superseded by inner grace), provided spiritual justification for free enterprise. Larzer Ziff argues that the supporters of Anne Hutchinson against charges of heresy were predominantly people who stood to gain by a relaxation of economic regulation by the Massachusetts government. *Puritanism in America*, 63–77.

41. Edwards, "Faithful Narrative," 67.

42. Gura writes that it is the "publick patriotism" through which personal ambitions might enrich public coffers—and not religious piety—which is heralded by Mather as the new basis for good leadership. "Cotton Mather's *Life of Phips*," 71.

TWO: Making Much of Nothing in the Chesapeake

1. Dumbleton, "Paper-Mill," 523. None of the July 26, 1744, issues of the *Virginia Gazette* is extant today. Dumbleton's poem was, however, reprinted in the August 1744 issue of the *American Magazine*, and a modern edition is available in Silverman, *Colonial American Poetry*.

2. In his study of "The Paper-Mill" Robert D. Arner has judged that the poem "incorporates into its imagery and ideology the essential assumptions of the British mercantile system." In a relationship similar to that of colony to metropolis, the townspeople furnish the paper maker with raw materials (rags) and also eventually provide the market for his manufactured goods (writing paper, reading material). This imagery, Arner writes, consequently works in tension with the poem's praise of colonial industry, which would have helped free the colony from dependence on British paper manufacturers. "Sources and Significance," 199.

3. Dumbleton, "Paper-Mill," 523.

4. I have in mind Jack P. Greene's "declensional" and "developmental" paradigms for understanding New England and the Chesapeake, respectively. Greene writes, "If, in the century after 1660, the societies of the orthodox puritan colonies seemed to many of their leading figures to be coming apart, those of the Chesapeake colonies appeared to be coming together." *Pursuits of Happiness*, 81.

5. For accounts of this regional literature, see Lemay, *Men of Letters*; and Nichols, "Tobacco and the Rise of Writing."

6. Greene, *Pursuits of Happiness*, 85.

7. Lemay, *Men of Letters*, 112. Michael Warner has discussed how printed representation reinforced republican ideals of political representation in the late eighteenth century. Drawing from Jürgen Habermas's paradigm of a "public sphere," Warner describes an eighteenth-century transformation from a "world in which power embodied in special persons is represented before the people to one in which power is constituted by a discourse in which the people are represented." *Letters of the Republic*, 39.

8. Markland, "Typographia," 10–11.

9. Warner observes that this poem's epigraph from Cicero confirms that the "light of letters" saves exemplary literature from obscurity: "Pleni sunt omnes Libri, plenae sapientum voces, plena Exemplorum vetustas; quae jacerent in Tenebris omnia, nisi Literarum Lumen accederet" (All literature and the voices of wisdom abound with ancient and noble examples that would lie in darkness if the light of letters did not fall upon them). He concludes that the passage from Cicero contrasts the "useful literature of public life with the private indulgence of the bookish recluse," while Markland, on the other hand, celebrates all letters for their usefulness. It is worth emphasizing that print makes this usefulness possible. While the legislative manuscripts are certainly not private or indulgent, they cannot serve their purpose until print makes them publicly accessible. Warner, *Letters of the Republic*, 29.

10. Nichols, "Tobacco and the Rise of Writing," 17.

11. *Proposals for a Tobacco-Law*, 3.

12. Cooke, *Sotweed Redivivus*, 4; hereafter cited as *SR*. I have used the original pagination of the 1730 edition as preserved in the reprint.

13. John Van Horne makes this point about the term *project* in an essay on Benjamin Franklin. "Collective Benevolence and the Common Good," 426–427.

14. Many readers of the poem have concluded that this portrait satirizes the images of a New World Eden which filled European promotional literature. In his study of Maryland literature, however, Lemay has also argued that the satire is twofold, mocking New World manners but also the condescending English attitude toward the colonies and the "ignorance and credulity of anyone believing such nonsense." *Men of Letters*, 92.

15. Cooke, *Sot-Weed Factor*, 20. I have used the original pagination of the 1708 publication as preserved in the reprint. All references are to the first edition.

16. Cooke, *Sot-Weed Factor*, 20–21.

17. Large-scale planters who could afford to ship their own tobacco often let small-scale planters piggyback and ship tobacco along with theirs. This system, however, was costly for the small-scale planter, and, as a result, "factors" tried to corner this market and come to the colonies to deal directly with them. Factors, therefore, were often disparaged as interlopers, and this disdain is clear in the opening lines of the poem, in which the speaker describes himself as short on cash and friends. *The Sot-Weed Factor* satirizes the crude manners of the colony, but, like Samuel Butler's poem, it also pokes fun at the protagonist.

18. More recently, anthropologists have argued that classical economics continues to shape Westerners' perceptions—or misperceptions—of barter exchange.

19. Smith, *Wealth of Nations*, 17.

20. Goux, *Coiners of Language*. Goux is primarily concerned with a concept of the "general equivalent," which is grounded in an Aristotelian standard that makes different things commensurable and is essential to Karl Marx's account of the genesis of money. The logic of this equivalent, Goux argues, is at work even when the values in question are not economic. In Freudian and Lacanian psychology, for example, the Father is the equivalent of subjects and the phallus the equivalent of objects; in Derridean logocentrism, language is the equivalent of signs.

21. Simmel, *Philosophy of Money*, 146.

22. In chapter 3 of volume 1 of *Capital*, Marx writes, "The first main function of gold is to supply commodities with the material for the expression of their values, or to represent their values as magnitudes of the same denomination, qualitatively equal and quantitatively comparable. It thus acts as a universal measure of value, and only through performing this function does gold, the specific equivalent commodity, become money" (188).

23. Franklin, *Nature and Necessity*, 345.

24. Randolph, *Letter to a Gentleman*, 15; my emphasis.

25. The drafts of this preface were written on the flyleaves of Cooke's volume of Sir Edward Coke's *Second Part of the Institutes of the Lawes of England* (1642). In chapter 3 of *Ebenezer Cooke: The Sot-Weed Canon* Edward H. Cohen reprints all four drafts and discusses them in detail. Cohen observes that the prefaces allude to the Conflagration Act, which mandated the burning of inferior-grade tobacco, and other methods aimed at improving the local tobacco trade.

26. Cooke, *Sotweed Factor*, 3d ed., 25.

27. Some readers have questioned whether the autograph preface can be legitimately attributed to Cooke. Cohen takes up this question in his study and concludes that it is Cooke's work. For my purposes, whether the apology is or is not the recant of Cooke himself, the relationship between the preface and the first edition seems to confirm Jack Greene's sense that Maryland's "new Creole elite," having been "stung by metropolitan condescension," aimed to improve the region's political and cultural life. The preface of the revised poem strikes me as an attempt to alleviate the sting of the original. Greene, *Pursuits of Happiness*, 85.

28. Franklin, *Nature and Necessity*, 351.

29. *Maryland Gazette*, April, 8-15, 1729.

30. "Circular Letter," 438; my emphasis.

31. Shields, *Oracles of Empire*, 57. Shields writes that hundreds of plays, tracts, and poems mocked the frivolity, immorality, and psychotropic effects of tobacco. But the "single aspect of tobacco that did not lend itself to humor was the economic effect of tobacco trade on the colonies. Because the economic welfare of populations hung on this issue, the tobacco trade inspired serious literary reflections" (58).

32. Sweet, *American Georgics*; Beverley, *History and Present State*, 314.

33. Beverley, *History and Present State*, 319.

34. Beverley, *History and Present State*, 71.

35. For a discussion of Beverley's critique of tobacco monoculture, see chap. 4 in Sweet, *American Georgics*. Beverley believed this monoculture had "reached an economic limit," Sweet writes, and he proposed that Virginia address this problem through economic diversification and "environmental management" aimed at compensating for the exhaustion of natural resources. Sweet, *American Georgics*, 76.

36. Beverley, *History and Present State*, 319, 285.

37. Borden, *Address to the Inhabitants*, 5, 6, 7, 8.

38. Borden, *Address to the Inhabitants*, 8.

39. Lewis, "Food for Criticks," 1-2, 80, 131, 134, 137-138. References are to line numbers in Lemay, *Early American Reader*. The poem originally appeared in the May 1730 issue of the *Maryland Gazette*, but no copy is extant today. Versions of the poem appeared later in the *New England Weekly Journal* (June 28, 1731) and the *Pennsylvania Gazette* (July 17, 1732). Lemay's reprint is based on the version in the *Pennsylvania Gazette*.

40. Again, Beverley's history identifies a similar problem among the colonists. In comparing the tobacco-growing methods of Indians and colonists, he records that Indians spend less time and use fewer procedures for tobacco cultivation, while the colonists sacrifice leisure to make "a heavy Bustle with it now, and can't please the Market neither." Beverley, *History and Present State*, 145.

41. Lewis, "To His Excellency," vii. I have used the original pagination of the 1728 edition as preserved in the reprint.

42. Lewis, "To His Excellency," vii, ix. Shields observes that, though Cooke and Lewis both reflected on the colony's economic problems, they endorsed fundamentally different solutions. Cooke favored self-imposed measures to limit tobacco supply (an inspection act, legal limitations on production, and the substitution of a tobacco medium with a paper medium), while Lewis favored intervention by leaders in the imperial hierarchy. Shields, *Oracles of Empire*, 60.

43. Chris Beyers finds that these lines urge planters to act because nothing will be done for them. I agree that the perspective is that of the planter and that the concerns of others are not accounted for, but I believe that the poem insists earnestly, if naively, on its own civic-mindedness. When the planter says he has the goal "that we may the better thrive; / Which is the Business of the *Hive*," I take that to be a communal hive and not a Mandevillian hive (*SR* 16). In his *Address to the Inhabitants of North Carolina* William Borden invokes a similar image, comparing his colony to a hive of mutually dependent bees working for the preservation and support of one another. Beyers, "Ebenezer Cooke's Satire."

44. As Kathryn L. Behrens explains, the act put a duty on exported tobacco in order to provide for a sinking fund. This duty was to be collected and sent in bills of exchange to three trustees, who were merchants of London charged to invest the money in capital stock of the Bank of England and hold it for the province. When bill holders finally redeemed the paper money, the government then drew on these trustees, who were to sell as much of the bank stock as was necessary to pay them. Behrens, *Paper Money in Maryland*.

45. See Schweitzer, "Economic Regulation and the Colonial Economy." The Inspection Act of 1747 would primarily serve large-scale planters, further concentrating wealth in their hands and inspiring a class of elites to replicate English culture in the New World by pouring energy and money into elaborate architecture and displays of wealth. Molded by England's Country ideology, this new planter moved personal autonomy to the center of his concerns and saw debt, government and personal, as a sign of weakness. This is not to say that this new large-scale planter was debt-free himself. Far from it, he was continually subject to the seasonal fluctuations of the agricultural market, buying this year's goods with the profits from next year's crop and never knowing what price his consigned tobacco would fetch in the European markets. He needed credit as the stopgap between seasons and yet did not want to acknowledge that he was anybody's debtor. The result, T. H. Breen writes, was an elaborate unwritten "etiquette of debt" through which debts were understood as personal favors and no one was to be publicly pressed for repayment or castigated for tardiness or default—until, that is, the imperial economic crises following the French and Indian War led British merchants to come calling for payment in the 1760s and 1770s. If we need to understand the Puritan's response to debt in light of a theology that emphasized that human autonomy was an illusion, we need also to understand the late-eighteenth-century planter's response to debt in light of his need to believe that autonomy was possible. This new planter simply did not want to see himself as part of a growing web of financial obligations. Speaking of William Byrd II and other Tidewater planters, Breen writes, "By the 1760s the image of the independent Virginian lodged in his plantation fortress had become something of a cliché, a self-deception that contained a good measure of defensiveness." *Tobacco Culture*, 86.

PART TWO: The Price of Independence

Epigraphs: Continental bill of credit (eight dollars), April 11, 1778; *Adventures of a Continental Dollar,* 265; Galbraith, *Money,* 45.
1. "Speech of a Member," 412–413.
2. Webster, "Principles of Government and Commerce," 44.

3. Cathy Matson approximates that between 1777 and 1779 Congress issued $191 million in bills of credit (Continental dollars), and between 1776 and 1778 it issued $67 million in loan office certificates. "Revolution," 366. In addition to these national currencies, states issued about two hundred million dollars of their own bills.

4. State governments issued their own paper money to finance the war. Beginning in 1776, Congress also established loan offices in several states to sell interest-bearing bonds that would mature at a future date. Although these government bonds were intended to be investment securities, they often circulated as a medium. Ferguson, *Power of the Purse*, 35. The Bank of North America and the Bank of the United States—established in 1781 and 1791, respectively—also issued circulating notes. These banks were technically private, as they were secured by subscriptions of individuals such as Thomas Paine and Robert Morris; nevertheless, people tended to associate the soundness of the bills with government credibility. For a comprehensive history of Revolutionary and postwar finance, see Ferguson, *Power of the Purse*; and Anderson, *Price of Liberty*.

5. Paine, *American Crisis VII*, 151. Paine was fond of distinguishing between the American debt and the British debt. In the same *Crisis* pamphlet he writes that America "neither raised money by taxes, nor borrowed it upon interest, but created it." But the paper money raised for military costs was indeed a loan—as the bills were issued for redemption at a future date—and certainly taxed those who were paid in bills that quickly depreciated (149).

6. "Paper Money once more" (1787 version), 483.
7. Ramsey, *History of the American Revolution*, 459.
8. "Circular Letter," 410.
9. Dreiser, *Financier*, 71.

THREE: Benjamin Franklin's Projections

1. Franklin, *Autobiography*, 54; hereafter cited parenthetically as *ABF* in the text.
2. Hamilton to Robert Morris, 605.
3. Mitchell Breitwieser and William Spengemann find that Franklin constructs a persona who is representative more in this first sense of the term. In the words of Breitwieser, Franklin "aspires to representative personal universality," creating a rhetorical personality by cultivating "characteristics he felt were in accord with what the age demanded." Franklin's *Autobiography*, according to Spengemann, attempts to "represent the conclusions of his experience as being universally true and hence applicable to every life, rather than peculiar to his own case." Breitwieser, *Price of Representative Personality*, 171; Spengemann, *Forms of Autobiography*, 55.
4. See Franklin's "Dissertation on Liberty and Necessity" for his discussion of the contrast between the "necessity" of circumstances fixed and determined (especially by providential design) and the "liberty" of human transgression. For discussions of Franklin's economic ideas, see Mott and Zinke, "Benjamin Franklin's Economic Thought;" and Carey, *Franklin's Economic Views* (esp. the chaps. on "Paper Money" and "Value and Interest").
5. Franklin, "Scheme for Supplying the Colonies," 53.
6. Franklin, "Legal Tender of Paper Money," 34.
7. Franklin to Samuel Cooper, 356.
8. According to numismatist Eric Newman, Franklin culled all of the 1775 "devices"

from emblem and motto books in Philadelphia at the time. See Newman's essay "Franklin Making Money More Plentiful" for a discussion of Franklin's work as a currency designer and printer.

9. Franklin, "Account of the Devices," 734.
10. Franklin, "Account of the Devices," 735.
11. See Beard, *Economic Interpretation of the Constitution of the United States;* and, for a counterargument, see Gordon Wood's "Interests and Disinterestedness in the Making of the Constitution."
12. Paine, *American Crisis XIII,* 232; *American Crisis V,* 121; *American Crisis III,* 98; *American Crisis I,* 55. Historians T. H. Breen and Timothy Hall detect a similar democratic impulse in the debates over colonial New England money. Many New Englanders, they write, "accommodated themselves to the demands of a new liberal society in which reasoning, well-informed, free individuals determined the ultimate sources of social authority," making the debates over money a "genuinely radical moment in the history of American thought." Breen and Hall, "Structuring Provincial Imagination," 1411.
13. Paine, *American Crisis I,* 50.
14. Paine, *American Crisis I,* 51; *American Crisis V,* 113; *American Crisis IV,* 102.
15. Humphreys, "Address to the Armies," 230.
16. Humphreys, "Address to the Armies," 231.
17. Shell, *Money, Language, and Thought,* 53–54.
18. Franklin to William Jackson, 220.
19. "Use and Abuse of Mottos," 588–589. Franklin's "Account of the Devices" originally appeared in the *Pennsylvania Gazette* in September 1775 but was reprinted in the *Pennsylvania Magazine* in December of that year. This rebuttal appeared in the magazine's 1775 supplement.
20. Burroughs, *Memoirs,* 61–62. In *Given Time: 1. Counterfeit Money* Jacques Derrida raises a different, but related, objection to any tidy distinction between real and counterfeit paper money. Once there is capital and credit, he writes, this distinction blurs: so-called real money that both "produces interest without labor" and depends on faith would seem to be counterfeit. Derrida, *Given Time,* 124.
21. "Representation and Remonstrance," 28.
22. Larzer Ziff has attributed the anxiety over print technology to changing notions of economic values and the fear that abstract selves created in print would proliferate alongside abstract forms of wealth. In this exchange the two fears are one and the same, as the monetary instrument is also an autobiographical persona. Ziff, *Writing in the New Nation.*
23. "Answer of Continental Currency," 113; "Reply of Continental Currency," 77; "Paper Money, Raised from the Dead, Speaketh for Itself!" 294; "Paper Money Once More Speaketh for Itself!" (1786 version), 372; "Paper Money Once More Speaketh for Itself!" (1787 version), 482.
24. Newman, *Early Paper Money,* 21.
25. Bruce H. Mann writes that "assignability," which promotes economic efficiency by depersonalizing the relationship between debtor and creditor, is part of the "social cost of commercialization." When a debt is assignable, the debtor's promise circulates as currency—regardless of who the bearers are—until the promise is presented finally for payment. Mann, *Republic of Debtors,* 12.
26. Christopher Looby writes that Keith's deferral could serve as an emblem for the

Autobiography as a whole because Franklin's writing enacts a similar postponement: a "real, integral Franklin," he writes, "is promised but never produced." To this analysis I would add that Franklin depicts reading as a process that often requires an acceptance of textual deferral—a willingness to be deferred. Looby, *Voicing America*, 123.

27. Lemay, "Franklin's *Autobiography* and the American Dream," 352.

28. It is worthwhile to compare Franklin's quest for freedom with that of Equiano. Franklin can write openly about having violated the terms of the apprenticeship. Equiano's attempts at emancipation, however, place him in a double bind with which Franklin would not have to contend. In order to parlay his loans into the profits he will use to redeem himself, Equiano must maintain credibility in the eyes of the white men with whom he conducts business and of the master who will eventually grant him the option of purchasing his freedom. This feat requires that he remain a slave, for his flight would compromise the precious reputation he has worked to cultivate and hopes to exploit after emancipation. Like the slave narrative Houston Baker has described, Equiano's memoir acknowledges that the economics of slavery "*must be mastered* before liberation can be achieved," and I would stress that this mastery entails Equiano's careful maintenance of his credibility through obedience. Equiano must gain credit with white men, as well as white readers of his narrative, by rejecting the option of running away from any master who treats him reasonably well. Baker, *Blues, Ideology, and Afro-American Literature*, 37.

29. The editors of the Norton edition of the *Autobiography*, J. A. Leo Lemay and P. M. Zall, write that Mickle was, in fact, "optimistic enough to have built a new stable only eight years earlier." They also note that Franklin opened his business just after a depression and currency depreciation lasting from October 1727 to January 1728. Lemay and Zall, *Autobiography*, 190, 47.

30. Looby, *Voicing America*, 110.

31. Warner, *Letters of the Republic*, 81; Rice, *Transformation of Authorship*, 47; Ward, "Making of an American Character," 137–138.

32. Morgan, *Benjamin Franklin*, 29.

33. My interpretation of the Thomas Bond episode would also challenge Rice's claim that "Franklin's philosophy of print bears an uncanny similarity to the fin de siècle sociologist Georg Simmel's monumental study of the philosophy of money." Money, according to Simmel, standardized indebtedness, making it quantifiable, numerically discharged, and *not* a function of social biases. With the introduction of money, in other words, individuals were freed from the unpredictable, idiosyncratic dependencies of social obligations. Rice argues that, like money, Franklin's textual self-representation frees him from subjective evaluations based on social biases: "interpersonal relationships are evacuated of their emotional or psychological constituents," he writes, "replaced by their objectified 'values' in terms of either currency . . . or textuality." I, too, find an "evacuation of personality" and a "recession of the corporeal writer" in those moments when Franklin disguises his name, but I also find that this trend simply does not continue in the narration after Franklin's retirement. Once he enjoys prominence in Philadelphia circles, Franklin's public projects stand to *gain* from such biases. Rice, *Transformation of Authorship*, 60, 63, 66.

34. Rice, *Transformation of Authorship*, 54.

35. Hamilton to Robert Morris, 605.

36. Anderson, *Price of Liberty*, 16. Men such as Morris would have an incentive to do so because a stronger public credit would boost the value of their individual holdings: "No paper credit," Hamilton wrote, can be substantial or durable, which has not funds, and which does not unite, immediately, the interest and influence of the moneyed men, in its establishment and preservation." Hamilton to Robert Morris, 620.

37. For a discussion of the ways in which Franklin reconciles self- and civic interests, see Zuckerman, "Doing Good While Doing Well."

38. Franklin, "Argument for Making the Bills of Credit," 13.

FOUR: Performing Redemption on the National Stage

1. *International Encyclopedia of Communications*, s.v. "Performance," 262.
2. Tanselle, *Royall Tyler*, 22–23.
3. Pressman, "Class Positioning and Shays' Rebellion," 89.
4. "Paper Money, raised from the dead," 294.
5. Trumbull, *M'Fingal*, 4.944, 4.972, 4.974. Numbers refer to canto and line.
6. Trumbull, *M'Fingal*, 4.997–1000.
7. To the outrage of creditors Rhode Island had adopted such a program, requiring by law that creditors redeem their war currency for a new paper currency that quickly lost its value. Because the creditors had, in general, not paid full value in the first place, those who were not personally invested tended to accept the program. For a discussion of Shays's Rebellion, see the chapter "The Economics of Disunion" in Ferguson, *Power of the Purse*.
8. James Madison was one of the most prominent proponents of a plan to split the redemption value between current and original bill holders. While many have considered his advocacy to be the result of humanitarian thinking, Ferguson has argued, instead, that Madison's proposition was politically expedient. It was Hamilton who insisted most vehemently that compensating original bill holders was impracticable and dishonorable; his was the opinion that ultimately prevailed. Ferguson, *Power of the Purse*, 297–299.
9. "Affecting and True Story," 130.
10. Tyler, *Contrast*, 56; hereafter cited parenthetically as C.
11. Although she takes a different approach to the play, Trish Loughran also reads *The Contrast* in the context of this critical period, characterizing the play as an "artifact of Articles-era dissent." Focusing on the play's treatment of regional contrasts (particularly between New York and Massachusetts), Loughran argues that Tyler's concern is "the problem of how, within the emerging language of nationalist unity, to make sense of profound regional or local differences" ("First American Contrasts," 237, 238).
12. Davidson, *Revolution and the Word*, 213; Meserve, *Emerging Entertainment*, 98; Pressman, "Class Positioning and Shays' Rebellion," 88. In *Cato's Tears and the Making of Anglo-American Emotion* Julie Ellison writes that Manly is typical of the "sensitive veterans" who populated early national literature. Embodying both "virtue and obsolescence," this veteran is often adrift in postrevolutionary culture (148).
13. In "*The Contrast*: The Problem of Theatricality and Political and Social Crisis in Postrevolutionary America" John Evelev makes a similar point when he writes that "Manly's abstractly-defined economically reputable character marks him as a business-

like man ('a man of punctuality') who carefully attends to his own interests." Evelev's concern, however, is more Tyler's depiction of commercial self-interest than his treatment of debt repayment and credibility (84).

14. Franklin, *Nature and Necessity*, 350; Franklin, *Autobiography*, 30; Stiles, "United States Elevated," 30; Washington, "Circular Letter," 24; Tyler, *Algerine Captive*, 76; Webster, "Essay on Credit," 3.

15. Pocock, *Virtue, Commerce, and History*, 114.

16. See Weyler, "'Speculating Spirit,'" for a discussion of the distinctions made between prudent and reckless speculation in early American fiction.

17. Appleby, *Capitalism and a New Social Order*, 15. There has been much debate over the role of liberal and classical ideas in the new republic. One particularly fruitful, and now well-known, debate occurred between Appleby and Lance Banning in the *William and Mary Quarterly* in 1986. See Banning, "Jeffersonian Ideology Revisited"; and Appleby, "Republicanism in Old and New Contexts."

18. Smith-Rosenberg, "Domesticating 'Virtue,'" 165–166.

19. Davidoff and Hall, *Family Fortunes*, 205.

20. My emphasis.

21. "On Public Faith," 405.

22. Riesman, "Money, Credit, and Federalist Political Economy," 140.

23. Paine, "Common Sense on Paper Money," 449, 450; Hamilton to Robert Morris, 623; Barton, *Observations On The Nature And Use of* Paper-Credit, 16, 23; "On establishing a Sinking Fund," 489.

24. Trumbull, *M'Fingal*, 4.975–982.

25. These financial thinkers all proposed, in one form or another, a national bank. Robert Morris's plan for the Bank of North America and Alexander Hamilton's plan for the Bank of the United States were realized in 1781 and 1791, respectively. Both plans, which borrowed from Richard Price's 1772 scheme to retire the English public debt and the English system of centralized banking in general, also called for a sinking fund. The government was to call in all outstanding public securities and exchange them for new ones that bore non-compounded interest (the interest accrued regularly but only on the original amount). Meanwhile, the government would collect tax revenues and invest them in a sinking fund at a rate of compounded interest. The interest revenue generated by the sinking fund would be used to pay the interest due on the new securities; because the interest in the sinking fund was compounded, however, it would accrue at a faster rate than the interest accruing on the new securities. Over time, then, the extra revenue in the sinking fund could be applied toward the principal of the debt and eventually retire it completely.

26. Hamilton to Robert Morris, 631.

27. Richard Brown writes, "From the time that the Constitution was written, Shays's Rebellion has been regarded as a catalyst in the movement for the Constitution and for its ratification." Brown notes that George Washington, James Madison, the nineteenth-century historian George Bancroft, and twentieth-century historians such as Forrest McDonald, Jackson Turner Main, and Gordon Wood have concurred with this conclusion. Brown, "Shays's Rebellion and the Ratification," 113.

28. Matson, "Revolution, Constitution and New Nation," 384.

29. Manly's speechified language was also not lost on a reviewer for the *New York*

Daily Advertiser, who lamented that the hero's soliloquies were admirable in content but not plausible as human speech. Review of *The Contrast.*

30. Stein, "Royall Tyler and the Question," 467; Richards, *Theater Enough,* 10; Fliegelman, *Declaring Independence,* 87.

31. Agnew, *Worlds Apart,* 60.

32. Evelev interprets Jonathan's night at the theater differently. He argues that Jonathan's mistaking the stage for real life actually exposes the "essentially theatrical nature of that real life" and challenges any neat distinction between American naturalness and European artificiality. As a result, the episode "problematizes the effort to simply define postrevolutionary social experience." Evelev believes this is not necessarily Tyler's intention so much as a reflection of the limitations of "postrevolutionary American nationalism." "*The Contrast:* The Problem of Theatricality," 90, 94.

33. Pressman, "Class Positioning and Shays' Rebellion," 100.

34. Stabile, *Origins of American Public Finance,* 3.

35. Barton, *Observations on the Nature and Use of Paper-Credit,* 39–40.

PART THREE: Bonds of the New Nation

Epigraphs: Holmes, arithmetic book; Jefferson, *Anas,* 345; Capra, dir., *It's a Wonderful Life.*

1. Hamilton, "Public Credit," 298; Hamilton, *Federalist* 35, 168.

2. Brown, *Power of Sympathy,* 58. In her study of sympathy and the early American novel Julia Stern points out that in Brown's *Ormond* moments of fellow feeling can actually be opportunities for the enfranchised elite to indulge in emotion and congratulate themselves for compassionate behavior. When Harrington sympathizes with a black female slave, he is voyeuristically viewing her from a distance and not, by virtue of his more powerful position, able to identify with her. That this display of sympathy is indulgent and voyeuristic, however, does not seem to be something that the novel itself acknowledges. Stern, *Plight of Feeling,* 23–25.

3. See Haskell, "Capitalism and the Origins of the Humanitarian Sensibility," for an account of capitalism's link to late-eighteenth-century humanitarianism. Haskell locates the rise of reform movements, particularly abolitionism, in a market mentality. Specifically, he argues that the market's elevation of "promise-keeping" to a "supreme moral and legal imperative" encouraged a new "scrupulosity in the fulfillment of ethical maxims." In addition, market transactions, which could make one's actions consequential in faraway places, "inspired people's confidence in their power to intervene in the course of events" (146, 148).

4. See especially Wood's discussion entitled "Interests" in *Radicalism of the American Revolution.* The political thinkers of the 1780s and 1790s were certainly not the first to validate personal interests or contemplate how they might serve public ends. Albert O. Hirschman observed that earlier moral philosophers, unlike those following a Country tradition, considered "interests" a rational form of self-love which was distinct from the irrational and destructive "passions"; these rational interests, he writes, could be called upon to counterbalance any passions that could not be successfully repressed, transformed into public virtues, or neutralized by other passions. Hirschman, *Passions and the Interests.*

5. The term *Revolutionary generation* designates an elite class of thinkers. Gary B. Nash has shown that the lower and middle ranks of colonial society took their inspiration from grassroots movements rather than from Country ideology. See, in particular, Nash, "Social Change"; and *Urban Crucible*.

6. Burstein, "Political Character of Sympathy," 629.

7. Fichtelberg, *Critical Fictions*, 73–82; Melville, *Confidence-Man*, 153.

8. Melville, *Moby-Dick*, 255. For Emerson these entanglements provided the figure of lamentable interdependence. Melville's merged individuality becomes for Emerson simply the loss of autonomy: "Society is a joint-stock company," he writes in "Self-Reliance," "in which the members agree, for the better securing of his bread to each shareholder, to surrender the liberty and culture of the eater. The virtue in most request is conformity. Self-reliance is its aversion." Emerson describes a Lockean social compact but emphasizes the price of conformity over the profit of security. Actual financial structures might compromise one's autonomy, but Emerson is primarily concerned that all of society, by requiring that individuals compromise liberty and culture, operates similarly. "Self-Reliance," 134.

FIVE: *Arthur Mervyn* and the Reader's Investments

1. Carey, *Short Account*, 10–12. As Philip Gould observes, even the medical theories about the plague's origins connect the disease to urban life and commerce. These theorists, dubbed "contagionists," surmised that commerce had brought the epidemic to the city's landing from the Caribbean. Those dubbed "climatists," who thought the plague had originated locally, tended to emphasize the unsanitary conditions of Philadelphia's densely populated commercial center. Gould, "Race, Commerce, and the Literature of Yellow Fever." See Powell, *Bring Out Your Dead*, for an account of these various theories.

2. Recently, Bryan Waterman has argued that the critical tendency to see contagion as a metaphor obscures the extent to which the fever is a "literal medical crisis" and *Arthur Mervyn* is a novel that should be read in relation to the era's medical debates. "*Arthur Mervyn*'s Medical Repository," 219.

3. There have been many interpretations of the plague's meaning in this novel. Reading the novel as a response to both the American and French revolutions, for example, Robert Levine argues that "the language describing the fever episodes works in alarmist fashion to present yellow fever as a form of silent subversion portending revolutionary upheaval." Shirley Samuels writes that many Americans found significance in the fact that the pestilence of 1793 coincided with the French Reign of Terror and the rise of Jacobinism, associated, in turn, with unleashed democracy, sexual promiscuity, and the destruction of family in the United States. Of the many ways illness has been read as a metaphor in this novel, two are particularly relevant to my own line of analysis: one way is to see this corruption as an erosion of republican disinterest; the other is to see it as an erosion of humanitarian fellow feeling—the "liberal sympathy," as Julia Stern puts it, that is hindered by a male-oriented civic ideology stressing disinterest. My own inclination is to read contagion as a metaphor for the corruption of republican disinterest but also to conclude that this corruption promotes the fellow feeling that Stern finds absent in Brown's novels. Levine, "Arthur Mervyn's Revolution," 151; Samuels, "Infidelity and Contagion," 190; Stern, *Plight of Feeling*.

4. Within the context of eighteenth-century classicism, according to J.G.A. Pocock, the pestilential imagery proves particularly apt. Republican thinking, he writes, always included the disturbing suggestion that civic virtue was susceptible to decay and eventual mortality. Once begun, its corruption was contagious and unstoppable: "If the individual was to be virtuous, he must live in a virtuous city; in a corrupt city, the individual himself must be corrupted." Pocock, *Virtue, Commerce and History,* 97.

5. Carl Ostrowski and Elizabeth Jane Wall Hinds, for example, have both argued that the novel depicts the advent of economic liberalism and the decline of classical republicanism. Hinds, however, finds that Mervyn embodies a positive form of self-interest, whereas Ostrowski emphasizes liberalism's corruptive qualities. Hinds, *Private Property;* Ostrowski, "'Fated to Perish by Consumption.'"

6. Wood, *Radicalism,* 255–258.

7. Hamilton, "Public Credit," 298–299.

8. Brown contributed the first installment to the inaugural issue of the *Weekly Magazine* on February 3, 1798. The twelve subsequent installments were published weekly over the next three months.

9. The narrator draws a clear distinction between debtors who are insolvent and unable to pay (in which case imprisonment does not act as a deterrent and proves an unenlightened means of dealing with crime) and debtors who are able and unwilling to pay. The narrator is certainly an able debtor, though he has also fallen into debt for reasons beyond his own means. The reader is left wondering whether to disapprove of his actions.

10. Brown, "Man at Home," 38, 36, 37. The narrator clearly equates mercantile curiosity with worldliness. He recalls that when he traded as a merchant his "curiosity as well as interest" prompted his decision to act as supercargo on the ship carrying his goods. His desire to see the world and his willingness to undertake risky enterprise fostered his "adventurousness" and "roving disposition" (45–46).

11. Brown, "Man at Home," 46. In another essay, "Alliance between Poverty and Genius," Brown writes, "The truest stimulus to literary efforts, in writing, it has been long ago observed, is necessity." But, while wealth does not befit one for literary endeavor, nor does poverty: "It is the middle class that produces every kind of worth in the greatest abundance." Brown, "Alliance," 145–146.

12. Brown, "Man at Home," 43.

13. While delay provokes curiosity, according to the narrator, the "curiosity is proportioned, among other circumstances, to the shortness of the interval, and thus slightness of the bar between us and knowledge." In other words, the closer the narrator comes to discovery, the greater his curiosity. Brown, "Man at Home," 43.

14. Brown, "Man at Home," 69–70.

15. Brown, "Difference," 84.

16. Brown, "Thoughts on American Newspapers," 99.

17. At times in *Arthur Mervyn* Mervyn even turns this scrutiny on himself, transforming his own lamentable paranoia into a tool of vigilant self-reflexiveness. Questioning his own suspicions of Clemenza's sexual propriety, for example, he notes, "From subsequent reflection, I have contracted a suspicion that the sentiment with which I regarded this lady was not untinctured from this source." Mervyn, then, contracts a suspicion about his own suspicions and justifies his own paranoia by suggesting it is a valuable form of self-scrutiny.

18. Brown, "Thoughts on American Newspapers," 98–100.

19. Anderson also argues that formal features of the novel, particularly omniscient narration and a temporal structure that captures simultaneity, allow readers to imagine themselves as members of a national or protonational community. In his examination of Anderson's impact on literary studies, Jonathan Culler reminds us that Anderson is not concerned with the nationalist content of novels—though the novel can certainly be put to ideological use—but, rather, with the form's ability to structure national consciousness. Anderson, *Imagined Communities;* Culler, "Anderson and the Novel."

20. Brown, "Thoughts on American Newspapers," 98.

21. Brown, *Arthur Mervyn,* 280; hereafter cited parenthetically as *AM.*

22. I should note the way in which Brown has fictionalized the events of 1793 for literary purposes. The pestilence motivated much philanthropy, especially on the part of doctors willing to treat the sick, and simultaneously brought out the self-interest of those eager to profit from the emergency (caretakers, undertakers, and grave diggers, for example, who charged exorbitant rates for their services). But, according to J. H. Powell, many members of the commercial class also used their own resources to help others.

23. Brown, "Man at Home," 52.

24. Hutcheson, Hume, and Smith were particularly interested in the feeling of approval or disapproval (or "moral sentiment") which arises when one sees or hears of the act in question. For these thinkers moral sentiment results either from the spectator's assessment of the action's ability to promote human welfare or from the spectator imagining himself or herself as the recipient of the action.

25. Smith, *Theory of Moral Sentiments,* 4.

26. Stern, *Plight of Feeling,* 6–7.

27. Stern, *Plight of Feeling,* 143.

28. In establishing the intellectual context of the novel, Tompkins cites a passage by the eighteenth-century Scottish historian William Robertson, who insisted that commerce would refine the manners of individuals, unite them through the common goal of supplying mutual wants, and dispose citizens to peace by linking their individual interests to public tranquillity. But what Tompkins misses in her reading of the novel is the crucial role of self-interest, which Robertson himself implies, in forging such communal ties; in fact, Robertson's explication of the pragmatic consequences of linking private and public interests would mesh easily with the philosophy of public banking.

29. Davidson, *Revolution and the Word,* 251.

30. Although far removed from the city, Hadwin's daughters are also susceptible to rumors, presumably because they are women of more delicate constitutions. Susan, whose romantic attachment to Wallace makes her particularly susceptible, awaits his daily letters with an "impatience and anxiety" that only increases with time and reads them finally in a "transport of eagerness" (*AM* 348).

31. Carey writes, "Great as was the calamity of Philadelphia, it was magnified in the most extraordinary manner. The hundred tongues of rumour were never more successfully employed, than on this melancholy occasion." *Short Account,* 34.

32. Brown, "Walstein's School," 35, 36, 37, 39.

33. Gilmore, "Literature of the Revolutionary and Early National Periods," 621.

34. Warner, *Letters of the Republic,* 150. Warner cites *Arthur Mervyn* as an example

of this attempt to create a work that is simultaneously privatized and publicly oriented, though his analysis follows a different line of thought from mine. He claims that Arthur indulges in repeated acts of disclosure (with the novel itself as the ultimate act of disclosure), and this publicity counters the threat of consuming privatization. The novel, he adds, offers readers the opportunity to claim Arthur's public success through private appropriation and participate imaginatively in a public order.

SIX: The Medium between Calculation and Feeling

1. Barnes, *States of Sympathy*, 2.
2. "Glass," 2.
3. As the various "female quixotes" of this era make clear, novels were accused of blurring the line between fantasy and reality and encouraging dangerously fanciful thinking in impressionable women readers. Catherine Ingrassia also documents the perceived link between economic speculation and novel *writing* among women. Alexander Pope, for example, draws a parallel between the threatening infusion of women writers into the literary marketplace and the advent of paper credit. "In representing the hack writers trying to sell their ever-increasing stockpiles of paper," Ingrassia writes, "Pope draws on the lingering suspicion about immaterial forms of literary and financial property, and his own ambivalence about the commercialization of literature and consumer culture." *Authorship, Commerce, and Gender*, 11.
4. Mary Poovey also argues that this association of women with volatility was embedded in the methods of double-entry bookkeeping developed earlier in the seventeenth century. These ordering methods, based on the idea that numerical entries could represent the transparent operations of a rule-bound market, were assumed beyond the bounds of female writing and thinking. Women, she argues, came to stand for the volatility generally associated with the mercantile class. Poovey, "Accommodating Merchants."
5. Terry Mulcaire has observed that Defoe, Joseph Addison, and the authors of *Cato's Letters* also express admiration for the amplitude and creativity of this feminized imagination. I have focused here on the negative ways that women were associated with credit because they are the ones to which Murray's own writing responds. Mulcaire, "Public Credit."
6. Pope, "To a Lady," 2273. Dutch Tulipomania inflated the price of rare tulip varieties, and, when the bubble burst in 1637, many merchants—especially those who had borrowed to purchase in the first place—were ruined financially.
7. Smith-Rosenberg, "Domesticating 'Virtue,'" 166; Weyler, "'Speculating Spirit,'" 208.
8. Hankins, *Science and the Enlightenment*, 2–3. In his description of the Protestant work ethic Max Weber called attention to this crucial distinction drawn by capitalist culture between rational and irrational forms of speculation. An individualistic capitalistic economy, he writes, is "rationalized on the basis of rigorous calculation, directed with foresight and caution toward the economic success," and this behavior is understood to contrast sharply with, among other things, the "adventurers' capitalism, oriented to the exploitation of political opportunities and irrational speculation." I would add that what rationalized certain forms of speculation in this era was not only their alignment with calculative skills but their masculinization and their detachment from an irrationality conventionally associated with the feminine. Weber, *Protestant Ethic*, 76.

9. Hankins, *Science and the Enlightenment*, 7.
10. Hume, *Enquiry Concerning Human Understanding*, 55. See pt. 1 of Patey, *Probability and Literary Form*, for a discussion of the changing concept of probability from the Renaissance to the Augustan era.
11. Locke, *Essay Concerning Human Understanding*, 405.
12. Hankins, *Science and the Enlightenment*, 179–181.
13. Wernick, "When the Bubble Burst," 158.
14. Norton, *Liberty's Daughters*, 118.
15. Unlike businesswomen such as Sarah Kemble Knight, who bought goods and trafficked them for a profit, Pinckney was interested in developing innovations within her line of business. I would characterize her as more aggressively enterprising because the ventures were riskier and the money she stood to gain or lose was considerably higher.
16. Pinckney to Miss Bartlett (1), 35.
17. Pinckney to Miss Bartlett (2), 38.
18. Murray to John Murray, 349.
19. Murray to Mr. J., 146.
20. When writing to a Mr. Parkman, a man of "mercantile knowledge," to ask advice on investing, she makes the curious request that "this application, or any transaction it may originate, may be considered as a secret, even from Mr. Murray, as her plan is, in a day of adversity, to surprise him with an unexpected resource." Murray to Mr. Parkman, 39–40.
21. Murray, *Gleaner*, 709.
22. Murray, *Gleaner*, 138.
23. Murray, *Gleaner*, 728.
24. Murray, *Gleaner*, 139.
25. Murray to Eliza, 966.
26. Norton, *Liberty's Daughters*, 256; Kerber, "Daughters of Columbia," 27.
27. Rush, *Thoughts upon Female Education*, 27, 29.
28. See, in particular, the chapter "Republican Arithmetic" in Cohen, *Calculating People*.
29. Murray, "On the Equality of the Sexes," 550; Murray to Rev. Mr. Redding, 287. See Baym, "Between Enlightenment and Victorian," for a discussion of how this Cartesian concept influenced post-Revolutionary thought and how it was modified in the Victorian era.
30. Murray, "On the Equality of the Sexes," 552.
31. Locke, *Essay Concerning Human Understanding*, 402–403.
32. Murray, *Gleaner*, 142–143.
33. Murray, *Gleaner*, 145, 144.
34. Murray, *Gleaner*, 147, 148.
35. Murray, *Gleaner*, 143, 145.
36. Murray, *Gleaner*, 728.
37. Murray, *Gleaner*, 28–29.
38. Murray to D. Rogers, 70.
39. Ditz, "Shipwrecked"; Murray, letter to Winthrop Sargent, 54; Murray, letter to Mrs. Gardiner, 74.
40. Skemp, *Judith Sargent Murray*, 50.
41. Murray, *Traveller Returned*, 642, 646.
42. See, for example, Murray, letter to Sally Wood, 231.

43. Baym, intro., *Gleaner*, ix.
44. Murray to [?], October 6, 1808, 61.
45. Murray, "On the Equality of the Sexes," 554.
46. Bloch, "Gendered Meanings of Virtue," 56. If, as Davidoff and Hall write, women were considered "the embodiment of both the positive and negative qualities [tenderness and capriciousness] associated with irrationality," Murray insists that the former is inborn and the latter only the result of poor education. Davidoff and Hall, *Family Fortunes*, 27.
47. Murray, *Medium*, 555.
48. Murray, *Medium*, 554.
49. Mulcaire argues that the figure of Credit represents as feminine the "social capital" that results when social relations themselves become "resources for individuals in the pursuit of their interests." In this way commerce is understood as having a refining influence on human interactions. Mulcaire, "Public Credit," 1035.
50. Murray, *Medium*, 580, 588, 546, 547, 589. Elsewhere Murray spoke also of a happy medium between behaviors that were either too tempered or too uncontrolled. In a letter to a young girl, Anna, she wrote, "I would not have the Maid I love reserved, and censorious like the Prude, nor would I have her fanatical, inconstant, or unmeaning, like the Coquet—Could I define the happy mean, I would present it to her as a treasure with which I would conjure her never to part." Murray to Anna, 38.
51. Murray, *Medium*, 572, 612.
52. Murray, *Medium*, 594.
53. Murray to "Sir," 79–80. In this letter she actually describes six hundred dollars in interest-bearing notes and three hundred dollars in deferred stock.
54. Hamilton, *Federalist* 31, 148; *Federalist* 30, 145; *Federalist* 31, 149.
55. Murray to Wood, 228.

EPILOGUE: Headwork, Literary Vocation

Epigraph: Thoreau, "Life without Principle," 748.
1. Cooper, *Pioneers*; Melville, "Happy Failure"; Stowe, *Uncle Tom's Cabin*, 209. Other literary scholars have made their own claims about this literature's concern with an unstable paper credit culture and its ability to elicit the worst of human traits. Marc Shell argues that Edgar Allan Poe's "Goldbug" depicts a Mephistophelean conversion of paper to gold. Walter Benn Michaels reads Nathaniel Hawthorne's *House of the Seven Gables* as an escapist fantasy about inviolable property rights in a time of rampant land speculation. Shell, *Money, Language, and Thought*; Benn Michaels, *Gold Standard and the Logic of Naturalism*; Poe, "Goldbug"; Hawthorne, *House of the Seven Gables*.
2. Crèvecoeur, *Letters*, 48.
3. Ziff, *Writing in the New Nation*, 29; Rice, *Transformation of Authorship*, 111.
4. Crèvecoeur, *Letters*, 48–49.
5. Crèvecoeur, *Letters*, 195.
6. While the Aeolian lyre was a popular subject for poetry, it was not until the nineteenth century, according to M. H. Abrams, that it also became the figure of the poetic mind. *Mirror and the Lamp*, 51.
7. Melville, "Rip Van Winkle's Lilac," 565.
8. Gilmore, "Literature," 661.

9. Irving, "Rip Van Winkle," 1063; Gilmore, "Literature," 671; Irving, "Rip Van Winkle," 1063.

10. Irving, *Money-Diggers*, 449, 451.

11. Irving, *Money-Diggers*, 474, 456, 489; Henretta, *Evolution of American Society*, 7; Irving, *Money-Diggers*, 489.

12. Irving, *Money-Diggers*, 444. In exchange for revealing to Tom Walker the whereabouts of a buried treasure, the Devil requires that Walker be his moneylender. Walker's usury preys upon those who have gone bankrupt on account of such schemes in colonial Massachusetts: "It was a time of paper credit. The country had been deluged with government bills, the famous Land Bank had been established; there had been a rage for speculating; the people had run mad with schemes for new settlements; for building cities in the wilderness; land-jobbers went about with maps of grants, and townships, and Eldorados, lying nobody knew where, but which everybody was ready to purchase. In a word, the great speculating fever which breaks out every now and then in the country, had raged to an alarming degree, and every body was dreaming of making sudden fortunes from nothing. As usual the fever had subsided; the dream had gone off, and the imaginary fortunes with it; the patients were left in doleful plight, and the whole country resounded with the consequent cry of 'hard times.'" Irving, *Money-Diggers*, 444.

13. Irving, *Money-Diggers*, 434.

14. Neider, intro., *Complete Tales of Washington Irving*, xxxi.

15. Thoreau, *Walden*, 303. In a similar vein Thoreau also writes, "if one advances confidently in the direction of his dreams, and endeavors to live the life which he has imagined, he will meet with a success unexpected in common hours." Again, aspiration and imagination are the first steps toward realization. Today an imperative derived from this sentence is used frequently by self-help gurus and financial planners: "Go confidently in the direction of your dreams and live the life you've imagined."

Bibliography

Abrams, M. H. *The Mirror and the Lamp.* New York: Norton, 1958.
Adams, John. Letter to F. A. Vanderkemp, February 16, 1809. In *Works of John Adams,* edited by Charles Francis Adams, 9:608–610. Boston, 1856.
"The Adventures of a Continental Dollar," chap. 1. *United States Magazine* (June 1779): 264–268.
"An Affecting and True Story." *American Museum, or, Universal Magazine* 7:3 (March 1790): 129–32.
Agnew, Jean-Christophe. *Worlds Apart: The Market and the Theater in Anglo-American Thought, 1550–1750.* Cambridge: Cambridge University Press, 1986.
Anderson, Benedict. *Imagined Communities: Reflections on the Origin and Spread of Nationalism.* 2d ed. London: Verso, 1991.
Anderson, William G. *The Price of Liberty: The Public Debt of the American Revolution.* Charlottesville: University Press of Virginia, 1983.
"Answer of Continental Currency to the Representation and Remonstrance of Hard Money." *United States Magazine; a Repository of History, Politics and Literature* (March 1779): 110–121.
Appleby, Joyce. *Capitalism and a New Social Order: The Republican Vision of the 1790s.* New York: New York University Press, 1984.
———. *Economic Thought and Ideology in Seventeenth-Century England.* Princeton, N.J.: Princeton University Press, 1978.
———. "Republicanism in Old and New Contexts." *William and Mary Quarterly,* 3d ser., 43 (1986): 20–34.
Arner, Robert D. "The Sources and Significance of Joseph Dumbleton's 'The Paper-Mill': Augustan American Poetics and the Culture of Print in Colonial Williamsburg." In *Finding Colonial Americas: Essays Honoring J. A. Leo Lemay,* edited by Carla Mulford and David S. Shields, 199–224. Newark: University of Delaware Press, 2001.
Bailyn, Bernard. *The Ideological Origins of the American Revolution.* Cambridge: Harvard University Press, 1967.
Baker, Houston A., Jr. *Blues, Ideology, and Afro-American Literature: A Vernacular Theory.* Chicago: University of Chicago Press, 1984.
Banning, Lance. "Jeffersonian Ideology Revisited: Liberal and Classical Ideas in the New American Republic." *William and Mary Quarterly,* 3d ser., 43 (1986): 3–19.
Barnes, Elizabeth. *States of Sympathy: Seduction and Democracy in the American Novel.* New York: Columbia University Press, 1997.
Barton, William. *Observations On The Nature and Use of Paper-Credit; And The Peculiar Advantages to be Derived from It, in North-America.* Philadelphia, 1781.

Baym, Nina. "Between Enlightenment and Victorian: Toward a Narrative of American Women Writers Writing History." *Critical Inquiry* 18:1 (Fall 1991): 22–41.

———. Introduction to *The Gleaner*, by Judith Sargent Murray, iii–xx. Schenectady, N.Y.: Union College Press, 1992.

Beard, Charles. *An Economic Interpretation of the Constitution of the United States*. New York: Macmillan, 1941.

Beeman, Richard, Stephen Botein, and Edward C. Carter II, eds. *Beyond Confederation: Origins of the Constitution and American National Identity*. Chapel Hill: University of North Carolina Press, 1987.

Behrens, Kathryn L. *Paper Money in Maryland, 1727–1789*. Baltimore: Johns Hopkins Press, 1923.

Bell, Ian. "The Hard Currency of Words: Emerson's Fiscal Metaphor in Nature," *ELH* 52:3 (Fall 1985): 733–753.

Bell, Michael Davitt. "Conditions of Literary Vocation." In *The Cambridge History of American Literature, Vol. 2: Prose Writing, 1820–1865*, edited by Sacvan Bercovitch, 9–123. Cambridge: Cambridge University Press, 1994.

Bercovitch, Sacvan. *The American Jeremiad*. Madison: University of Wisconsin Press, 1978.

———. "'Delightful Examples of Surprising Prosperity': Cotton Mather and the American Success Story." *English Studies* 51 (1970): 40–43.

———. *The Puritan Origins of the American Self*. New Haven, Conn.: Yale University Press, 1975.

Beverley, Robert. *The History and Present State of Virginia*. 1705. Edited by Louis B. Wright. Chapel Hill: University of North Carolina Press, 1947.

Beyers, Chris. "Ebenezer Cooke's Satire, Calculated to the Meridian of Maryland." *Early American Literature* 33 (1988): 62–85.

Bloch, Ruth H. "The Gendered Meanings of Virtue in Revolutionary America." *Signs: Journal of Women in Culture and Society* 13:1 (Fall 1987): 37–58.

Borden, William. *An Address to the Inhabitants of North Carolina; Occasioned by the Difficult Circumstances the Government Seems to Labour under, for Want of a Medium, or Something to Answer in Lieu of Money*. Williamsburg, 1746.

Brackenridge, Hugh Henry. *Modern Chivalry, Containing the Adventures of Captain John Farrago and Teague O'Regan, His Servant*. 1792, 1793, and 1797. Vols. 1–4. Edited by Lewis Leary. New Haven, Conn.: College and University Press, 1965.

Brantlinger, Patrick. *Fictions of State: Culture and Credit in Britain, 1694–1994*. Ithaca, N.Y.: Cornell University Press, 1996.

Breen, T. H. *Tobacco Culture: The Mentality of the Great Tidewater Planters on the Eve of the Revolution*. Princeton, N.J.: Princeton University Press, 1985.

Breen, T. H., and Timothy Hall. "Structuring Provincial Imagination: The Rhetoric and Experience of Social Change in Eighteenth-Century New England." *American Historical Review* 103:5 (December 1998): 1411–1439.

Breitwieser, Mitchell. *Cotton Mather and Benjamin Franklin: The Price of Representative Personality*. New York: Cambridge University Press, 1984.

Brown, Charles Brockden. "Alliance between Poverty and Genius." In *Literary Essays and Reviews*, 145–146.

———. *Arthur Mervyn; or Memoirs of the Year 1793*. 1799–1800. In *Three Gothic Novels*, edited by Sydney J. Krause, 229–637. New York: Library of America, 1998.

———. "The Difference between History and Romance." In Brockden Brown, *Literary Essays and Reviews*, 83–85.
———. *Literary Essays and Reviews*. Edited by Alfred Weber and Wolfgang Schäfer. Frankfurt: Peter Lang, 1992.
———. "The Man at Home." *Weekly Magazine*, February 3–April 28, 1788. In *The Rhapsodist and Other Uncollected Writings*, edited by Harry R. Warfel, 27–98. New York: Scholars' Facsimiles and Reprints, 1943.
———. *Ormond; or, The Secret Witness*. 1799. Edited by Mary Chapman. Peterborough, Ontario: Broadview Press, 1999.
———. "Thoughts on American Newspapers." In Brockden Brown, *Literary Essays and Reviews*, 95–100.
———. "Walstein's School of History, from the German of Krants of Gotha." In Brockden Brown, *Literary Essays and Reviews*, 31–39.
Brown, Richard D. "Shays's Rebellion and the Ratification of the Federal Constitution in Massachusetts." In *Beyond Confederation*, 113–127.
Brown, William Hill. *The Power of Sympathy*. 1789. In *The Power of Sympathy and The Coquette*, edited by Carla Mulford, 1–103. New York: Penguin, 1996.
Burroughs, Stephen. *Memoirs of the Notorious Stephen Burroughs of New Hampshire*. 1858. New York: Dial Press, 1924.
Burstein, Andrew. "The Political Character of Sympathy." *Journal of the Early Republic* 21:4 (Winter 2001): 601–632.
Carey, Lewis J. *Franklin's Economic Views*. Garden City, N.Y.: Doubleday, Doran and Co., 1928.
Carey, Mathew. *A Short Account of the Malignant, Fever Lately Prevalent in Philadelphia*. 2d ed. Philadelphia, 1793.
"A Circular Letter from the Congress of the United States of America to Their Constituents." *United States Magazine; a Repository of History, Politics and Literature* (October 1779): 408–410, 436–438.
Cohen, Edward H. *Ebenezer Cooke: The Sot-Weed Canon*. Athens: University of Georgia Press, 1975.
Cohen, Patricia Cline. *A Calculating People: The Spread of Numeracy in Early America*. Chicago: University of Chicago Press, 1982.
"Common Sense, in Dishabille, No. V: The Castle in the Air." *New Star; a Republican Miscellaneous, Literary Paper* (August 15, 1797): 149–150.
"Considerations on the use and abuse of Mottos." *Supplement to the Pennsylvania Magazine* (1775): 587–589.
Continental bill of credit (eight dollars). April 11, 1778. University of Notre Dame, Department of Special Collections (Project of the Robert H. Gore Numismatic Endowment).
Cooke, Ebenezer. *The Sot-Weed Factor; or, a Voyage to Maryland, &c.* 1708. In Steiner, *Early Maryland Poetry*, 11–32.
———. *The Sotweed Factor, or Voiage to Maryland. The Third Edition, Corrected and Amended*. In *The Maryland Muse*. Annapolis, 1731.
———. *Sotweed Redivivus: Or the Planters Looking-Glass*. 1730. In Steiner, *Early Maryland Poetry*, 35–52.
Cooper, James Fenimore. *The Pioneers*. 1823. Edited with an introduction by James D. Wallace. Oxford: Oxford University Press, 1991.

Crèvecoeur, J. Hector St. John de. *Letters from an American Farmer.* 1781. In *Letters from an American Farmer and Sketches of Eighteenth-Century America,* edited with an introduction by Albert E. Stone, 33–227. New York: Penguin, 1986.

Culler, Jonathan. "Anderson and the Novel." *Diacritics: A Review of Contemporary Criticism* 29:4 (Winter 1999): 20–39.

Davidoff, Leonore, and Catherine Hall. *Family Fortunes: Men and Women of the English Middle Class, 1780–1850.* Chicago: University of Chicago Press, 1987.

Davidson, Cathy. *Revolution and the Word: The Rise of the Novel in America.* New York: Oxford University Press, 1986.

Davies, Glyn. *A History of Money: From Ancient Times to the Present Day.* Cardiff: University of Wales Press, 1994.

Davis, Andrew McFarland, ed. *Colonial Currency Reprints, 1682–1751.* 4 vols. New York: B. Franklin, 1971.

Defoe, Daniel. *An Essay upon Projects.* Edited by Joyce D. Kennedy, Michael Seidel, and Maximillian E. Novak. New York: AMS Press, 1999.

———. *Robinson Crusoe.* 1719. Edited by Michael Shinagel. New York: Norton, 1994.

Derrida, Jacques. "Différance." Translated by Alan Bass. In *Deconstruction in Context: Literature and Philosophy,* edited by Mark C. Taylor, 396–420. Chicago: University of Chicago Press, 1986.

———. *Given Time I: Counterfeit Money.* Translated by Peggy Kamuf. Chicago: University of Chicago Press, 1992.

Dickson, P.G.M. *The Financial Revolution in England: A Study in the Development of Public Credit, 1688–1756.* London: Macmillan, 1967.

Ditz, Toby L. "Shipwrecked; or, Masculinity Imperiled: Mercantile Representations of Failure and the Gendered Self in Eighteenth-Century Philadelphia." *Journal of American History* 81:1 (June 1994): 51–80.

Dreiser, Theodore. *The Financier.* 1912. New York: Meridian, 1995.

Dumbleton, Joseph. "The Paper-Mill, Inscrib'd to Mr. Parks." *Virginia Gazette,* July 26, 1744. In *American Magazine* (August 1744), 523.

Dunn, Elizabeth. "'Grasping at the Shadow': The Massachusetts Currency Debate, 1690–1751." *New England Quarterly* 71:1 (March 1998): 54–76.

Edwards, Jonathan. "A Faithful Narrative of the Surprising Work of God." 1737. In *A Jonathan Edwards Reader,* edited by John E. Smith, Harry S. Stout, and Kenneth P. Minkema, 57–87. New Haven, Conn.: Yale University Press, 1995.

Elliott, Emory. *Revolutionary Writers: Literature and Authority in the New Republic, 1725–1810.* New York: Oxford University Press, 1982.

Ellison, Julie. *Cato's Tears and the Making of Anglo-American Emotion.* Chicago: University of Chicago Press, 1999.

Emerson, Ralph Waldo. *Nature,* 1836. In *The Essential Writings of Ralph Waldo Emerson,* edited by Brooks Atkinson with an introduction by Mary Oliver, 3–39. New York: The Modern Library, 2000.

———. "Self-Reliance." 1841. In *The Essential Writings of Ralph Waldo Emerson,* edited by Brooks Atkinson with an introduction by Mary Oliver, 132–153. New York: Modern Library, 2000.

Equiano, Olaudah. *The Interesting Narrative of the Life of Olaudah Equiano, or Gustavus Vasa, the African.* 1794. In *The Interesting Narrative and Other Writings,* edited by Vincent Carretta. New York: Penguin, 1995.

Evelev, John. "*The Contrast:* The Problem of Theatricality and Political and Social Crisis in Postrevolutionary America." *Early American Literature* 31:1 (1996): 74–97.

Ferguson, E. James. "Currency Finance: An Interpretation of Colonial Monetary Practices." *William and Mary Quarterly*, 3d ser., 10:2 (April 1953): 153–180.

———. *The Power of the Purse: A History of American Public Finance, 1776-1790*. Chapel Hill: University of North Carolina Press, 1961.

Ferguson, Robert A. "The American Enlightenment, 1750–1820." In *The Cambridge History of American Literature: 1590–1820*, edited by Sacvan Bercovitch, 345–537. Cambridge: Cambridge University Press, 1994.

Fichtelberg, Joseph. *Critical Fictions: Sentiment and the American Market, 1780–1870*. Athens: University of Georgia Press, 2003.

———. "Word between Worlds: The Economy of Equiano's *Narrative*." *American Literary History* 5:3 (Fall 1993): 459–480.

Fiedler, Leslie. *Love and Death in the American Novel*. 1960. New York: Anchor Books, 1992.

Fliegelman, Jay. *Declaring Independence: Jefferson, Natural Language, and the Culture of Performance*. Stanford, Calif.: Stanford University Press, 1993.

Foster, Hannah Webster. *The Coquette; or, The History of Eliza Wharton*. 1797. Edited by Cathy N. Davidson. Oxford: Oxford University Press, 1986.

Foucault, Michel. *The Order of Things: An Archaeology of the Human Sciences*. New York: Random House, 1970.

Franklin, Benjamin. "Account of the Devices on the Continental Bills of Credit." *Pennsylvania Gazette*, September 20, 1775. In Lemay, *Writings*, 734–738.

———. "Argument for Making the Bills of Credit Bear Interest." 1764. In *Papers of Benjamin Franklin*, edited by Leonard Labaree, 11:11–18. New Haven, Conn.: Yale University Press, 1967.

———. *Autobiography: An Authoritative Text*. Edited by J. A. Leo Lemay and P. M. Zall. New York: Norton, 1986.

———. "Dissertation on Liberty and Necessity." 1725. In Lemay, *Writings*, 57–71.

———. "The Legal Tender of Paper Money in America." 1767. In *Papers of Benjamin Franklin*, edited by Leonard Labaree, 14:33–39. New Haven, Conn.: Yale University Press, 1970.

———. Letter to Samuel Cooper, April 22, 1779. In *The Papers of Benjamin Franklin*, edited by Barbara B. Oberg, 29:354–356. New Haven, Conn.: Yale University Press, 1992.

———. Letter to William Jackson, July 5, 1781. In *The Papers of Benjamin Franklin*, edited by Barbara B. Oberg, 35:219–220. New Haven, Conn.: Yale University Press, 1999.

———. *A Modest Inquiry into the Nature and Necessity of a Paper-Currency*. 1729. In Davis, *Colonial Currency Reprints*, 2:335–357.

———. "Poor Richard Improved, 1758" (including "The Way to Wealth"), Maxims. In Lemay, *Writings*, 1294–1304.

———. "Scheme for Supplying the Colonies with a Paper Currency." 1765. In *Papers of Benjamin Franklin*, edited by Leonard Labaree, 12:51–60. New Haven, Conn.: Yale University Press, 1968.

———. [Untitled]. *American Weekly Mercury*, March 27, 1729.

———. *Writings*. Edited by J. A. Leo Lemay. New York: Library of America, 1987.

Galbraith, John Kenneth. *Money: Whence It Came, Where It Went.* Rev. ed. Boston: Houghton Mifflin, 1995.

Garson, Robert. "Counting Money: The US Dollar and American Nationhood, 1781-1820." *Journal of American Studies* 35:1 (April 2001): 21-46.

Gilmore, Michael T. *American Romanticism and the Marketplace.* Chicago: University of Chicago Press, 1985.

———. "The Literature of the Revolutionary and Early National Periods." In *The Cambridge History of American Literature, 1590-1820*, edited by Sacvan Bercovitch, 539-693. Cambridge: Cambridge University Press, 1994.

"The Glass; or Speculation: A Poem." New York, 1791.

Gordon, John Steele. *Hamilton's Blessing: The Extraordinary Life and Times of Our National Debt.* New York: Penguin, 1997.

Gould, Philip. "Free Carpenter, Venture Capitalist: Reading the Lives of the Early Black Atlantic." *American Literary History* 12:4 (Winter 2000): 659-684.

———. "Race, Commerce, and the Literature of Yellow Fever in Early National Philadelphia." *Early American Literature* 35:2 (September 2000): 157-186.

Goux, Jean-Joseph. *The Coiners of Language.* Translated by Jennifer Curtiss Gage. Norman: University of Oklahoma Press, 1984.

Green, Joseph. "The *Dying Speech* of Old Tenor." Boston, 1750.

———. "A Mournful Lamentation For the sad and deplorable Death of Mr. Old Tenor." Boston, 1750.

———. "A Mournful Lamentation On the untimely Death of Paper Money." Wilmington, [Del.], 1781.

Greene, Jack P. *Pursuits of Happiness: The Social Development of Early Modern British Colonies and the Formation of American Culture.* Chapel Hill: University of North Carolina Press, 1988.

Gura, Philip F. "Cotton Mather's *Life of Phips*." In *The Crossroads of American History and Literature,* 64-78. University Park: Pennsylvania State University Press, 1996.

Habermas, Jürgen. *The Structural Transformation of the Public Sphere: An Inquiry into a Category of Bourgeois Society.* Translated by Thomas Burger. Cambridge, Mass.: MIT Press, 1991.

Hamilton, Alexander. Letter to Robert Morris, April 30, 1781. In *The Papers of Alexander Hamilton*, edited by Harold C. Syrett, 2:604-635. New York: Columbia University Press, 1961.

———. "Public Credit, Communicated to the Senate, 16 and 21 January, 1795." In *The Works of Alexander Hamilton*, edited by Henry Cabot Lodge, 3:199-301. New York: Haskell House, Publishers, 1971.

Hamilton, Alexander, James Madison, and John Jay. *The Federalist.* Introduction by William R. Brock. London: J. M. Dent, 1992.

Hammond, Bray. *Banks and Politics in America: From the Revolution to the Civil War.* Princeton, N.J.: Princeton University Press, 1957.

Hankins, Thomas L. *Science and the Enlightenment.* Cambridge: Cambridge University Press, 1985.

Haskell, Thomas L. "Capitalism and the Origins of the Humanitarian Sensibility" (pts. 1-2). In *The Antislavery Debate: Capitalism and Abolitionism as a Problem in Historical Interpretation*, edited by Thomas Bender, 107-160. Berkeley: University of California Press, 1992.

Hawthorne, Nathaniel. *The House of the Seven Gables.* 1851. Edited by Seymour Lee Gross. New York: Norton, 1967.
Heinzelman, Kurt. *The Economics of the Imagination.* Amherst: University of Massachusetts Press, 1980.
Henretta, James A. *The Evolution of American Society, 1700-1815: An Interdisciplinary Analysis.* Lexington, Mass.: D. C. Heath, 1973.
Hinds, Elizabeth Jane Wall. *Private Property: Charles Brockden Brown's Gendered Economics of Virtue.* Newark: University of Delaware Press, 1997.
Hirschman, Albert O. *The Passions and the Interests: Political Arguments for Capitalism before Its Triumph.* Princeton, N.J.: Princeton University Press, 1977.
Holmes, Alice Arnold. Arithmetic book. 1795. Manuscripts Department, American Antiquarian Society, Worcester, Mass.
Hume, David. *An Enquiry Concerning Human Understanding.* 1748. Amherst, N.Y.: Prometheus, 1988.
[Humphreys, David]. "Address to the armies of the united states of America." *American Museum; or, Repository of Ancient and Modern Fugitive Pieces &c* 1:3 (March 1787): 230-240.
Humphreys, David, Joel Barlow, John Trumbull, and Lemuel Hopkins. *The Anarchiad: A New England Poem.* 1786-1787. Edited by Luther G. Riggs and introduction by William K. Bottorf. Gainesville, Fla.: Scholars' Facsimiles and Reprints, 1967.
Ingrassia, Catherine. *Authorship, Commerce, and Gender in Early Eighteenth-Century England: A Culture of Paper Credit.* Cambridge: Cambridge University Press, 1998.
Innes, Stephen. *Creating the Commonwealth: The Economic Culture of Puritan New England.* New York: Norton, 1995.
International Encyclopedia of Communications. Edited by Erik Barnouw. New York: Oxford University Press, 1989.
Irving, Washington. "The Legend of Sleepy Hollow," from *The Sketch Book.* 1820. In *History, Tales and Sketches,* selections and notes by James W. Tuttleton, 1058-1088. New York: Library of America, 1983.
―――. *The Money-Diggers,* from *Tales of a Traveller.* 1824. In *The Complete Tales of Washington Irving,* edited by Charles Nieder, 427-490. New York: Da Capo Press, 1998.
―――. "Rip Van Winkle," from *The Sketch Book.* 1820. In *History, Tales and Sketches,* selections and notes by James W. Tuttleton, 767-785. New York: Library of America, 1983.
Isaac, Rhys. *The Transformation of Virginia, 1740-1790.* New York: Norton, 1988.
It's a Wonderful Life. VHS. Directed by Frank Capra. 1946. New York: Goodtimes Home Video Corporation, 1985.
Jefferson, Thomas. *The Anas, 1791-1806: Selections.* In *Public and Private Papers,* introduction by Tom Wicker and notes by Merrill D. Peterson, 335-370. New York: Library of America, 1990.
Kerber, Linda. "Daughters of Columbia: Educating Women for the Republic, 1787-1805." In *Toward an Intellectual History of Women: Essays by Linda K. Kerber,* 23-40. Chapel Hill: University of North Carolina Press, 1997.
Knight, Janice. *Orthodoxies in Massachusetts: Rereading American Puritanism.* Cambridge: Harvard University Press, 1994.
Knight, Sarah Kemble. *The Journal of Madam Knight.* 1825. In *Colonial American Travel Narratives,* edited with an introduction by Wendy Martin, with notes by Susan Imbarrato and Deborah Dietrich, 49-75. New York: Penguin, 1994.

Kramnick, Isaac. "The 'Great National Discussion': The Discourse of Politics in 1787." *William and Mary Quarterly*, 3d ser., 45:1 (January 1988): 3–32.

Lemay, J. A. Leo. "Franklin's *Autobiography* and the American Dream." In *Benjamin Franklin's Autobiography: An Authoritative Text, Backgrounds, Criticism*, edited by J. A. Leo Lemay and P. M. Zall, 349–360. New York: Norton, 1986.

———. *Men of Letters in Colonial Maryland*. Knoxville: University of Tennessee Press, 1972.

Levine, Robert. "Arthur Mervyn's Revolutions." *Studies in American Fiction* 12 (1984): 145–160.

Lewis, Richard. "Food for Criticks." In *An Early American Reader*, edited by J. A. Leo Lemay, 512–515. Washington, D.C.: U.S. Information Agency, 1988.

———. "To His Excellency Benedict Leonard Calvert, Governour, and Commander in Chief, in and over the Province of Maryland." 1728. In Steiner, *Early Maryland Poetry*, 59–61.

Locke, John. *An Essay Concerning Human Understanding*. 1690. Edited by A. D. Woozley. New York: Meridian, 1964.

Looby, Christopher. *Voicing America: Language, Literary Form, and the Origins of the United States*. Chicago: University of Chicago Press, 1996.

Loughran, Trish. "The First American Contrasts: Region and Nation under the Articles of Confederation." *Explorations in Early American Culture* 5 (2001): 230–259.

Madison, James. Letter to Thomas Jefferson, July 18, 1787. In *The Papers of James Madison*, edited by Robert A. Rutland and William M. E. Rachal, 10:105–106. Chicago: University of Chicago Press, 1977.

———. "Money." September 1779–March 1780. In *The Papers of James Madison*, edited by William T. Hutchinson and William M. E. Rachal, 1:302–310. Chicago: University of Chicago Press, 1962.

Mann, Bruce H. *Republic of Debtors: Bankruptcy in the Age of American Independence*. Cambridge: Harvard University Press, 2002.

Markland, J. "Typographia: An Ode on Printing," 1730. Roanoke, Va.: Stone, 1926.

Marshall, Gordon. *In Search of the Spirit of Capitalism: An Essay on Max Weber's Protestant Ethic Thesis*. New York: Columbia University Press, 1982.

Marx, Karl. *Capital: A Critique of Political Economy*, vol. 1. 1867. In *Capital, Volume 1*, translated by Ben Fowkes with an introduction by Ernest Mandel. New York: Penguin, 1976.

Maryland bill of credit (six dollars). April 10, 1733. University of Notre Dame, Department of Special Collections (Project of the Robert H. Gore Jr., Numismatic Endowment).

Mather, Cotton. *The Christian Philosopher*. Edited by Winton U. Solberg. Urbana: University of Illinois Press, 1994.

———. *Concio ad Populum. A Distressed People Entertained with Proposals for the Relief of Their Distresses*. Boston, 1719.

———. *Durable Riches. Two Brief Discourses, Occasioned by the* Impoverishing Blast of Heaven, *which the Undertakings of Men, both by Sea and Land, have met withal*. Boston, 1695.

———. *Ecclesia Monilia: The Peculiar Treasure of the Almighty King Opened; And the Jewels that are* made up *in it, Exposed*. Boston, 1726.

———. *Fair Dealing between Debtor and Creditor*. Boston, 1716.

———. *Lex Mercatoria, Or, the Just Rules of Commerce Declared*. Boston, 1705.
———. *Magnalia Christi Americana, Books I and II*. Edited by Kenneth B. Murdock. Cambridge: Harvard University Press, 1977.
———. A Man of his Word. *A very brief Essay on Fidelity in Keeping Promises and Engagements*. Boston, 1713.
———. *News from Robinson Cruso's Island*. Boston, 1720.
———. *Pascentius: A* Very Brief *Essay upon the Methods of Piety*. Boston, 1714.
———. *Pietas in Patriam: The Life of His Excellency Sir William Phips, Knt. Late Governour of New-England*. 1697. In *Selections from Cotton Mather*, edited by Kenneth Murdock, 150–283. New York: Hafner, 1960.
———. *Some Considerations on the Bills of Credit Now Passing in New-England*. Boston, 1690. In Davis, *Colonial Currency Reprints*, 1:189–195.
———. *Theopolis Americana. An Essay on the Golden Street of the Holy City*. Boston, 1710.
———. *The True Riches: A Present of Glorious and Immense Riches, Plainly and Freely Tendered unto Those That Are Willing to Accept of Them*. Boston, 1724
———. The Voice of God in a Tempest. *A Sermon Preached in the Time of the Storm*. Boston, 1723.
Matson, Cathy. "The Revolution, Constitution and New Nation." In *The Cambridge Economic History of the United States*, edited by Stanley L. Engerman and Robert E. Gallman, 1:363–401. Cambridge: Cambridge University Press, 1996.
McCusker, John. *Money and Exchange in Europe and America, 1600–1775: A Handbook*. Chapel Hill: University of North Carolina Press, 1978.
McCusker, John, and Russell R. Menard. *The Economy of British America, 1607–1789*. Chapel Hill: University of North Carolina Press, 1985.
McIntyre, Ruth A. *Debts Hopeful and Desperate: Financing the Plymouth Colony*. [Plymouth, Mass.]: Plimoth Plantation, 1963.
Melville, Herman. *Bartleby, the Scrivener*. 1853. In *Melville's Short Novels*, edited by Dan McCall, 39–74. New York: Norton, 2001.
———. *The Confidence-Man: His Masquerade*, 1857. Edited by Hershel Parker. New York: Norton, 1971.
———. "The Happy Failure: A Story of the River Hudson." 1854. In *Great Short Works of Herman Melville*, edited by Warner Berthoff, 179–186. New York: Harper and Row, 1969.
———. *Moby-Dick; or, the Whale*. 1851. Edited by Harrison Hayford and Hershel Parker. 2d ed. New York: Norton, 2002.
———. "Rip Van Winkle's Lilac." In *Tales, Poems, and Other Writings*, edited by John Bryant, 557–565. New York: Modern Library, 2002.
Meserve, Walter J. *An Emerging Entertainment: The Drama of the American People to 1828*. Bloomington: Indiana University Press, 1977.
Michaels, Walter Benn. *The Gold Standard and the Logic of Naturalism*. Berkeley: University of California Press, 1987.
Miller, Perry. *The New England Mind: From Colony to Province*. Cambridge: Harvard University Press, 1953.
More, Thomas. *Utopia*. Translated and edited by Robert M. Adams. 2d ed. New York: Norton, 1992.
Morgan, Edmund S. *Benjamin Franklin*. New Haven, Conn.: Yale University Press, 2002.

Mott, Tracy, and George W. Zinke. "Benjamin Franklin's Economic Thought: A Twentieth Century Appraisal." In *Critical Essays on Benjamin Franklin*, edited by Melvin H. Buxbaum, 111–127. Boston: G. K. Hall, 1987.

Mulcaire, Terry. "Public Credit; or, The Feminization of Virtue in the Marketplace." *PMLA* 114:4 (October 1999): 1029–1042.

Murray, Judith Sargent. *The Gleaner*. 1798. Introduction by Nina Baym. Schenectady, N.Y.: Union College Press, 1992.

———. Letter to [?], October 6, 1808, Letterbook 15:61–62. In Murray Papers.

———. Letter to Anna, July 3, 178[?], Letterbook 2:38–41. In Murray Papers.

———. Letter to D. Rogers, March 5, 1786, Letterbook 3:68–73. In Murray Papers.

———. Letter to Eliza, November 26, 1804, Letterbook 12:965–967. In Murray Papers.

———. Letter to John Murray, January 29, 1791, Letterbook 5:348–349. In Murray Papers.

———. Letter to Mr. J., September 5, 1798, Letterbook 10:146–148. In Murray Papers.

———. Letter to Mr. Parkman, August 17, 1808, Letterbook 15:39–40. In Murray Papers.

———. Letter to Mrs. Gardiner, March 5, 1786, Letterbook 3:73–76. In Murray Papers.

———. Letter to Rev. Mr. Redding, May 7, 1801, Letterbook 11:285–289. In Murray Papers.

———. Letter to Sally Wood, November 25, 1800, Letterbook 11:225–233. In Murray Papers.

———. Letter to "Sir," December [?], 1808, Letterbook 15:79–80. In Murray Papers.

———. Letter to Winthrop Sargent, January 31, 1786, Letterbook 3:52–55. In Murray Papers.

———. *The Medium* (also titled *Virtue Triumphant*). 1795. In *Gleaner*, 543–614.

———. Murray Papers of the Mississippi Department of Archives and History. Collection no. Z/1827.000/M.

———. "On the Equality of the Sexes." 1790. In *Early American Writing*, edited by Giles Gunn, 548–555. New York: Penguin, 1994.

———. *The Story of Margaretta*. In *Selected Writings of Judith Sargent Murray*, edited by Sharon M. Harris, 153–272. New York: Oxford University Press, 1995.

———. *The Traveller Returned*. 1796. In *Gleaner*, 637–682.

Nash, Gary B. "Social Change and the Growth of Prerevolutionary Urban Radicalism." In *The American Revolution: Explorations in the History of American Radicalism*, edited by Alfred F. Young, 3–36. DeKalb: Northern Illinois University Press, 1976.

———. *Urban Crucible: The Northern Seaports and the Origins of the American Revolution*. Cambridge: Harvard University Press, 1986.

Neider, Charles. Introduction. *The Complete Tales of Washington Irving*, edited by C. Neider, xi–xxxvii. New York: Da Capo Press, 1998.

Nettels, Curtis. *The Money Supply of the American Colonies before 1720*. New York: A. M. Kelley, 1973.

Newman, Eric P. *The Early Paper Money of America*, 3d ed. Iola, Wisc.: Krause Publications, 1990.

———. "Franklin Making Money More Plentiful." *Proceedings of the American Philosophical Society* 115:5 (October 1971): 341–349.

———, ed. *Studies on Money in Early America*. New York: American Numismatic Society, 1976.

New News from Robinson Cruso's *Island, In a Letter to a Gentleman at* Portsmouth. Boston, 1720. In Davis, *Colonial Currency Reprints* 2:127–135.
Nichols, Capper. "Tobacco and the Rise of Writing in Colonial Maryland." *Mississippi Quarterly* 50 (Winter 1996–97): 5–17.
Nicholson, Colin. *Writing and the Rise of Finance: Capital Satires of the Early Eighteenth Century.* Cambridge: Cambridge University Press, 1994.
Norton, Mary Beth. *Liberty's Daughters: The Revolutionary Experience of American Women, 1750–1800.* Boston: Little, Brown, 1980.
"On establishing a Sinking Fund in Pennsylvania." *American Museum; or, Repository of Ancient and Modern Fugitive Pieces &c* 1:6 (June 1787): 487–491.
"On Public Faith." *American Museum; or, Repository of Ancient and Modern Fugitive Pieces &c* 1:5 (May 1787): 405–409.
Osteen, Mark, and Martha Woodmansee. "Taking Account of the New Economic Criticism: An Historical Introduction." In *The New Economic Criticism,* edited by Martha Woodmansee and Mark Osteen, 3–50. London: Routledge, 1999.
Ostrowski, Carl. "'Fated to Perish by Consumption': The Political Economy of *Arthur Mervyn.*" *Studies in American Fiction* 32:1 (Spring 2004): 3–20.
Paine, Thomas [1694–1757]. *A Discourse Shewing That the real first Cause of the Straits and Difficulties of this Province of the* Massachusetts Bay, *is it's* Extravagancy, *& not* Paper Money. 1721. In Davis, *Colonial Currency Reprints,* 2:279–300.
Paine, Thomas [1737–1809]. *American Crisis.* 1776–1783. In *The Life and Major Writings of Thomas Paine,* edited by Philip S. Foner, 47–239. New York: Citadel Press, 1974.
———. "Common Sense on Paper Money." *Pennsylvania Packet,* November 7, 1786. In *Worcester Magazine,* 2:37, December 8, 1786, 449–450.
———. *Rights of Man.* 1791–1792. In *The Life and Major Writings of Thomas Paine,* edited by Philip S. Foner, 241–458. New York: Citadel Press, 1974.
"Paper Money once more speaketh for itself!" *Worcester Magazine* 2:31, November 1, 1786, 372–373.
"Paper Money once more speaketh for itself!" *Worcester Magazine* 2:40, January 1, 1787, 482–484.
"Paper Money, raised from the dead, speaketh for itself!" *Worcester Magazine* 1:25, September 15, 1786, 294.
Patey, Douglas. *Probability and Literary Form: Philosophic Theory and Literary Practice in the Augustan Age.* New York: Cambridge University Press, 1984.
Perkins, Edwin J. *American Public Finance and Financial Services, 1700–1815.* Columbus: Ohio State University Press, 1994.
Pinckney, Eliza Lucas. Letter to Miss Bartlett (1). 1742. In *The Letterbook of Eliza Lucas Pinckney, 1739–1762,* edited by Elise Pinckney, 34–35. Chapel Hill: University of North Carolina Press, 1972.
———. Letter to Miss Bartlett (2). 1742. In *The Letterbook of Eliza Lucas Pinckney, 1739–1762,* edited by Elise Pinckney, 38–39. Chapel Hill: University of North Carolina Press, 1972.
Pitkin, Hanna. *Fortune Is a Woman: Gender and Politics in the Thought of Niccolò Machiavelli.* Berkeley: University of California Press, 1984.
Pocock, J.G.A. *Virtue, Commerce and History: Essays in Political Thought and History, Chiefly in the Eighteenth Century.* Cambridge: Cambridge University Press, 1985.

Poe, Edgar Allan. "The Goldbug." 1843. In *The Selected Writings of Edgar Allan Poe*, edited by G. R. Thompson, 321–348. New York: Norton, 2004.

Poovey, Mary. "Accommodating Merchants: Accounting, Civility, and the Natural Laws of Gender." *differences: A Journal of Feminist Cultural Studies* 8:3 (Fall 1996): 1–20.

Pope, Alexander. *The Dunciad.* In *The Norton Anthology of English Literature*, edited by M. H. Abrams et al., 5th ed., 1:2290–2296. New York: Norton, 1986.

———. "To a Lady: Of the Characters of Women." In *The Norton Anthology of English Literature*, edited by M. H. Abrams et al., 5th ed., 1:2271–2278. New York: Norton, 1986.

Powell, J. H. *Bring Out Your Dead: The Great Plague of Yellow Fever in Philadelphia in 1793.* Philadelphia: University of Pennsylvania Press, 1949.

Pressman, Richard. "Class Positioning and Shays' Rebellion: Resolving the Contradictions of *The Contrast.*" *Early American Literature* 21:2 (Fall 1986): 87–102.

Proposals for a Tobacco-Law, in the Province of Maryland. Annapolis, 1726.

Ramsey, David. *The History of the American Revolution.* 1789. Edited by Lester Cohen. 2 vols. Indianapolis: Liberty Classics, 1990.

Randolph, Peyton. *A Letter to a Gentleman in* London, *from* Virginia. Williamsburg, 1759.

"Reply of Continental Currency to the Representation and Remonstrance of Hard Money." *United States Magazine; a Repository of History, Politics and Literature* (February 1779): 72–81.

"The Representation and Remonstrance of Hard Money. Addressed to the People of America." *United States Magazine; a Repository of History, Politics and Literature* (January 1779): 28–31.

Review of *The Contrast. New York Daily Advertiser,* April 18, 1787.

Rice, Grantland S. *The Transformation of Authorship in America.* Chicago: University of Chicago Press, 1997.

Richards, Jeffrey H. *Theater Enough: American Culture and the Metaphor of the World Stage, 1607–1789.* Durham, N.C.: Duke University Press, 1991.

Riesman, Janet A. "Money, Credit and Federalist Political Economy." In Beeman et al., *Beyond Confederation*, 128–161.

Rinehart, Lucy. "A Nation's 'Noble Spectacle': Royall Tyler's *The Contrast* as Metatheatrical Commentary." *American Drama* 3:2 (Spring 1994): 29–52.

Roll, Eric. *A History of Economic Thought.* 5th ed. London: Faber and Faber, 1992.

Rowson, Susanna. *Charlotte Temple.* 1794. Edited by Cathy N. Davidson. Oxford: Oxford University Press, 1986.

Rush, Benjamin. *Thoughts upon Female Education, Accommodated to the Present State of Society, Manners, and Government in the United States of America.* 1787. In *Essays on Education in the Early Republic*, edited by Frederick Rudolph, 25–40. Cambridge: Harvard University Press, 1965.

Samuels, Shirley. "Infidelity and Contagion: The Rhetoric of Revolution." *Early American Literature* 22:2 (September 1987): 183–191.

Schweitzer, Mary McKinney. "Economic Regulation and the Colonial Economy: The Maryland Tobacco Inspection Act of 1747." *The Journal of Economic History* 40:3 (September 1980): 551–569.

The Second Part of South-Sea Stock. Being an Inquiry into the Original of Province Bills *or* Bills of Credit. 1721. In Davis, *Colonial Currency Reprints*, 2:303–332.

Shell, Marc. *Money, Language, and Thought: Literary and Philosophical Economies from the Medieval to the Modern Era.* Berkeley: University of California Press, 1982.
Sheridan, Richard Brinsley. *The School for Scandal.* 1821. In *The School for Scandal and Other Plays,* edited by Eric Rump, 187–279. New York: Penguin, 1988.
Sherman, Sandra. *Finance and Fictionality in the Early Eighteenth Century: Accounting for Defoe.* Cambridge: Cambridge University Press, 1996.
Shields, David S. *Oracles of Empire: Poetry, Politics, and Commerce in British America, 1690–1750.* Chicago: University of Chicago Press, 1990.
Silverman, Kenneth, ed. *Colonial American Poetry.* New York: Hafner, 1968.
———. *The Life and Times of Cotton Mather.* New York: Harper and Row, 1984.
Simmel, Georg. *The Philosophy of Money.* 2d ed., 1907. Edited by David Frisby and translated by Tom Bottomore and David Frisby. London: Routledge, 1978.
Skemp, Sheila L. *Judith Sargent Murray: A Brief Biography with Documents.* Boston: Bedford, 1998.
Smith, Adam. *An Inquiry into the Nature and Causes of the Wealth of Nations.* 1776. Edited by Edwin Cannan. Chicago: University of Chicago Press, 1976.
———. *The Theory of Moral Sentiments.* 1759. New York: August M. Kelley Publisher, 1966.
Smith, John. *A Description of New England: Or the Observations, and Discoveries, of Captain John Smith (Admirall of that Country) in the North of America, in the Year of Our Lord 1614.* 1616. In *Captain John Smith, Works, 1608–1631,* edited by Edward Arber, pt. 1, 175–229. Westminster: Archibald Constable and Co., 1895.
Smith, Venture. *A Narrative of the Life and Adventures of Venture, A Native of Africa.* 1798. In *Unchained Voices: An Anthology of Black Authors in the English-Speaking World of the Eighteenth Century,* edited by Vincent Carretta, 369–387. Lexington: University of Kentucky Press, 1996.
Smith-Rosenberg, Carroll. "Domesticating 'Virtue': Coquettes and Revolutionaries in Young America." In *Literature and the Body: Essays on Populations and Persons,* edited by Elaine Scarry, 160–184. Baltimore: Johns Hopkins University Press, 1988.
"Speech of a Member of the General Court of Massachusetts, on the Question whether the Public Securities should be redeemed at their Current Value." *American Museum; or, Repository of Ancient and Modern Fugitive Pieces &c* 1:5 (May 1787): 412–417.
Spengemann, William C. *The Forms of Autobiography: Episodes in the History of a Literary Genre.* New Haven, Conn.: Yale University Press, 1980.
Stabile, Donald R. *The Origins of American Public Finance: Debates over Money, Debt, and Taxes in the Constitutional Era, 1776–1836.* Westport, Conn.: Greenwood Press, 1998.
Steele, Richard. *The Spectator,* no. 167. In *The Spectator,* edited by Donald F. Bond, 2:157–160. Oxford: Clarendon, 1965.
Stein, Roger B. "Royall Tyler and the Question of Our Speech." *New England Quarterly* 38:4 (December 1965): 454–474.
Steiner, Bernard C., ed. *Early Maryland Poetry: The Works of Ebenezer Cook, Gent, Laureat of Maryland, with an Appendix Containing The Mousetrap.* Baltimore: Maryland Historical Society, 1900.
Stern, Julia A. *The Plight of Feeling: Sympathy and Dissent in the Early American Novel.* Chicago: University of Chicago Press, 1997.
Stiles, Ezra. *The United States elevated to Glory and Honor.* New Haven, Conn., 1783.

Stone, Albert E. Introduction. *Letters from an American Farmer and Sketches from an American Farmer*, by J. Hector St. John de Crèvecoeur, 7–25. New York: Penguin, 1986.
Stowe, Harriet Beecher. *Uncle Tom's Cabin: or, Life among the Lowly*. 1852. Edited by Elizabeth Ammons. New York: Norton, 1994.
Sweet, Timothy. *American Georgics: Economy and Environment in Early American Literature*. Philadelphia: University of Pennsylvania Press, 2002.
Tanselle, G. Thomas. *Royall Tyler*. Cambridge: Harvard University Press, 1967.
Taylor, Edward. *The Poems of Edward Taylor*. Edited by Donald E. Stanford. Chapel Hill: University of North Carolina Press, 1960.
Thompson, E. P. "Eighteenth-Century English Society: Class Struggle without Class?" *Social History* 3:2 (May 1978): 133–165.
Thompson, James. *Models of Value: Eighteenth-Century Political Economy and the Novel*. Durham, N.C.: Duke University Press, 1996.
Thoreau, Henry David. "Life without Principle." 1863. In *Walden and Other Writings*, edited by Brooks Atkinson, 745–769. New York: Modern Library, 2000.
———. *Walden*. In *Walden and Other Writings*, edited by Brooks Atkinson, 1–312. New York: Modern Library, 2000.
Tompkins, Jane P. *Sensational Designs: The Cultural Work of American Fiction, 1790–1860*. Oxford: Oxford University Press, 1985.
Trumbull, John. *M'Fingal*. In *The Satiric Poems of John Trumbull*, edited by Edwin T. Bowden, 101–212. Austin: University of Texas Press, 1962.
Tyler, Royall. *The Algerine Captive; or, the Life and Adventures of Doctor Updike Underhill*. 1797. Introduction and notes by Caleb Crain. New York: Modern Library, 2002.
———. *The Contrast, A Comedy; in Five Acts: Written by a Citizen of the United States*. Philadelphia, 1790.
Van Horne, John C. "Collective Benevolence and the Common Good in Franklin's Philanthropy." In *Reappraising Benjamin Franklin*, edited by J. A. Leo Lemay, 425–440. Newark: University of Delaware Press, 1993.
Vespucci, Amerigo. From *The First Four Voyages of Amerigo Vespucci*. London, 1885. In *Utopia*, translated and edited by Robert M. Adams. 2d ed. New York: Norton, 1992.
Ward, John William. "Benjamin Franklin: The Making of an American Character." *Red, White and Blue: Men, Books and Ideas in American Culture*, 125–140. Oxford: Oxford University Press, 1969.
Warner, Michael. *The Letters of the Republic: Publication and the Public Sphere in Eighteenth-Century America*. Cambridge: Harvard University Press, 1990.
Washington, George. "A Circular Letter from his Excellency General Washington." Annapolis, 1783.
Waterman, Bryan. *Arthur Mervyn*'s Medical Repository and the Early Republic's Knowledge Industries. *American Literary History* 15:2 (Summer 2003): 213–247.
Weber, Max. *The Protestant Ethic and the Spirit of Capitalism*. 1904–1905. Translated by Talcott Parsons. London: Routledge, 1992.
Webster, Noah. "Principles of Government and Commerce." 1788. In *Collection of Essays and Figitiv Writings. On Moral, Historical, Political and Literary Subjects*, 38–44. Boston, 1790.
———. "Remarks on the Manners, Guvernment, and Debt of the United States." 1787. In *Collection of Essays and Figitiv Writings. On Moral, Historical, Political and Literary Subjects*, 81–118. Boston, 1790.

Webster, Pelatiah. *An Essay on Credit*. Philadelphia, 1786.
Wernick, Robert. "When the Bubble Burst, All of England Wound up Broke." *Smithsonian* 20:9 (December 1989): 155–165.
Weyler, Karen. "'A Speculating Spirit': Trade, Speculation, and Gambling in Early American Fiction." *Early American Literature* 31:3 (1996): 207–242.
Wilson, Thomas Frederick. *The Power "To Coin" Money: The Exercise of Monetary Powers by the Congress*. Armonk, N.Y.: M. E. Sharpe, 1992.
Winthrop, John. *A Model of Christian Charity*. In *The Norton Anthology of American Literature*, 4th ed., edited by Nina Baym et al., 1:170–180. New York: Norton, 1994.
Wise, John [as Amicus Patriae]. *A Word of Comfort to a Melancholy County. Or the Bank of Credit Erected in the Massachusetts-Bay*. 1721. In Davis, *Colonial Currency Reprints*, 2:159–223.
Witherspoon, John. *Essay on Money as a Medium of Commerce; With Remarks on the Advantages and Disadvantages of Paper admitted into general Circulation*. Philadelphia, 1786.
Wood, Gordon S. "Interests and Distinterestedness in the Making of the Constitution." In Beeman et al., *Beyond Confederation*, 69–109.
———. *The Radicalism of the American Revolution*. New York: Knopf, 1991.
Ziff, Larzer. *Puritanism in America: New Culture in a New World*. New York: Viking, 1973.
———. *Writing in the New Nation: Prose, Print, and Politics in the Early United States*. New Haven, Conn.: Yale University Press, 1991.
Zuckerman, Michael. "Doing Good While Doing Well: Benevolence and Self-Interest in Franklin's *Autobiography*." In *Reappraising Benjamin Franklin*, edited by J. A. Leo Lemay, 441–451. Newark: University of Delaware Press, 1993.

Index

Page numbers for illustrations are in *italics*.

Abrams, M. H., 191n6
"Account of the Devices on the Continental Bills of Credit" (Franklin), 74–75
Adams, John, 7
Address to the Inhabitants of North-Carolina, An (Borden), 58
Adventures of a Continental Dollar, The, 63
Agnew, Jean-Christophe, 110
Algerine Captive, The (Tyler), 104–5
Alsop, George, 45
American Crisis (Paine), 78–79, 180n5
American Revolution: economic aspects of, 3, 5, 68; paper money and, 64–65, 73, 180nn3–4
Americans: Crèvecouer's archetypal, 23; pre- vs. post-Revolutionary meaning of term, 3; self-concept of, 5; theatricality in early culture, 110, 185n32
American Weekly Mercury, 1, 73
Anarchiad, The (Connecticut Wits), 12–13, 99, 100, 170n17
Anderson, Benedict, 126, 188n19
antinomianism, 175n40
Appleby, Joyce, 106
Arner, Robert D., 176n2
Arthur Mervyn; or Memoirs of the Year 1793 (Brown), 119–36; benevolence vs. corruption in, 131–32; commercial bonds in, 131; contagion as metaphor in, 120, 186nn2–3, 188n22; loss of innocence in, 127; narratives in, 132–36; reading in, 120–22, 125, 133–36; republicanism in, 120, 128; rumor in, 132–33; self-interest in, 126–36; social function of, 121–22; storytelling in, 127; sympathy in, 120, 130–32, 135–36; vulnerability in, 120, 128–29, 187nn4–5

authorship: copyright laws and, 165–66; emergence as profession, 157–58; as headwork, 158, 162; and writing as speculation, 159–62, 165–66. *See also* writing
Autobiography of Benjamin Franklin, The, 71–95; autobiographical persona, 72, 89–91, 180n3 (chap. 3); on nation's credit rating, 71; projections in, 80, 88; and reader's suspension of disbelief, 80; rhetorical strategies, 72; sea voyage in, 37; on value of debt, 14, 64, 71–72, 84–88. *See also* Franklin, Benjamin

Bailyn, Bernard, 114
Baker, Houston, 182n28
banknotes, 6–7. *See also* paper currency
banks and banking: Bank of England, 6, 34, 114; Bank of North America, 78, 121, 180n4, 184n25; Bank of the United States, 6–7, 180n4, 184n25; Free Banking Era, 11; government-chartered, for funding public debt, 107, 108; and Hamilton's national bank plan, 107, 114, 184n25; land banks, 38, 173n14; multiplicative, 13–14; and Philadelphia debates on national banks, 120–21; Second Bank of the United States, 11
Barlow, Joel, 12
Barnes, Elizabeth, 138
barter, 49, 50, 51, 54
Barth, John, 47
Bartlett, Mary, 142
Barton, William, 107–8, 112
Bartram, John, 161
Baym, Nina, 151
Beard, Charles, 78
Behrens, Kathryn L., 179n44
Bell, Ian, 170n14

Bell, Michael Davitt, 165, 166
benevolence, 131–32, 150, 154–55, 156
Bercovitch, Sacvan, 17, 28, 33, 174n24
Beverley, Robert, 57–58, 178n35, 178n40
Beyers, Chris, 179n43
bills of credit. *See* paper currency
Blackleg (land swindler), 100
Bloch, Ruth H., 152
Bond, Thomas, 90, 182n33
Borden, William, 58–59
Bordley, Thomas, 45
borrowing: agrarian, 111; Franklin on, 14, 64, 71–72, 84–88; managed, 111–12; self-determination and, 14–15, 70; strategic, 69; success and, 64. *See also* credit; indebtedness; public debt
Brackenridge, Hugh Henry, 2, 102
Bradford, William, 22, 37
Brantlinger, Patrick, 171n20
Breen, T. H., 175n35, 179n45, 181n12
Breitwieser, Mitchell, 40, 180n3 (chap. 3)
Brown, Charles Brockden, 3, 114, 116; on commercial mind, 122–24, 187nn9–11, 187n13; on curiosity, 122–24; "The Difference between History and Romance," 124; "The Man at Home," 122–24, 129; on the novel, 121–25; "Thoughts on American Newspapers," 125–26; "Walstein's School of History," 134. *See also Arthur Mervyn; or Memoirs of the Year 1793* (Brown)
Brown, Richard, 184n27
Brown, William Hill, 114, 137
Bryan, William Jennings, 54
Bubble Acts, 22
Burroughs, Stephen, 81–82
Burstein, Andrew, 116
"Busy-Body" (Franklin), 169 (epigraph)
Byrd, William, 172n16

Calvert, Benedict Leonard, 59
Calvinism, 173n19
capitalism, 4–5, 173n19, 185n3
Carey, Mathew, 119, 132–33
cash, definition, 7
castle building: Irving's fiction celebrating, 162; paper money as, 1–2; speculation as, 14–15; Steele on, 6; Thoreau on, 6, 166–67
Chesapeake colonies, 43–62, 176n4; Cooke on economic reform of, 48–50; crude state of letters in, 60–61; ecological destruction in, 56–59; paper money in, 44, 61; printing press and social transformation of, 45–46; tobacco as medium of exchange in, 44, 46, 53–54
Christian Philosopher, The (Mather), 29
Civil War (U.S.), 11
Cohen, Edward H., 177n25, 178n27
Cohen, Patricia Cline, 145–47
coinage, 9–10, 50–51, 170n10. *See also* money
colonization: British mercantilism and, 20, 65; expansion and public debt, 64–65; Franklin on, 73; paper currency and, 19–20, 21, 22, 29. *See also* Chesapeake colonies; Massachusetts; New York; Puritanism
commercial mind, Brown on, 122–24
commercial relations and sociality, 117, 186n8, 188n28
Committee of Inspection and Observation (Philadelphia), 16, 171n30
community development, 2, 3, 15, 27, 30, 44, 88, 171n28
compassion. *See* sympathy
Confidence-Man (Melville), 117
conjecture, 123, 124–25
Connecticut Wits, 12–13
"Considerations on the Use and Abuse of Mottos," 81
Constitution (U.S.), 11, 78, 109, 170n15, 184n27
Continental Congress, 64
Continental dollars: funding Revolutionary War, 64–65, 180nn3–4; Humphreys' defense of, 79; issuance of, 64, 180n3 (chap. 2); mottoes and images, 74–75, 76–77, 115, 180n8 (chap. 3); postwar redemption of, 98–99, 183nn7–8; speculation in, 99
Contrast, The (Tyler), 3, 4, 64, 96–112; main chance in, 104–6; manliness in, 105–6; performance in, 94, 97, 103, 109–11; public credibility in, 101–3, 109; punctuality in, 96, 104–5; regional differences in, 183n11; as response to postwar credit crisis, 96–97; *The School for Scandal* as model for, 101, 104; sentimental patriotism in, 112, 183n12; Shays's rebellion and, 101; theatricality in, 110, 183n13, 185n32
conversion: of paper money, 8–9, 13–14, 31–39;

performance and, 107–8; religious/financial analogy, 31–39
Cooke, Ebenezer: autograph preface to *The Sot-Weed Factor*, 52, 177n25, 178n27; on economic reform, 48–50; on "headwork," 159; *The Sot-Weed Factor*, 47–49, 52, 177n14, 177n17; *Sotweed Redivivus*, 44, 47–48, 52–57, 159
Cooper, James Fenimore, 158
copyright laws, 165–66
Coquette, The, 131
corruption: Hamilton on, 113–14; public debt as, 115; strengthening social bonds, 114–17, 120; sympathy and, 126–32
Cotton, Elizabeth, 35
Cotton, John, 27
counterfeiting, 66, 82, 181n20
credit: definition, 7, 16, 105; Hamilton on interdependence of credit system, 113; Marxism on, 17; necessity for farmers, 111; paper (*see* paper currency); performance and, 109; public, 16, 17, 72–73 (*see also* public credibility); punctuality and, 106; superfluous vs. necessary use of, 14; women and, 138–41. *See also* borrowing
Crèvecoeur, J. Hector St. John, 23–24, 157, 159–62, 166
Culler, Jonathan, 188n19
curiosity, 122–23, 124, 187n10, 187n13
currency. *See* paper currency
Currency Acts, 38, 65

Davidoff, Leonore, 106, 191n46
Davidson, Cathy N., 131
debt. *See* borrowing; indebtedness; public debt
Declaration of Independence, 78
deferral, textual, 181n26
Defoe, Daniel, 22, 34, 37, 48, 88, 140
dependence. *See* interdependence, financial
depreciation, 8, 68–69, 73, 79, 93, 106–7
Derrida, Jacques, 181n20
Description of New England (Smith), 19
despair, 4, 34, 35, 37, 41
"Devil and Tom Walker, The" (Irving), 164, 165, 192n12
"Difference between History and Romance, The" (Brown), 124
disinterest, 2, 114–17, 131, 154

Ditz, Toby L., 151
Don Quixote (Cervantes), 14
Dorval; or, The Speculator (Wood), 101
Dreiser, Theodore, 69
Dumbleton, Joseph, 43–44, 45, 176nn1–2
Dunciad, The (Pope), 12, 13, 170n19, 171n20
"*Dying Speech* of Old Tenor, The" (Green), 19

ecological destruction, 56–57
economic man, 105, 140–41
education of women, 145–47
Edwards, Jonathan, 37, 41–42
Elliott, Emory, 131
Ellison, Julie, 183n12
Emerson, Ralph Waldo, 10–11, 170n14, 186n8
emotions, prediction of, 142
empirical observation, 141
Enlightenment, 141
Enquiry Concerning Human Understanding (Hume), 142
entrepreneurial spirit, 23–24, 190n15
environmental protection, 56–57
Equiano, Olaudah, 24–25, 182n28
Essay Concerning Human Understanding (Locke), 142
Essay upon Projects (Defoe), 34, 48, 88
Evelev, John, 183n13, 185n32
exchange media: alternatives to metal, 21–23; commodities as, 50, 51, 53, 58, 177n20; dematerialized, benefits of, 29, 54–55, 58; tobacco as, 20, 44, 46, 53–54

Fair Dealing between Debtor and Creditor (Mather), 28
faith: civic, 2; economic, 34–35, 80; in paper money, 16–17, 32; religious, 41–42; success as reward for, 39; as virtue, 94, 95
"Faithful Narrative of the Surprising Work of God" (Edwards), 41
family dramas, 138
farmers, and credit, 111
Federalist, The (Hamilton), 113, 155–56
federal powers, scope of, 98, 156
Ferguson, Robert, 172n14
Fichtelberg, Joseph, 117
Fiedler, Leslie, 131
financial speculation. *See* speculation, financial

Financier, The (Dreiser), 69–70
Findley, William, 121
fiscal responsibility, heroism as, 96
Fliegelman, Jay, 110
"Food for Criticks" (Lewis), 59, 178n39
Forlorn Hope (newspaper), 116
Foster, Hannah, 137
Franklin, Benjamin: "Account of the Devices on the Continental Bills of Credit," 74–75; autobiographical persona, 72, 89–91, 180n3 (chap. 3); on depreciation, 73, 93; on economic faith, 80, 94–95; on indebtedness, 7c, 84–87; industrialization and, 4; *A Modest Inquiry into the Nature and Necessity of a Paper-Currency*, 51, 71, 72–73; mottoes and images for Continental dollars, 74–75, 76–77, 180n8 (chap. 3); on paper currency, 1, 13–14, 72–74; on public credit, 72–73, 90–93; on reputation as asset, 71; on symbolism of money, 51; on writing effecting economic change, 75, 78. See also *Autobiography of Benjamin Franklin, The*
Free Banking Era, 11
French and Indian War, 92

Galbraith, John Kenneth, 63
Garson, Robert, 171n28
gender typing, virtue and, 106
general or common equivalent, 50–51, 177n20
Gilmore, Michael T., 135, 163
"Glass; or Speculation, The," 139–40
Gleaner, The (Murray), 137, 144, 147–50
"Goldbug, The" (Poe), 191n1
Gooch, William, 46
Gould, Philip, 172n14, 186n1
Goux, Jean-Joseph, 50, 177n20
government, representative, 113
Great Awakening, 38, 41, 175n35
Green, Joseph, 19, 64
Greene, Jack P., 45, 176n4
Gresham's Law, 30, 55
Gura, Philip, 37, 174n21, 176n42

Habermas, Jürgen, 125, 176n7
Hall, Catherine, 106, 191n46
Hall, Timothy, 175n35, 181n12
Halley's comet, 141

Hamilton, Alexander, 72; on contingencies and government powers, 156; on corruption, 113–14; on interdependence of credit system, 113; monetary thinking of, 92, 97; national bank plan, 6, 107, 114, 184n25; on public debt, 15, 16; on redemption of war currency, 183n8; on sympathy, 4, 113
Hammond, Bray, 22
"Happy Failure, The" (Melville), 158
Hariot, Thomas, 45
Haskell, Thomas L., 185n3
Hawthorne, Nathaniel, 191n1
headwork. *See* authorship
"Hell Gate" (Irving), 165
Henretta, James, 24, 164
heroism, as fiscal responsibility, 96
Hinds, Elizabeth Jane Wall, 187n5
Hirschman, Albert O., 185n4
history, Brown on, 124
History and Present State of Virginia (Beverley), 57–58
History of the American Revolution (Ramsey), 68–69
Holmes, Alice Arnold, 113
Hopkins, Lemuel, 12
House of the Seven Gables, The (Hawthorne), 191n1
humanitarianism, and capitalism, 185n3
Hume, David, 9, 130, 142, 188n24
Humphreys, David, 12, 79–80
Hutcheson, Francis, 130, 188n24

Ichabod Crane, 162, 163
imaginary money, 7, 169n7
imagination, 6
immigration, indebtedness and, 23–24
indebtedness: assignability of, 181n25; avoidable vs. unavoidable, 122, 150–52, 187n9; immigration and, 23–24; punishment of debtors, 122, 187n9; as slavery, 116. *See also* borrowing; public debt
independence and debt, 65, 66–67, 85
Ingrassia, Catherine, 189n3
Innes, Stephen, 174n20
insolvency. *See* indebtedness
interdependence, financial, 17, 27, 113, 115, 138, 151–52, 186n8

Interesting Narrative (Equiano), 24–25
investment: financial and emotional, 16; reading and, 120, 131–33; women and, 138–40, 145, 152–53, 156
Irving, Washington: on authorship, 158, 162–63; on enterprising individuals, 159; *The Money-Diggers*, 163–65, 192n12; *Tales of a Traveller*, 166; on writer as speculator, 157–58, 166
Isaac, Rhys, 25
It's a Wonderful Life, 113

Jackson, Andrew, 11
Jack Tar (sailor), 100
James, Abel, 88
Jefferson, Thomas, 113
jeremiad, 17, 28, 31

Kerber, Linda, 146
"Kidd the Pirate" (Irving), 165
Knight, Janice, 32
Knight, Sarah Kemble, 190n15

land, 14, 105, 114, 127, 140, 164
land clearing, slash-and-burn, 56–57
language, analogies between money and, 10–13, 170n12
Law, John, 9
legal language, 12
Lemay, J. A. Leo, 85, 177n14, 182n20
Letters from an American Farmer (Crèvecoeur), 23–24, 157, 159–62, 166
Letters of the Republic, The (Warner), 5
Levine, Robert, 186n3
Lewis, Richard, 59–60, 178n39, 178n42
Lex Mercatoria (Mather), 28
Life of Phips (Mather), 4, 28, 33–42; acceptance of unknowing in, 39–40; epistemological anxiety in, 42; lack of faith in paper money in, 33–34; preparationist sensibilities in, 32; resistance to despair as theme in, 34, 35, 41; speculative ventures in, 33–34; success in, 33, 36–37, 39; treasure hunt metaphor in, 35–36
"Life without Principle" (Thoreau), 157
literature: changing definitions of, 5; Chesapeake, 59–60; economics and, 3–5, 47, 75, 78–80, 170n12; romance, 124, 157, 158
Locke, John, 9, 142, 147

Looby, Christopher, 88, 181n26
Loughran, Trish, 183n11

Machiavelli, republicanism and, 140
Madison, James, 7, 97, 106–7, 183n8
Magaw, Samuel, 145–47
Magnalia Christi Americana (Mather), 4, 27
"main chance," 40, 104–6, 175n39
"Man at Home, The" (Brown), 122–24, 129
Mann, Bruce H., 181n25
Man of His Word, A (Mather), 28
"man of punctuality," 104–5
Markland, J., 46
Marshall, Gordon, 173n19
Marx, Karl, 3, 17, 51, 64–65, 177n20, 177n22
Maryland Gazette, 45, 51, 83–84
masculinity, 105–6, 140–41, 161
Massachusetts: issuance of paper currency, 6–7; retirement of colonial bills of credit, 19; "Sword in Hand" currency, 66; views of paper money in, 29–31, 181n12
mathematics, women's education and, 146
Mather, Cotton, 3, 4; *The Christian Philosopher*, 29; defense of witchcraft trials, 175n38; economic vision of, 27–28; elegy for Elizabeth Cotton, 35; *Fair Dealing between Debtor and Creditor*, 28; financial conundrums as exemplum, 35, 174n24; financial entanglements, 172n4; financial metaphors, 38–39; on godly capitalism, 28–29; *Lex Mercatoria*, 28; *Magnalia Christi Americana*, 4, 27; monetary policy of, 173n7; on natural disasters, 37–38; on paper money, 29–30; *Pascentius: A Very Brief Essay upon the Methods of Piety*, 38–39; on potentiality, 25; on public debt, 20, 28–32; on public patriotism, 176n42; on secularization of New England, 33, 174n21; *Some Considerations on the Bills of Credit Now Passing in New-England*, 28, 29, 30; on unleashed self-interest, 41. See also *Life of Phips*
Mather, Nathaniel, 41
Matson, Cathy, 109, 180n3 (chap. 2)
McCusker, John, 169n7
Medium, The (Murray), 138, 152–54
Melville, Herman, 117, 162, 186n8
mercantilism, British, 20, 65
metals, precious, 7, 10, 29, 30, 170n10

214 Index

Metamorphoses (Ovid), 43
metaphors: contagion, 186n2; financial, 35–36, 38–39, 174n27, 174–75n28, 175n29
M'Fingal (Trumbull), 98, 108
Michaels, Walter Benn, 191n1
Mickle, Samuel, 87, 94, 119
Miller, Perry, 31
Milton, John, 12–13
misers, 51–52
Moby-Dick (Melville), 117
"Model of Christian Charity" (Winthrop), 28
Modern Chivalry (Brackenridge), 2, 102
Modest Inquiry into the Nature and Necessity of a Paper-Currency, A (Franklin), 51, 71, 72–73
money: Congressional powers to issue, 170n15; imaginary vs. real, 7, 169n7; language and, 10–13, 170n12; national identity and, 171n28; philosophy of, 182n33; symbolism of, 9–10, 13, 50–52, 177n20. *See also* coinage; paper currency
"Money" (Madison), 106–7
Money-Diggers, The (Irving), 163–65, 192n12
moral economy, 16
More, Thomas, 22
Morgan, Edmund S., 90
Morris, Robert, 93, 107, 180n4, 183n36, 184n25
mottoes, currency, 74–75, 76–77, 180n8 (chap. 3)
"Mournful Lamentation For the sad and deplorable Death of Mr. Old Tenor, A" (Green), 64
"Mournful Lamentation On the untimely Death of Paper Money, A" (Green), 64
Mulcaire, Terry, 189n5, 191n49
multiplicative banking, 13–14
Murray, John, 137, 144
Murray, Judith Sargent, 17, 114, 116, 137–56; on benevolence, 150, 154–55, 156; on debt, 150–52; on female circumspection, 147–50; on financial speculation, 150, 155–56; *The Gleaner* essays, 137, 144, 147–50; on instability of women's lives, 144–45; marriage to John Murray, 137, 144; marriage to John Stevens, 137; *The Medium*, 138, 152–54; "On the Equality of the Sexes," 146–47, 152; on rationality of women, 149; refusal to apologize for entrepreneurism, 144; *The Story of Margaretta*, 138; struggle with debt, 137, 150–51; on sympathy in women, 152; *The Traveller Returned*, 138, 151; on women's education, 145–47; on women's intellectual equality, 138–39, 152

narratives, 132–36
Nash, Gary B., 186n5
national debt. *See* public debt
National Debt Clock, 15
natural resources, protection of, 56–57
Nature (Emerson), 10–11
Neider, Charles, 166
Nettels, Curtis, 172n6
New Economic Criticism, The (Osteen and Woodmansee), 170n12
New-England Courant, 43
Newman, Eric, 180n8 (chap. 3)
New News from Robinson Cruso's Island (1720), 30, 173n11
newspapers, 125–26
Newton, Isaac, 142
New World experience: British mercantilism and, 20; chattel slavery in, 24–25, 172n14; and entrepreneurial values, 23–24; and monetary media, 22–23
New York, colonial paper currency, 21
Nichols, Capper, 47
Nixon, Richard, 7
Norton, Mary Beth, 142, 146
novels: Brown on, 121–22; in early America, 135; negative influence on women, 140; speculation and, 122–25, 189n3

observation, 131, 141
"Observations on the Nature and Use of Paper-credit" (Barton), 107
"On Public Spirit in Regard to Public Works" (Savage), 90
"On the Equality of the Sexes" (Murray), 146–47, 152
Osteen, Mark, 170n12
Ostrowski, Carl, 187n5
Ovid, 43

Paine, Thomas [1694-1757], 28, 173n16
Paine, Thomas [1737-1809]: *American Crisis*, 78–79, 180n5; on American vs. British debt, 180n5; call for government-chartered bank,

107, 180n4; on funding of independence, 65; on popular sovereignty, 68, 92; support of public credit, 78–79

paper currency: advantages of, 55–57; in *The Anarchiad* satire, 12–13; banknotes vs., 6–7; as castle building, 1–2; in Chesapeake, 54–55, 61; in colonial period, 19–20, *21*, 22, 29; counterfeit, *66*, 82, 181n20; Currency Acts and, 38, 65; depreciation of, 68–69; as detachment of symbol and referent, 7, 10; economic transformation and, 2–3; eighteenth-century views of, 1–3; Emerson on, 10–11; Franklin on, 1, 13–14, 72–74; funding Revolutionary War, 64–65, 180nn3–4; as legal tender, 6–7, 29, 170n15, 172n6; in *Life of Phips*, 33–34; Mather on, 29–30; of New York, *21*; opposition to, 30–31, 173n14; of Pennsylvania, 72; permanently circulating, 108; popular sovereignty and, 68; in postwar period, 98; private commercial paper, 7; protection of natural resources, 56–57; as public debt, 1–2; redemption of, 8–9, 98–99, 183nn7–8; replacing barter, 51; of South Carolina, *67*; states issuing, 180n4; "Sword in Hand" bill (Massachusetts), *66*; taxation vs., 64; unbacked, 10–11, 16; veterans and, 100–101. *See also* Continental dollars

"Paper-Mill, The" (Dumbleton), 43–44, 176nn1–2

Paradise Lost (Milton), 12

Parks, William, 43, 45, 46, 47

Pascentius: A Very Brief *Essay upon the Methods of Piety* (Mather), 38–39

patriotism, wartime economy and, 68

Pennsylvania, paper money of, 72

performance, 3, 94, 97, 103, 106–11

personal wealth, concepts of, 2

Philadelphia, 16, 120–21

Philosophy of Money, The (Simmel), 50

Phips, William: acceptance of unknowing, 39–40, 175n37; discovery of Spanish shipwreck, 33; economic faith of, 34, 92; ending witchcraft debacle, 39–40; historical significance of, 33; military expedition to Quebec, 29; resignation to economic uncertainty, 40–41; treasure hunt and religious faith, 36–37, 39. *See also Life of Phips* (Mather)

Pinckney, Eliza, 142–44, 190n15

Pioneers, The (Cooper), 158

Pitkin, Hanna, 140

Pocock, J.G.A., 105, 114, 140–41, 187n4

Poe, Edgar Allen, 191n1

Poovey, Mary, 189n4

Pope, Alexander, 12, 13, 140, 170n19, 171n20, 189n3

Potter, William, 9

Power of Sympathy, The (Brown), 114

precious metals, 7, 10, 29, 30, 170n10

predestination, 31–32

preparationism, Puritan, 32, 35–36

Pressman, Richard, 98, 109

printing and print media: fears about, 82, 83, 181n22; influence on public credibility, 78; social transformation and, 44, 45, 47, 176n7

probability, 141–42

projection, 48, 80, 88, 130

Protestant Ethic and the Spirit of Capitalism, The (Weber), 173n19

public credibility: debt redemption and, 96, 97; performance and, 106, 109; prominent individuals supporting, 72, 92–93; punctuality and, 104–5, 106; as theme for *The Contrast*, 101–3, 109; writers supporting, 17, 78–80

public debt: benefits of, 20, 157; colonial expansion and, 64–65; communal identity and, 3; compromising national self-determination, 65; economic growth and, 15; government-chartered banks funding, 107, 108; Hamilton on, 15, 16; literature supporting, 157; Marxist thought and, 3, 64–65; Mather on, 28–32; moral objections to, 30–31; national credibility and, 69, 96, 100; paper currency as, 1–2; payment of interest and, 108; performance and, 109; permanent, as asset, 97; state credibility and, 63; strategic borrowing and, 69; Webster on, 63

public securities, 16

punctuality, 104–5, 106

Puritanism, 27–42; Calvinism and capitalism, 173n19; grace as discovery of treasure, 35–36; Mather's economic vision for, 27–28; paper money and theology, 28–32; preoccupation with self-assessment, 36; preparationism in, 32, 35–36, 174n20; secularization of, 33, 174n21. *See also* colonization

Ramsey, David, 68–69
Randolph, Peyton, 51–52
rationality, 29, 52, 141, 149, 155
Recoinage Act of 1696 (England), 9
redemption. *See* conversion
reform movements, 185n3
representation, 4, 7–10, 51, 72
"Representation and Remonstrance of Hard Money," 81–82
republicanism, 120, 128, 140
resistance to despair, 34, 35, 41
Revere, Paul, 66
revivals, 38, 41, 175n35
Revolutionary generation, 116, 186n5
Revolutionary War: economic aspects of, 3, 5, 7, 68, 100–101; paper money funding, 64–65, 180nn3–4
Ricardo, David, 13
Rice, Grantland S., 89–90, 159, 182n33
Richards, Jeffrey, 110
Riesman, Janet, 106–7
Rip Van Winkle, 162–63
"Rip Van Winkle's Lilac" (Melville), 162
risk, 1, 14, 157; Franklin on, 75, 94–95; as intellectual pursuit, 159–62; masculinity and, 104–5; Murray on, 149–51; New World and, 19, 24; women's aversion to, 161–62
Robertson, William, 188n28
Robinson Crusoe (Defoe), 22, 37
Rogers, Thomas, 16, 171n30
Roll, Eric, 171n23
romance (literature), 124, 157, 158
Rowson, Susanna, 137
Rush, Benjamin, 146

Samuels, Shirley, 186n3
Savage, Richard, 90
School for Scandal, The (Sheridan), 101, 103–4
Second Bank of the United States, 11
self-assessment, Puritan, 36
self-interest: communal ties and, 16, 114–17, 120, 188n28; curiosity and speculation as byproducts of, 126, 187n17; economic, plague and, 128–29; in *Life of Phips*, 41
sentimentality, 117, 188n24
Sermon, Joseph, 17, 171n30

Shays, Daniel, 98, 99
Shays's rebellion: as catalyst for Constitution, 109, 184n27; outbreak of, 98–99; significance of, 100; Tyler's role in suppressing, 97–98
Shell, Marc, 9, 80, 191n1
Shields, David S., 56, 178n31, 178n42
Short Account of the Malignant Fever (Carey), 119, 132–33
Silverman, Kenneth, 37, 172n4, 175n38
Simmel, Georg, 50, 182n33
Skemp, Sheila, 151
slash-and-burn agriculture, 56–57
slavery: debt as, 116; narratives of, 24–25; as permanent condition, 25, 172n16; as speculation, 5, 24, 172n14; tobacco cultivation and, 56
Smith, Adam, 13–14, 50, 69, 130, 142, 188n24
Smith, John, 19, 45
Smith, Venture, 24, 172n14
Smith-Rosenberg, Carroll, 106
Some Considerations on the Bills of Credit Now Passing in New-England (Mather), 28, 29, 30
Sot-Weed Factor, The (Cooke), 47–49, 177n14, 177n17; revisions of, 52, 177n25, 178n27
Sotweed Redivivus (Cooke), 44, 47–48, 52–57, 159
South Carolina, paper currency, 67
South Sea Company, 22, 140, 171n4
speculation: castle building as, 14–15; in novels, 122–25, 189n3; rationality and, 141, 155; sympathy and, 155; writing as, 159–62, 165–66
speculation, financial: cerebral nature of, 6, 139–40, 166; conjecture in, 6, 123–24, 147; in Continental dollars, 99; credit used for, 150; culture of, 4–5; gender and, 105, 140–41; Murray on, 150, 155–56; rational vs. irrational, 189n8; reckless vs. prudent, 14–15, 105, 141; self-interest in, 126, 187n17; slavery as, 24, 172n14; in tulips, 189n6; by women entrepreneurs, 143–44; women's condition and, 138; writing as, 157–58, 159–62
Spengemann, William, 180n3 (chap. 3)
Stamp Act (1765), 65
Steele, Richard, 6
Stein, Roger B., 109
Stern, Julia, 131, 185n2, 186n3
Steuart, James, 9
Stevens, John, 137

stock-jobbing, 5, 101, 139, 164
Story of Margaretta, The (Murray), 138
Stowe, Harriet Beecher, 154
suspension of disbelief, 41, 80
Sweet, Timothy, 57, 178n35
symbolism, 9–10, 13, 50–52, 177n20
sympathy: in *Arthur Mervyn,* 126–32, 136; compassion and, 130, 185n2; credit-based, 113–14, 185n4; as feminized zone of imagination, 131; financial dependence and, 138; Hamilton on, 4; observation and, 131; speculation and, 155; of women, 152

Tales of a Traveller (Irving), 166
taxation, paper currency vs., 64
Taylor, Edward, 35–36, 174n27, 174–75n28, 175n29
theatricality, 109–11, 183n13, 185n32
Theopolis Americana (Mather), 28
Theory of Moral Sentiments (Smith), 130–31
Thompson, E. P., 16
Thoreau, Henry David, 157, 192n15; on castle building, 6, 166–67; nonmonetary goals of writing, 158, 166
"Thoughts on American Newspapers" (Brown), 125
"To a Lady: Of the Character of Women" (Pope), 140
tobacco: Chesapeake overdependence on, 56–57, 178n35; as commodity vs. medium, 53–54; ecological impact of cultivation, 59, 178n40; economic impact of, 56, 178n31; literary culture and, 47; as medium of exchange, 20, 44, 46, 53–54; as morally suspect crop, 55–56; paper currency impact on, 55–56; slavery and, 56
Tobacco Inspection Act, 47, 179nn44–45
Tompkins, Jane, 131, 188n28
Traveller Returned, The (Murray), 138, 151
treasure, 35–36, 133, 164–65, 192n12
Trumbull, John, 12, 98–99, 108
tulip speculation, 189n6
Tyler, Royall: *The Algerine Captive,* 104–5; military service of, 97–98. See also *Contrast, The* (Tyler)
"Typographia" (Markland), 46, 176n9

Uncle Tom's Cabin (Stowe), 158
United States Constitution, 11, 78, 109, 170n15, 184n27
Utopia, 22

Van Horne, John, 177n13
Vaughan, Benjamin, 88, 94–95
Vespucci, Amerigo, 22
veterans, Revolutionary, 100–101, 183n12
Virginia Gazette, 45
virtue, 106, 152
Virtue Triumphant. See *Medium, The* (Murray)

Walden (Thoreau), 6, 166
"Walstein's School of History" (Brown), 134
Ward, John William, 90
Warner, Michael, 5, 135, 176n7, 176n9, 188n34
wartime economy, patriotism and, 68
Washington, George, 104
Waterman, Bryan, 186n2
Wealth of Nations, The (Smith), 13
Weber, Max, 28, 32, 173n19, 189n8
Webster, Noah, 7, 63
Webster, Pelatiah, 105, 106
Weyler, Karen, 141
"What Is an American?" (Crèvecoeur), 23–24
Winthrop, John, 27, 42
Wise, John, 6, 28
witchcraft trials, 39–40, 175n38
Witherspoon, John, 7, 15
"Wolvert Webber, or the Golden Dreams" (Irving), 163–64
women: circumspection of, 147–50; credit and, 138–41; education of, 145–47; as entrepreneurs, 142–44, 190n15; intellectual equality of, 138–39, 152; mathematics and, 146; novel reading and, 140; rationality of, 142–43, 149; risk aversion of, 161–62; sympathy of, 139, 152; volatility of, 140, 189n4; as writers, 189n3
Wood, Gordon S., 114, 115, 120, 121
Wood, Sally S.B.K., 101, 156
Woodmansee, Martha, 170n12
Worcester Magazine, 82–83, 98
Worlds Apart (Agnew), 110

writing: analogy to speculation, 157–58; effecting economic change, 5, 47, 75, 78–80; as vocation, 157. *See also* authorship
Writing in the New Nation (Ziff), 2

yellow fever epidemic (Philadelphia, 1793), 119–29, 186n1; credit economy and, 120; fictionalization in *Arthur Mervyn*, 120, 188n22; gossip and rumor in, 132–33

Zall, P. M., 182n29
Ziff, Larzer, 2, 81, 159, 175n40, 181n22

www.ingramcontent.com/pod-product-compliance
Lightning Source LLC
Chambersburg PA
CBHW021757230426
43669CB00006B/103